ENCYCLOPEDIA

OF THE

EXQUISITE

NAN A. TALESE | DOUBLEDAY

NEW YORK LONDON TORONTO

SYDNEY AUCKLAND

ENCYCLOPEDIA

OF THE

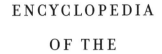

EXQUISITE

AN ANECDOTAL HISTORY OF
ELEGANT DELIGHTS

JESSICA KERWIN

JENKINS

Illustrations by Elizabeth Haidle
Book design by Pei Loi Koay

LIBRARY OF CONGRESS CATALOGING-IN-PUBLICATION DATA
Jenkins, Jessica Kerwin
Encyclopedia of the exquisite : an anecdotal history of elegant delights /
Jessica Kerwin Jenkins.—1st ed.
p. cm.
Includes bibliographical references.
(alk. paper)
1. Curiosities and wonders. I. Title.
AG243.K447 2010
001.94—dc22   2010003191

ISBN 978-0-385-52969-3

PRINTED IN THE UNITED STATES OF AMERICA

1 3 5 7 9 10 8 6 4 2

First Edition

For Nico

I don't know what I may seem to the world, but, as to myself, I seem to have been only like a boy playing on the seashore, and diverting myself in now and then finding a smoother pebble or a prettier shell than ordinary, whilst the great ocean of truth lay all undiscovered before me.

—SIR ISAAC NEWTON

Great effort has been made to be certain that all the information found in this book is factual, accurate, and up-to-date, as well as amusing. Notification of any errors or inaccuracies would be greatly appreciated: queries@encyclopediaoftheexquisite.com.

ENCYCLOPEDIA

OF THE

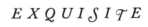

EXQUISITE

INTRODUCTION

This book first took form in my grade-school jewelry box, designed to look like a small birdcage with a faux canary swinging behind brass bars. In its shallow drawer I kept a prism that made rainbows, two Mexican pesos, an unusually large acorn cap, a miniature seashell, the face of my father's old Timex, and a sample vial of Patou's Joy—all my treasures.

The word "exquisite" comes from the Latin verb *exquirēre*, to search out, or to seek. It means uncommon delicacies, carefully selected, and the kind of beauty that can "excite intense delight or admiration," as explained in *The Oxford English Dictionary*. For many years, I wrote for a slick magazine, trying my best to invoke that sense of delight by lending a fashion designer's story haute romance, giving a new shop an old pedigree, or dusting off an antique idea to make it sparkle anew. Becoming part of the luxe fantasy was as easy as swiping a credit card. That is, if you could afford it. But in real life, in my life, I didn't make enough to land the fancy trinkets I wrote about. I was Holly Golightly with my nose pressed against the glass.

While those years taught me to recognize beauty of all kinds, to respect it, and to allow myself the time to ponder the exquisite, by contrast, this book is an ode to life's many luxuries that don't require much spending. It's about how knowing the royal lineage of a common Bartlett pear or the origins of the top hat can make you feel rich, and about how learning the history of the Japanese kimono or of confetti can turn the world vast and strange.

The earliest encyclopedias, like Pliny the Elder's thirty-seven-volume *Natural History* (first century AD), celebrated nature's marvels, describing fantastic creatures of Africa and Asia, incredible gemstones, and miraculous plants. Similarly, Renaissance authors compiled books of knowledge with an exotic bent, like cabinets of curiosities assembled by the nobility. They're brimming with mysterious artifacts, religious relics, and intriguing clockworks, presented alongside the occasional unicorn tusk. This spirit of renewing old sources of beauty guided my search.

My encyclopedia is also like its predecessors in that its scope is far-flung, extravagant, and maybe a little eccentric. And like those early books, it's also very personal. Wikipedia represents the accumulated knowledge of the general public. These entries sprang directly from a file I kept on my desk, bulging with scribbled scraps, Xeroxed articles, quotes, and curious images I'd come across—anything that lit a spark, or excited "intense delight." In my mind I called the collection "Why I Like It Here," "here" meaning on the planet. If I was having a bad day, flipping through the file could sweep me into a dreamy demimonde where things didn't seem so bad.

Yet, unlike the couture collections and black-tie balls I wrote about for my job, many of these pieces of ephemera illuminated an esoteric world independent of big-ticket luxury, and one that gave off an aura of wonder that was even more beguiling. I've often found myself defending frivolity when in serious-minded company. This book is an homage to frivolity—though again, I don't mean the empty gesture of spending too much: doing something frivolous means doing something pretty and purposeless. And what better reason to do something than for no reason at all? I believe it's essential.

At every step along the way, the obscure, exquisite, and twinkling facts I gleaned filled my notebooks, fueled my imagination, and delivered an exhilaration that splurging on some new bauble could never do. To me these carefully compiled tales of folly are the treasures that make it all worthwhile.

AEROSTATION

The art of hot-air ballooning

By 6 A.M. carriages blocked the road from Paris to Versailles, where a fire raged in the château's courtyard one September morning in 1783. Black smoke funneled into a heaving aerostatic machine, the bulk of it painted blue with gold curlicues. The hot-air balloon, as it is now known, was slowly swelling and coming to life.

King Louis XVI and Marie Antoinette stood by. People crowded the streets watching the sky. Spectators climbed onto nearby roof-tops and filled every window of the château, as attendants placed a trio of passengers into the balloon's basket—a duck, a sheep, and a rooster, history's first aeronauts. Up they went, drifting for eight minutes before sinking into the woods, where a recovery crew on horseback raced to find them. Dazed, but otherwise unharmed, the pilgrims were presented to the king, who was so pleased he promptly ordered the creatures cooked for his dinner.

The balloon, invented by the enterprising French brothers Joseph-Michel Montgolfier (1740–1810) and Jacques-Étienne

Montgolfier (1745–1799), was inspired, Joseph claimed, by seeing Madame Montgolfier's chemise fluttering as it dried near the fire. A month after the first flight, it was the first contraption to ferry humans into the "aerian ocean," when the twenty-six-year-old daredevil Pilâtre de Rozier (1754–1785) rose to a height of eighty feet in a Montgolfier balloon held in place by ropes.

Still, no one had flown untethered. The king had decreed that

only a condemned inmate could fly freely, in exchange for a pardon. But, working his connections at court, de Rozier convinced King Louis that aerostation was safe, and Louis watched from below in the Bois de Boulogne park as Rozier and his aristocratic copilot the Marquis d'Arlandes (1742–1809) climbed aboard their aerostatic machine.

They lifted off without a sound. "I was surprised at the silence and the absence of movement which our departure caused among the spectators," wrote the marquis, who, admittedly, wasn't a great pilot. "I was still gazing, when M. Rozier cried to me—'You are doing nothing, and the balloon is scarcely rising a fathom.'" The two grabbed pitchforks and shoveled hay into the fire that kept their balloon filled with hot air, rising again. But only for a moment. The marquis took another break to stare at the marvelous Seine below. "'If you look at the river in that fashion you will be likely to bathe in it soon,' cried Rozier. 'Some fire, my dear friend, some fire!'" They fell toward the Paris rooftops, just missing the bell towers of Saint-Sulpice.

One of Benjamin Franklin's (1706–1790) more skeptical friends doubted the usefulness of the balloon, but Franklin, who was also watching the scene from below in the Bois that day, shot back, "What is the use of a newborn baby?" In truth, the hot-air balloon was impossible to steer, but it was lovely. Aerostation became all the rage. "We think of nothing here at present but of flying," wrote one observer. "The balloons engross all attention."

Eleven days later, a crowd of 400,000 turned out to see French physicist Jacques Charles (1746–1823) and his assistant Noël Robert take off from the Tuileries to ride in the boat-shaped wicker basket of their speedy hydrogen-powered aerostatic machine. The duo waved banners as they floated over the countryside and shouted to the astonished people below. "We cried, *'Vive le Roi!'*" wrote Charles. The people below shouted back, "My good friends, have you no fear? Are you not sick? How beautiful it is! Heaven preserve you! *Adieu*, my friends!" The pilots landed two hours and twenty-seven miles later, along the way dropping a blanket onto the dome of a church for fun.

In flying, Charles found perfect bliss. "How great is our good fortune!" he told Robert. "I care not what may be the condition of the earth; it is the sky that is for me now."

ALFRESCO

Out in the fresh air

Poised between civilization and the wild, picturesque picnicking and outdoor dining alfresco—"in the fresh air," as the Italians say—offered stiff, cinched Victorians a chance to escape the city and to breathe. Chaperones kept an eye on young picnickers, but "even the rigidest disciplinarian will romp a little when there is green grass underfoot and a blue sky overhead," as one writer pointed out. Alfresco etiquette was as loose as the tone of the sunny invitations. "Dear Jo, What ho!" began one fictional epistle, sent to *Little Women*'s Jo March and her sisters. "Some English boys and girls are coming to see me tomorrow, and I want to have a jolly time. If it's fine, I'm going to pitch my tent at Longmeadow, and row up the whole crew to lunch and croquet;—have a fire, make messes, gypsy fashion, and all sorts of larks."

Bolstered by flirtation, sunshine, and good food, the ancient Romans began the grand tradition. Average citizens celebrated festivals under giant tents, in imitation of the nomadic kings of the East, who traveled in sprawling tented cities. The wealthy put on deluxe banquets in their gardens, as rich Florentines of the Renaissance era would later do. During the Renaissance, even alfresco meals were exactingly formal. Servants hauled out a giant sideboard, and every dish on the long stone table was arranged symmetrically on top of a triple layer of fine damask cloth, right down to the perfumed finger bowls. The French took a self-consciously laid-back approach, heading outdoors in the eighteenth century with their fêtes champêtres, rosy pastoral parties celebrated by painters like Watteau, Fragonard, and Boucher. Silken Parisian ladies and their gallants ate at tables brought into the Tuileries, then lazed under the trees by the Seine.

At the end of the nineteenth century, before air-conditioning kept people indoors and before Prohibition corked the good times, the alfresco meal took on a dazzling urban veneer at New York's flourishing rooftop cabarets. "From early June until late September nightfall brings to birth a new and fairy city on hotel tops," one journalist wrote, "a city of pleasure, of suave shaded lights, of tinkling fountains, of gay music, song and dancing, of luxurious food and wine."

At the block-long roof garden above Oscar Hammerstein's Olympia Music Hall, swans glided on a faux lake and lovers cooed in the arbors under three thousand twinkling lights. The rooftop at the nearby Republic was done up like a Dutch farm, complete with a mini-windmill, a duck pond, and two live cows stationed outside a miller's cottage where a stork's nest was perched on the chimney. The most fabled of New York's alfresco spots, however, was the sprawling pleasure garden atop the Hotel Astor on Times Square, which opened in 1905 and accommodated five thousand guests. Gazebos, mossy grottoes, and thousands of blooms—roses, Virginia creeper, moonflowers, and fuchsias—turned the place into paradise. Fountains sprayed water into the air. Fish swam in the lily pool, and the white-columned promenade ran on for a quarter of a mile.

With the addition of a glass-roofed restaurant situated under a waterfall, the Astor was still thriving in 1920. "Every New Yorker," the *New York Times* reported that summer, "and every stranger in New York who can possibly make it is trying to get on some roof somewhere, somehow."

AMORINI AND PUTTI

Cupids, cherubs; and baby angels

The tumbling swarms of pudgy pink cupids fluttering through the artwork of the Renaissance and Baroque eras are known both as amorini, a diminutive of the Italian *amore*, or love, and as putti, a diminutive of *putus*, Latin for "boy child." But their origins are as old as antiquity. Delivering messages for the Greek gods, the fleets of flying babies first took to their wings on the crowded sarcophagi of the fourth century BC. Known as *erotes*, these guardian sprites protected living humans, then ushered their souls to heaven. Putti were pix-ies with a taste for the finer things in life. They frolicked, boxed, wres-tled, blew horns, or bowled hoops. They hauled heavy garland swags, celebrating wine's delicious in-toxication and the heft of the harvest, or otherwise ca-vorted around, dancing like dervishes.

Recast as angels, cherubs flit-ted through early Christian imag-ery, though they fell out of favor during the Middle Ages, when artists took celestial inspiration from goddesses in long flowing gowns instead. They reappeared during the Renaissance, when the sculptor Donatello (1386–1466) fashioned a new breed of naughty putti as brazen as their bacchanalian ancestors. Most often, however, then as now, the amorini stood for earthly love in the form of Cupid, setting lovers aflame with mini-torches and targeting their hearts with his arrows.

Cupid hit a bull's-eye in 1464, when Bartolomeo Benci, a young lover from Donatello's hometown of Florence, fell in with Love's winged crew. At carnival time, Benci costumed himself as Signor Amante (the inamorato), wearing a set of wings over his fashionable armor, and led through the streets a horse-driven love-themed carnival car mobbed with amorini figurines and topped with the image of a bleeding heart. A cavalcade of some 150 young men paraded behind him, and when they reached his sweetheart Marietta's house they sang and shouted Love's praises. Then, to prove the fierceness of his affection, Benci, with a sweeping gesture, threw his wings into the car and caused the whole thing to burst into flames, setting off devices that shot exploding arrows from the amorini's tiny bows into the night sky. "And so it burned, and with such great shouting and thundering that the noise rose even to the stars," wrote one witness. "One arrow indeed flew into the house of said lady, so that it was said that one had entered into her heart, a sign of her compassion for the said lover." Having made his point plain, Benci took his leave, coaxing his horse backward until they were out of sight, never once turning his back on his beloved. We can only assume that they lived happily ever after.

ATTITUDES

Bodily postures and poses implying an action or mental state

Although the auburn-haired muse Emma Hamilton (1765–1815) wasn't born wealthy, bright, or ambitious, she made the most of her statuesque assets, posing for Regency England's artists as a stand-in for ancient heroines—a fresh-faced Circe, a coy Medea, and, most often, a frolicsome bacchante. Artist George Romney (1734–1802), smitten, called Hamilton "superior to all womankind," and during her early days in London he painted the runaway teenager dozens of times. His work was well received, but by transforming her goddess routine into a live performance—nimbly reenacting a brisk series of classical poses, her "Attitudes"—Hamilton caused a sensation across Europe.

A blacksmith's daughter turned professional beauty, she worked her way through a string of aristocratic lovers before winding up in louche Naples as mistress to Sir William Hamilton (1730–1803), the recently widowed British ambassador. Sir William, whose keen eye for antiquities supplied treasures to the British Museum, hosted a constant stream of well-heeled visitors at his Palazzo Sessa overlooking the sea. He played tour guide, taking guests to Pompeii, and stepped in as an interior designer, fueling the taste for Greek revivalism by brokering antiques deals.

Doing her part to entertain their visitors, Emma slipped into a white gown and, working a shawl or a prop tambourine, posed rapid-fire in imitation of well-known Greek and Roman statues. She buried her face in sorrow one moment and flung out an arm in vamped victory the next. The legend of her Attitudes spread. "Sir William has actually married his gallery of statues," Horace Walpole (1717–1797) said of their 1791 nuptials. Sir William was sixty to Emma's twenty-six.

At the height of her reputation, Hamilton was, as the visiting poet Johann Wolfgang von Goethe (1749–1832) put it, "the universal prototype for heroines, muses and demigoddesses." Artist Élisabeth Vigée-Lebrun (1755–1842), another lover of Greek art, just arrived from Paris, painted Emma as a bacchante and as Ariadne in 1790. But while she appreciated Emma's antiquated beauty, Vigée-Lebrun judged Emma as having no style and "very little wit."

Frankly, most sophisticates found her less than scintillating company. "No Grecian or Trojan princess could have had a more perfect or commanding form," admitted Georgiana Cavendish, Duchess of Devonshire (1757–1806), though Emma was, she added, "coarse and vulgar." William, Lord Beckford (1760–1844), called her "not at all delicate, ill-bred, affected." Elizabeth Vassall Fox, Lady Holland (1770–1845), criticized Emma's lower-class accent. "Just as she was lying down, with her head reclining upon an Etruscan vase to represent a water-nymph, she exclaimed in her provincial dialect 'Don't be afreared Sir Willum I'll not crack your joug,'" Holland huffed. "I turned away disgusted."

The Hamiltons took their act on the road at the turn of the century, touring Europe with Admiral Nelson, Emma's lover, and inciting gossip along the way. Before long, however, both men were dead, and Emma arrived alone on French artist Vigée-Lebrun's London doorstep.

Vigée-Lebrun was more successful than ever, having recently left Catherine the Great's St. Petersburg court. Emma was obese, alcoholic, and desperate. Out of pity, the artist invited her former model to perform at a party for some visiting French nobles. Though Emma's drinking shocked the Duc de Bourbon, once more her Attitudes did not fail. "She went from sorrow to joy, from joy to dread, so well and with such swiftness that we were all amazed," Vigée-Lebrun wrote in her memoirs.

Nineteenth-century dance masters laid the foundation of classical ballet—another dynamic series of postures—on Hamilton's Attitudes and the evocative poses she lifted from antiquity.

BLACK

Black, the timeless color of mourning and of elegant restraint, is also the color of resistance, worn head to toe by both seventeenth-century religious reformers and 1960s-era revolutionaries. In imitation of the strict Catholic Spanish court of the 1600s, nobles across Europe adopted an austere all-black wardrobe, an unwavering sobriety carried on by Dutch merchants and English Puritans. Perky brights offended God, argued the Protestants, and anyone who wore them was "but a blowne bladder, painted over with so many colours, stuft full of pride and envy," as one grumbled.

Centuries later, black epitomized the ascetic reserve so admired by Victorians. First among them, of course, was Queen Victoria (1819–1901), who buttoned herself into mourning clothes at age forty-two, when Prince Albert died, and was still dressed in black forty years later at her death. "A mourning dress does protect a woman while in deepest grief against the untimely gayety of a passing stranger," one etiquette writer explained in 1884. "It is a wall, a cell of refuge." Inspired by their queen, proper widows throughout the era shrouded themselves in black for two and a half years, from their black dresses to black gloves, and from jewelry made from jet—carved black coal—to black bonnets with crape streamers, and black veils. Their petticoats were slotted with black ribbon. Their stationery was bordered in black. Some even dressed their beds in black. And widows were expected to remain at home, lest seeing a mourner at a party snuff out everyone else's fun.

But when mourning dresses began to follow fashion more closely in the 1860s, black took on a theatrical new edge. French actress Sarah Bernhardt (1844–1923), who kept an ebony coffin in her bedroom and lay in it "to learn my parts," liked to wear black velvet gowns onstage. Silent-movie vamp Theda Bara (1885–1955) dressed in black to play the femme fatale, as did the film noir vixens who followed. All this set the stage for the success of Coco Chanel's now-iconic Little Black Dress of the 1920s.

Few have worn black to better dramatic effect, however, than the women of the Black Panthers did in the 1960s, standing together at a rally shaking their fists in the air in sleek black skirts and knee-high boots with their Afros coaxed high, embodying the Black Is Beautiful ideal. Kathleen Cleaver (1945–), a diplomat's daughter, dropped out of Barnard College to join the Student Nonviolent Coordinating Committee, and married founding Panther Eldridge Cleaver a year later. "At the time we weren't running around thinking 'we look cool,'" she remembered. "That wasn't on the top of our minds." Cleaver's style was cool by necessity, as her limited wardrobe consisted of only one black dress, one black jacket, and one black skirt.

With the release of style-heavy films such as *Cleopatra Jones*, *Shaft*, and *Superfly*, the Panthers' rebellious look turned trendy and nearly overshadowed their political agenda. But by then the real revolutionaries had moved on. Eldridge had been shot by California police. The Panthers' slick separatist style was too easy to target. "The orders went out for everybody just to wear regular clothes," said Cleaver. "We didn't want to encourage police by standing out. So we just stopped wearing that stuff."

BLANCMANGE

A milky, sweet, almond-flavored pudding

Blancmange tastes like heaven. Creamy, fluffy, and sweet, it's an old-fashioned white pudding flecked with ground almonds and scented with rose water. It's easy enough to make, but it's a little ritzy, too. Back in the fourteenth century, when going on a pilgrimage was rough and hiring a private chef for the trip was expensive, blancmange was one of the delicacies that made doing so worthwhile. Geoffrey Chaucer's Cook in *The Canterbury Tales*, a rowdy, ribald Londoner, is known for his nasty temper and his questionable hygiene, but is redeemed by his blancmange: "That he made with the best."

The dish, originally thickened with capon or chicken bones, probably came from Arabia to medieval Europe via Spain and appears in some of the oldest existing French cookbooks, grease-spattered manuscripts detailing refined menus of the fourteenth and fifteenth centuries, when aristocrats developed a taste for sugar. (Its name—whether blankmange, blancmanger, or blanc-mange—comes from the French: white, *blanc*, and to eat, *manger*.)

Naturally, France's first true culinary star, chef Antonin Carême (1784–1833), was big on blancmange. Carême, a Left Bank urchin abandoned during the Revolution, cooked his way to the top with a chip on his shoulder, and, at the height of his career, created the wedding cake for Napoleon and his empress. His heavy, two-volume *Le Pâtissier royal parisien* includes his recipe for blanc-mange, which, at its best, is lighter than a crème brulée but richer than a mousse. When making the dessert at Château Rothschild, Carême pressed almond milk through a piece of silk. He spooned alternate layers of creamy pudding and fresh orange marmalade into hollowed-out orange peels, then arranged his clever concoctions into pyramids garnished with laurel leaves.

The fanciful dessert did not die with Carême. Like the famed chef, American photographer Solomon Carvalho (1815–1897) was devoted to blancmange. In 1853 he was invited by explorer John Frémont to document an expedition from Missouri to the Pacific, and, despite being a novice to the trail, signed on for the five-month trip. In the Rocky Mountains that winter, when temperatures fell to thirty degrees below zero and the snow was neck-high, food rations ran dangerously low. The men butchered their horses for meat when the time came. Then they took a solemn pledge not to eat each other.

On New Year's Day, Carvalho, born in Charleston, South Caro-

lina, did both Chaucer's English pilgrims and the French chef Carême proud. Hidden in his luggage were two tin boxes: one filled with preserved eggs, the other with powdered milk. He mixed the contents together with arrowroot to thicken it, boiled up some snow, and made for the starving crew "as fine a blancmange as ever was *mangéd* on Mount Blanc," he wrote to his wife. "The satisfaction and astonishment of the whole party cannot be portrayed when I introduced, as dessert, my incomparable blancmange . . ."

Blancmange

from Dorie Greenspan's *Paris Sweets: Great Desserts from the City's Best Pastry Shops*

1 packet (2½ tsp) powdered gelatin

3 tbs cold water

1½ cups chilled heavy cream

¾ cup whole milk

¾ cup ground blanched almonds

½ cup sugar

2 to 3 tbs kirsch or to taste

1 peach, peeled, pitted, and cut into small dice

2 slices canned or fresh pineapple, cut into small dice

½ cup strawberries, preferably fraises des bois, hulled and halved (if using larger berries, cut them into small dice)

1. Have ready an (8x2-inch) round cake pan or springform pan, preferably nonstick. Fill a large bowl with ice cubes and cold water and set out a smaller bowl that fits into this ice-water bath.

2. Sprinkle the gelatin over the cold water. When it is soft and spongy, heat it for 15 seconds in a microwave oven to liquefy it (or do this stovetop); set aside. Whip the chilled heavy cream until it holds medium-firm peaks; refrigerate.

3. Bring the milk, almonds, and sugar to a boil in a medium saucepan over medium heat, stirring occasionally to make certain the sugar dissolves. At the boil, pull the pan from the heat and stir in the dissolved gelatin, as well as the kirsch. Pour this into the set-aside small bowl and set the bowl into the ice-water bath. Stir regularly, and lift the bowl out of the ice bath as soon as the mixture cools and starts to thicken.

4. Working with a flexible rubber spatula, fold in the whipped cream. Still working with the spatula and a light touch, fold in the fruit. Scrape the blancmange into the pan and refrigerate for at least 2 hours or for up to 24 hours.

5. To serve, unmold the cake onto a cake plate. (If you've used a cake pan, the easiest way to unmold the blancmange is to dunk the pan into a sink full of hot water. If you've used a springform, warm the sides of the pan with a hairdryer before opening the latch.)

Keeping: Once assembled, the blancmange can be stored in the refrigerator, away from foods with strong odors, for 1 day, although it is preferable to serve it the day it is made.

THE BOB

A women's style of short haircut

"Do you think I ought to bob my hair, Mr. Charley Paulson?"
Charley looked up in surprise.
"Why?"
"Because I'm considering it. It's such a sure and easy way of
attracting attention."

So wrote the twenty-four-year-old F. Scott Fitzgerald (1896–1940), conjuring Bernice, a society belle on her way to becoming "a society vampire" in his story "Bernice Bobs Her Hair," published in 1920, when a woman's threat to visit the barbershop for a bob stupefied, and when the sight of her there could draw a crowd.

History credits French libertines with inventing the scandalous hairstyle, cut sharp and short at the jawline. Take, for example, the eurhythmic dancer Caryathis, who, when rejected by a would-be lover, lopped off her tresses in a fit of heartbreak in 1913, and inspired her dance student Coco Chanel to do the same. Across the ocean in America, where short hair and short skirts defined an audacious new breed of coquette called the flapper, incredulous style watchers traced the bob's origins to bolshevism. Intellectual Russians on the run adopted the style "for convenience in disguising themselves when the police trailed them," the *New York Times* explained. Once they'd escaped, they settled in Greenwich Village, where they were imitated by artists like Clara Tice, who bobbed her hair in 1908. (In the seventeenth century, "bobbed" described a short traveling wig, and later the blunt cut of a horse's tail.)

A lithe American dancer, Irene Castle (1887–1918), popularized the racy hairstyle in the United States. Castle and her dashing husband, Vernon, known for their smooth tango and mincing maxixe, were ballroom idols when she gave herself a drastic pre-appendectomy haircut, making headlines in 1914. "I just couldn't stand the thought of having strange nurses and attendants fussing over my head," she said. "The next week, 250 women had their hair cut. The week after it was 2500—and then it was impossible to keep count." A ribbon decorated with pearls—soon called the Castle band—held flyaway locks in place, as did the newly invented "bob pin."

As popular as it was, the look was still controversial. Conservative matrons played it both ways, wearing bobbed wigs. Others suffered. One foreign correspondent explained that the bob offered her "comfort for the first time in my life," free from the burden of styling her long, unruly hair. Still, she grew it out before returning home from covering the war in France.

"My husband is numbered among the group opposed to bobbed hair."

Opposition was formidable. Schoolteachers, nurses, shopgirls, and railroad office workers were prohibited from wearing the cut in various regions. "If a girl goes so far as to bob her hair, her work will probably be affected and she could not give 100 per cent efficiency," argued a Baltimore insurance executive, convinced a bob demonstrated a distracting vanity. Newly shorn teens explained their haircuts to parents and policemen with "Jack-the-Clipper" tales. A Bronx girl said a highwayman seized her on the street and chopped her hair, while an eighteen-year-old in Queens claimed "an Italian man of 50" had snipped off her flaxen braids.

Modernization called for drastic measures. The story of Fitzgerald's Bernice grew from a pointed ten-page letter he'd written from Princeton at age nineteen to his sister Annabel, then fourteen, instructing her on how to become a fascinating, modern woman. He told her to groom her eyebrows, choose jaunty hats, refine her awkward walk, and kid the boys, while cultivating a "pathetic, appealing" expression to win them over (head hung, staring up directly into their eyes). "You have beautiful hair," he conceded, assessing her best traits. "You ought to be able to do something with it."

BON CHRÉTIEN

The most commonly grown variety of pear in the Western world

We assume Eve served Adam an apple, though the book of Genesis never actually names the forbidden fruit. Mightn't it have been a juicy pear? The pear has a democratic, sober reputation, but its easy-bruising delicacy makes it all the sweeter—and that much more tempting.

The Bon Chrétien, a singularly delicious pear brought in 1481 by Saint Francis of Paola (1416–1507) from the saint's home in Calabria all the way to the sickbed of Louis XI (1423–1483) in France, was later named the "good Christian" in the saint's honor, or so the story goes. The variety was later called Williams' Bon Chrétien, or the Bartlett, after its first distributors in England and the United States. But by any name, it is tender, perfectly granular—and juicy.

The saint's reputation preceded him in France. Francis, a precocious hermit, retired to a cave at age fourteen and quickly began racking up miracles after his six-year stint in solitude: he strolled into a blazing furnace without getting burned; resuscitated a favorite lamb by calling its name; and cured the paralyzed and the blind. Disciples followed his pious example, refusing meat, eggs, or milk. His fame grew, and soon enough Louis XI, determined to stave off death, summoned the miracle worker to his château at Plessis-les-Tours, though Francis refused to come until Pope Sixtus IV gave the order.

The king, lonely, isolated, and grim, let the world know he was alive by shopping—ordering horses from Naples, a leopard from the Duke of Ferrara, and reindeer from Scandinavia. No one was allowed to speak the word "death."

When Francis arrived at the château, after delivering two cities from the plague en route, the king asked him to work his magic. But Francis was frank. "The lives of kings are in the hands of God and have divinely appointed limits," he said, advising Louis to put his affairs in order and to prepare for death. Francis presented the king with a Calabrian pear he'd brought from home (pears can be kept for several months), and, eventually, they became friends. Louis ordered sweet oranges sent from Languedoc for the vegan saint. Soon after, the king died in Saint Francis's arms.

More than a century later, Francis's lingering reputation brought the French queen Anne of Austria to pray each week in the Paris chapel housing one of his vertebrae. She had yet to bear an heir to the throne after two decades of marriage, when she finally—miraculously—gave birth to Louis XIV, who took the crown at four years old and soon acquired his grandiose taste.

Thanks to innovative hothouse techniques, the royal gardener at Versailles,

Jean-Baptiste de La Quintinie (1624–1688), could accommodate Louis XIV's cravings for asparagus in December, peas in April, and strawberries nearly all year round. The Bon Chrétien pears that La Quintinie produced—prized distant cousins to the one Saint Francis delivered to Plessis-les-Tours—were so luscious that Louis gave the fruit to favorite courtiers as gifts. "One must agree," La Quintinie wrote, "that nature has not given us anything as beautiful and as noble to see as this pear." In 1996, Versailles gardeners reintroduced the Bon Chrétien pear to the château's celebrated kitchen garden, the Potager du Roi. Beyond Versailles, and better known as the Bartlett, it's the most widely grown pear in the Western world.

BOUDOIR

A woman's private lair

Lying in her bed, Catherine de Vivonne, Marquise de Rambouillet (1588–1665), oversaw France's first true salon, then called a *ruelle*, the name for the little alleyway between the bed and the wall where a lady's friends sat to chat with her while she lounged. The horizontal marquise, raised in genteel Italy, retired early from Henri IV's licentious Parisian court, claiming ill health, and established instead a weekly rendezvous of the city's brightest lights—Madame de Sévigné, Guez de Balzac, Richelieu, La Roche-foucauld—in her boudoir, the famed *chambre bleu*. There, she reigned for over forty years, surrounded by admirers, hundreds of lit candles, and baskets of fresh-cut flowers. The scene that was, as one habitué noted, "less crowded and more refined than that at the Louvre."

Rambouillet's cozy boudoir, built to encourage conversation, caused nothing short of a revolution in domestic architecture. Her rooms were more intimate than the grand halls in old-fashioned houses, and much easier to heat. And they were bright—accustomed to Italy's sun, the marquise had her windows enlarged and elongated to the floor. Queen Marie-Thérèse soon emulated Rambouillet's scheme—as did the rest of Paris—constructing, beyond Versailles' formal reception rooms, a *petit appartement* of her own, which included an intimate boudoir, a refuge from the rigors of court life.

Regal European bedrooms of the era were of two sorts: the rooms where the master or mistress of the house actually slept, and opulent rooms anchored by a *lit de parade*, an imposing canopied bed, where every morning a clutch of courtiers—sometimes as many as one hundred of them—gathered to watch their betters pretend to wake up. To be allowed such intimate contact with royalty was thought to be an honor. The boudoir was something in-between, a cozy, feminine hideaway where select friends were invited.

The word "boudoir" comes from the French verb *bouder*, to

brood or sulk, but in the eighteenth century it also became a place of pleasure. The grand courtesan Anne-Victoire Dervieux (1752–1826), supported in her prime by a consortium of dukes, was the daughter of a washerwoman. She made her stage debut as a dancer at thirteen, then switched to singing opera. Her town house perfectly matched her theatrical urge. Decorating her domain, Dervieux amassed 124 chairs, showed her collection of embalmed exotic birds behind glass, and devoted a whole room to her porcelain collection. Her bathroom was done in a Pompeian motif, while her formal *lit de parade* dripped with Persian fantasy—swagged in blue brocade and topped off with a spray of ostrich feathers, with the inside of its canopy lined in mirrors.

But a sumptuous boudoir—a "little temple of Venus," according to one lucky guest—was her sanctuary. Continuous mirrors covered the ceiling, walls, and the floor, "so two lovers could, in the midst of their voluptuous embrace, consider themselves in each attitude," wrote memoirist Antoine Caillot (1759–1830). Cushions strewn around the room were the plush weapons of her "amorous combats." Yet, as racy as it was, Dervieux's tantalizing boudoir set the tone "for young ladies of quality and bourgeois women of the better sort."

When one of those women, a duchess, wanted a firsthand glimpse of the place, she badgered her lover, who knew the courtesan, to get her inside. Thinking they were alone in the house, she offered her noisy opinion about Dervieux's infamous boudoir.

"Oh, this is too much," she shrieked. "It could only be equaled in the *Arabian Nights!*" Just then, a hidden door swung open, and there was the famous courtesan herself, laughing. "You are right," she announced, "and I doubt much whether you could offer anything half so charming." After years of pleasing the men around her and pillow fighting, Dervieux married her architect.

CAROUSEL

A tournament of horsemanship, or a merry-go-round ride

The carousel, that spinning joyride, with its gaudy flash and old-world pomp, has been around in one manner or another since at least the sixth century, when dizzy thrill-seekers rode in big twirling baskets tied to a strong center pole, as seen in a Byzantine bas-relief. Likewise, low-tech rides swung daring riders through the air in India, as well as in Turkey, where they competed in knocking the turban off the head of a man standing below.

Before the word "carousel" meant a ride, however, it described a different sort of amusement: a splashy chivalric pageant staged live on a vast field to showcase lavish displays of horsemanship, like the pretty war games put on by medieval Arabian warriors. Performing elaborate feats on horseback in the sixteenth century, brilliantly dressed nobles demonstrated their agility and prowess by jousting, or by lancing a gold ring while seated on horseback. At one of the most spectacular events, six hundred aristocratic riders competed in the courtyard of the Louvre in 1662, called the Place du Carrousel to this day, during a festival to celebrate the birth of Louis XIV's son, though, according to Voltaire, the king really staged the show to impress his teenage mistress. The fête was months in the planning, with five teams of horsemen all flamboy-antly costumed as Turks, Persians, Indians, American Indians, and ancient Romans. In decorous faux combat, they galloped toward one another in a newly built Roman amphitheater before fifteen thousand guests, firing brightly colored balls filled with perfume. In the midst of all the scented pageantry, Louis cantered out to play the part of the Roman emperor himself. The vividly colored trap-pings worn by their horses still festoon the mechanical carousel's carved horses hundreds of years later.

Young riders prepared for these grand displays by training with a prototype of the mechanical carousel. On real horses, they charged after a golden ring hanging from a hand-cranked wheel rotating overhead. Eventually, the game evolved into a horseless ride with carved animals perched on a turning platform, often powered by strong servants. And by the eighteenth century, such a device had become an eccentric extravagance. The Duke of Chartres installed one in his Parisian garden, the Parc Monceau, so his guests could ride on dragons or on little cushions held by sculpted Chinese attendants.

But even after the carousel ran on steam or electricity and became a more common sight around Paris, it retained its strange magic. Poet Rainer Maria Rilke (1875–1926) was hypnotized by the whizzing, turning carousel in the Jardin du Luxembourg while in one of his wistful moods. He wrote:

. . . And on the lion whitely rides a
    young
boy who clings with little sweaty hands,
the while the lion shows his teeth and tongue.

And now and then a big white elephant.

And on the horses swiftly going by
are shining girls who have outgrown this play;
in the middle of the flight they let their eyes
glance here and there and near and far away—

and now and then a big white elephant . . .

CHAMPAGNE

Sparkling white wine from the French region of Champagne

At the coronation of the sixteen-year-old Louis XIV (1638–1715), one of the locals at Reims, the capital of the Champagne region, told the new king, "Sire, we offer you our wines, our pears, our gingerbreads, our biscuits, and our hearts." "That, gentlemen," the cocky new king replied, "is the kind of speech I like."

What he didn't like, however, were bubbles in his wine, thought to be a flaw in the fermenting process until the blind Benedictine monk Dom Pierre Pérignon (1638–1715) gave sparkling champagne its big start, regulating the effervescence when he couldn't get rid of it.

All wines bubble naturally when the grapes are first pressed, but in colder regions, like Champagne, the yeasts that cause fizzing hibernate during the winter, waking up again in the spring to bubble anew. Champagne's wine came to life in March, and by summertime it was *"en furie."*

Because the highly pressurized bottles shattered at the

slightest provocation, champagne's prices soared. Winemakers sidled into their cellars wearing iron masks as a protection against exploding glass. One vineyard owner was left with just 120 bottles out of 6,000 after the rest were blown to smithereens in 1746.

Its explosive property aside, champagne wasn't an easy sell in the beginning. One winegrower proclaimed that froth was only appropriate in "beer, chocolate, and whipped cream." Doctors expounded on the dangers of drinking champagne. Others, such as professor Benigné Grenan, issued warnings in verse:

Lift to the skies thy foaming wine,
That cheers the heart, that charms the eye,
Exalt its fragrance, gift divine,
Champagne, from thee the wise must fly!
A poison lurks those charms below,
An asp beneath the flowers is hid.

Nevertheless, fizzy fans like Madame de Pompadour loved the delicacy of the drink. As Voltaire (1694–1778) put it, "This wine where sparkling bubbles dance/Reflects the brilliant soul of France." The Faculty of Medicine of Paris finally ruled in champagne's favor.

A good champagne, like those blended by Krug, is feathery with small bubbles and complex, revealing a taste that is tart like a green apple, flowery with roses and violets, sweet like roasted pineapple, and toasty as a golden brioche.

Technical advances kept bottles from bursting during the nineteenth century, which should have lowered prices, but by then champagne was draped in a luxe legend all its own. Its bubbles were synonymous with celebration, and were required to toast any important moment, from the launching of a boat to a marriage or the birth of a child.

Its pull was so strong that even Stalin couldn't resist. Under his guidance, Professor Frolov-Bagraev launched Soviet champagne—*Sovetskoe shampanskoe*—in Russia in the mid-1930s. Cheaply mass-produced, sugary, and still available today, it offered workers of all walks a sickly sweet taste of the good life.

CLAUDE GLASS

A convex hand mirror used to view landscapes

The English poet Thomas Gray (1716–1771) climbed onto a hilltop near the village of Keswick in 1769, and instead of simply taking in the view of the misty meadowland below, he took out his Claude glass, a convex, tinted mirror, something like a lady's compact, which artists and tourists kept close at hand in the late eighteenth century, convinced that the reflection of a pretty view was usually prettier than the view itself. In order to see the landscape in his mirror more clearly, Gray turned his back to the sight and aimed the Claude glass back over his shoulder, framing up "a picture, that if I could transmit it to you, & fix it in all the softness of its living colours, would fairly sell for a thousand pounds," he wrote to a friend. "This is the sweetest scene I can yet discover in point of pastoral beauty."

Like Gray, fastidious European aesthetes set out in pursuit of the sweetest scenery, armed both with clear colored glass filters that tinted their views pink, green, or blue, and with black-tinted Claude glass mirrors, which distorted the landscape, while seeming to improve it. Condensed in the smoky-hued mirror, almost any landscape turned into an unspoiled Shangri-la in miniature, a tiny glowing vista that conjured the idyllic pastoral paintings of the seventeenth-century painter Claude Lorrain. Claude, as he was called, wasn't known to use the device (though other artists used it as a drawing aid), but like the mirror named in his honor, Claude's work "conducts us to the tranquility of Arcadian scenes and fairyland," artist Joshua Reynolds (1723–1792) wrote. Nostalgic travelers like Goethe compared every attractive landscape they saw with Claude's sylvan dreamscapes, often preferring the painted version to reality. That is, until—like modern tourists wielding digital cameras—they took out their magic mirrors.

In the days before the camera, capturing and framing wild scenery in a Claude glass gave an artsy thrill. The rambling English vicar William Gilpin (1724–1804), calling himself a "picturesque traveler" in search of "visual effects," trekked all over southern England, watching the world go by in his mirror. "Shall we suppose it a greater pleasure to the sportsman to pursue a trivial animal, than it is to the man of taste to pursue the beauties of nature?" he wondered.

The mirrors remained popular until the mid-nineteenth century, when the formidable English art critic John Ruskin (1819–1900) held sway, blaming the painter Claude for his dreamy distortion of reality, and calling the Claude glass "one of the most pestilent inventions for falsifying Nature and degrading art which was ever put into an artist's hand." Instead, Ruskin recommended carrying a magnifying glass in one's pocket to examine the truth up close.

CONFETTI

Scraps of colored paper thrown during festive occasions

Throwing confetti wasn't always such dainty fun, though it began decorously enough. In medieval Italy, *confetti* meant candied spices or fruits—like the hard, sugarcoated almonds that Venetian traders brought back from the Far East. Wealthy families served confetti at first-rate feasts, and, during the Lenten Carnival, tossed it from their balconies to the eager throngs below. (The good stuff didn't shatter.) At baptisms and at weddings Italians still hand out powdery, sweet confetti bundled in pouches of ribbon-tied tulle, though it's now called *coriandoli*, to distinguish it from the cheap, rock-hard candy that masked combatants hurled at one another in mock battles during Carnival in the nineteenth century, when revelers caroused in open carriages, flinging it at each other with tin ladles.

Novelist Nathaniel Hawthorne (1804–1864) jumped into the fray in Rome, receiving "a handful of confetti, right slap in my face," as he wrote in his diaries in 1859. Courteous players threw bouquets at ladies, but when stockpiles of the genteel projectiles ran out, they grabbed dried peas, sawdust, eggs—anything. Hawthorne was hit with sugarplums, and took a blast of seeds. From his balcony, he bombarded the enemy in retaliation—and he loved it. "Though I pretended to take no interest in the matter, I could have bandied confetti and nosegays as readily and as riotously as any urchin there," he wrote.

Parisians played a polite version of the game with festive scraps of colored paper, but with an equal passion. An estimated 1.5 million pounds of paper confetti were sold in the days preceding Lent one year during the 1890s. Confetti blanketed the big boulevards, inches deep, like tutti-frutti snow, and everyone joined in—women and men, rich and poor—except policemen, who made the best targets.

That European sense of decorum vanished at New York's Coney Island during Carnival season in 1906. Young toughs lobbed handfuls of wet paper confetti at innocent bystanders and threw punches at one another, as the police station filled up with arrests. "The hand that flung confetti was not more than four inches from the victim's face," reported the *New York Times*. "There was malice in the thrust, and often the confetti was moistened so that it was quite compact."

In contemporary India, as nowhere else on earth, both the mirth and the menace of those confetti rites live on in the wild springtime festival of Holi, which women, men, and children of every caste celebrate by pelting one another with colored powders. (Historians link Holi to ancient Rome's Bacchanalia, which, in turn, gave rise to Carnival.) The play is particularly fierce in Varanasi, where younger children—and tourists confined to their hotels—battle one another from the tightly packed rooftops with colored water bombs, while teenage boys rampage through the labyrinthine alleyways below, armed with powders and water cannons, ruining their clothes, staining their skin, and leaving the city awash in a streaky rainbow.

But playing Holi is a rite of passage, for even the most dignified guests. During the festivities in Delhi in 1962, First Lady Jackie Kennedy visited Prime Minister Nehru, who later appeared at a press conference with a bright pink dab on the front of his otherwise pristine white jacket. "Jackie did it," he said with a grin.

COUNTESS DE CASTIGLIONE

A nineteenth-century Italian noblewoman of legendary beauty

The Countess de Castiglione (1837–1899), often called the most beautiful woman of her day, gave off a seductive magnetism still potent years after her death in the hundreds of portraits she commissioned. She was "immortal Venus, as deified by the brushstrokes and chisels of the great masters," in the eyes of her admirers.

The Florentine belle married a count at seventeen, then tumbled into a love affair with Vittorio Emanuele II of Savoia. When they were through, Prime Minister Camillo Cavour (1810–1861) sent her to Paris to win Napoleon III's support for his plan to unify Italy under Vittorio Emanuele's crown. "Succeed by whatever means you wish," the prime minister told her, "but succeed." At a garden party that summer, guests watched as the emperor disappeared with the dewy de Castiglione, not to return for several hours. Empress Eugénie turned pale and "betrayed not a little chagrin," as one witness put it. Napoleon backed Cavour's unification scheme. The affair lasted for a summer.

That year, de Castiglione, victorious, newly famous, and looking shy and sweet in a billowing taffeta gown, visited photographer Pierre-Louis Pierson for the first of many sessions in his studio. Posing there over the years, she staged her every fantasy, dressing up as a menacing Lady Macbeth, a powdered-wig princess, a tipsy barfly, a dour nun, and an odalisque. She pretended to be asleep, or terrified, or destitute, weeping into a handkerchief. She played the seductress, sprawled across a chaise longue wrapped in nothing but a striped sheet. She commissioned Pierson to photograph her bare feet and legs, a risqué indiscretion at the time.

She was nearly as theatrical in the ballroom, where she kept aloof from her admiring crowd. "Despite our indignation, I must swear that the sculptural beauty she revealed was so complete that there was nothing indecent about it," claimed Princess Pauline de Metternich (1836–1921). "One could call her a statue come to life." While some found her intolerable, others argued that de Castiglione's vanity was justified. "She was not vain, for her grounds were strong, but her self-appreciation was enormous, and her frankness in regard to her beauty most amusing," explained one admirer, noting that when she came into a party, the other guests stood on chairs to get a look. "These demonstrations never disturbed her equanimity—she was so accustomed to adulation that she would probably have been more embarrassed by the lack of them."

De Castiglione, who wouldn't play by the strict rules of the French court, wound up banished, though stories of her love affairs and her rare appearances at masquerade balls sent ripples through society. But when her legendary looks faded, she became a recluse. The walls of her apartment were painted black and the mirrors were removed. She only went out at night, heavily veiled, to walk her beloved Pekingese.

Before she died, the countess posed for a final photo session, re-creating the most important scenes from her modeling years. "The Eternal Father did not realize what He had created the day He brought her into the world," de Castiglione wrote, at age sixty, of her youthful self. "He formed her so superbly that when it was done He lost His head at the contemplation of this marvelous work."

COUNTESS DE CASTIGLIONE, POSTHUMOUSLY

"The life of this woman was nothing but a lengthy *tableau vivant*, a perpetual *tableau vivant*," wrote Count Robert de Montesquiou-Fezensac (1855–1921), the most fervent among the Countess de Castiglione's next generation of worshippers.

Montesquiou, a dandy whom Marcel Proust called a "professor of beauty," rushed to de Castiglione's apartment when he heard the countess was dead. He'd never met her alive, but he managed to peek inside her coffin before it was shut. "There was for me a flash of light in the brief glimpse of the pale, beautiful, noble, solemn face of death, on the point of vanishing forever," he remembered. At the auction of her estate, he feverishly pursued de Castiglione memorabilia, buying her pearl necklace, plaster casts of her hands and feet, a nightgown she wore during her summer with Napoleon, and amassing 434 of her photographic portraits, creating a shrine he called her "boudoir beyond the grave." "I wanted to pay tribute to the renunciation of beauty in its relation to what destroys it, to beauty's retreat from the injurious passage of time, to its confinement as age advances," he wrote in 1905.

In a similar fashion, the Italian eccentric the Marquesa Luisa Casati (1881–1957) fell under the spell of the countess. Casati inherited a fortune young and married a marquis, who left once he discovered just how quirky she was. She owned de Castiglione's fans, portraits, books, and her saltcellars, as well as a pair of sandals, which she wore around town. When Casati lost her fortune, she tried to sell photographer Cecil Beaton one of her last cherished mementos, a scrap from the queen-of-hearts costume de Castiglione once wore to a ball.

Like the countess, Casati doted on her Pekingese dogs. Like the countess, she posed for endless portraits. She once played de Castiglione for the night, hosting a costume ball in 1924, wearing a full-skirted tulle gown scattered with diamonds and carrying a silver hand mirror that had belonged to the countess and which was bought at Montesquiou's estate sale. She made her entrance with a clutch of torchbearers leading the way, even though, fearing fire, the director of the Paris Opéra, where the party was held, had banned any open flames. "If the Opéra burns," Casati assured him, "I'll pay for the damage."

Casati's Castiglione-collecting competitor was another extravagant Parisian, the Polish opera singer Ganna Walska (1887–1984), who landed the 434 photos previously kept by Montesquiou and currently owned by the Metropolitan Museum of Art. Walska, born to a humble family, married a series of thinking men and millionaires, including Alexander Cochran, known as the "richest bachelor in the world." One bought her a theater to sing in, but she didn't have the knack and critics let her know it. (Film historians say Walska inspired Orson Welles's rich, talentless singer in *Citizen Kane.*) Still, as the countess she wasn't half bad. Walska commissioned a play about de Castiglione's life and took the lead, wearing the countess's own dresses and jewelry.

At the end of her life, Walska, like the fabled de Castiglione, retreated from high society. But instead of painting her walls black at her thirty-seven-acre spread in Santa Barbara, California, Lotusland, the diva focused on her flamboyant garden, full of oversize aloes and towering cacti, and writhing with succulents and bromeliads. It's said she sold her jewelry to pay for rare cycad plants. She strolled nude down the garden path when she went for a moonlit dip in the pool. "I am an enemy of the average," she wrote.

CRICKETS

Chirping insects

Rubbing his ridged wings together, the male cricket sings at his best during the last month of his short life, according to the connoisseurs of insect music. Royal courtiers in China kept singing crickets as early as the eighth century, housing the insects they'd caught in small golden cages kept next to their beds. The craze spread, and soon aficionados hung prized crickets around their necks in carved walnut shell cages, a phenomenon that continued into the twentieth century, though even the hardiest cricket will not live much longer than a year. "In passing men in the street you may hear the shrill sound of the insect from its warm and safe place of refuge," reported the Asian scholar Berthold Laufer (1874–1934).

The treasured pets demanded meticulous care. The *Tsu chi king* (*Book of Crickets*), written by a thirteenth-century court official, suggested changing seasonal menus and offered cures for the sick insect. Professional cricket tenders looked after the most pampered flocks, which could include hundreds of chirping pets. The musicians spent their summers in cool pottery jars, decorated inside with tiny blue-and-white porcelain food dishes, and clay beds. During the winter they lived in gourds with fancy carved lids in ivory or sandalwood or jade, nestling into miniature cotton mattresses on cold nights. Cricket keeping wasn't necessarily a cheap hobby, however. The vogue for baroque cages drove some

Beijing nobles into bankruptcy at the end of the nineteenth century. Others lost it all gambling on high-stakes cricket fights. An especially valiant cricket was thought to be the incarnation of a great warrior and was buried in a miniature silver coffin with all due pomp and solemnity.

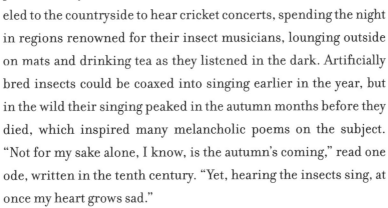

In Japan, listening to crickets was a more wistful pleasure. City dwellers traveled to the countryside to hear cricket concerts, spending the night in regions renowned for their insect musicians, lounging outside on mats and drinking tea as they listened in the dark. Artificially bred insects could be coaxed into singing earlier in the year, but in the wild their singing peaked in the autumn months before they died, which inspired many melancholic poems on the subject. "Not for my sake alone, I know, is the autumn's coming," read one ode, written in the tenth century. "Yet, hearing the insects sing, at once my heart grows sad."

As in China, Japan's markets rang out with singing varieties of all sorts. Tokyo's connoisseurs favored the *korogi* cricket, which, according to nineteenth-century émigré Lafcadio Hearn (1850–1904), sang "kiri-kiri-kiri-kiri!—koro-koro-koro-koro!—ghi-ï-ï-ï-ï-ï-ï!," and the *matsumushi*, whose tune resembled "the sound of an electric bell heard from a distance."

But the most revered insect musician was the *suzumushi*, whose bright song rang out like the bunches of little bells jangled by a dancing Shinto priestess, Hearn noted in his treatise on the subject. "Yes, my dwelling is old: weeds on the roof are growing," read a poem penned in that cricket's honor. "But the voice of the *suzumushi*—that will never be old!"

CUMULONIMBUS

A vast, extremely dense cloud, usually producing heavy storms

Though no one could have predicted the impact he'd have, amateur British meteorologist Luke Howard (1772–1864) changed the way we look at the sky. His cloud classification system in 1802 coined the Latin cloud names known today: cumulus (heaped), stratus (layered), cirrus (curl of hair), and nimbus (rain). The publication of the popular first *International Cloud Atlas* at the end of the nineteenth century expanded the system to encompass ten cloud types, including of course the vast, mountainous cumulonimbus, listed as Cloud Nine. Cumulonimbus was the fluffiest, most billowy and soft-looking, and, therefore, to the poetically minded, a place of bliss, though later editions of the *Atlas* bumped Cloud Nine to the tenth spot.

Howard, a pharmacist, wasn't the first to come up with such a scheme. Just the year before, French scientist Jean-Baptiste Lamarck (1744–1829) had published his own Linnaean cloud system, classifying the frothy formations that floated past his bedroom window during a prolonged illness. Lamarck used French names: *en voile* (hazy), *attroupés* (massed), *pommelés* (dappled), *en balayures* (brooms), and *groupés* (grouped). No one, however, seemed to notice his treatise on the subject.

Lamarck, professor of invertebrates at Paris's Jardin des Plantes, never had it easy. Fifty years before Charles Darwin's *On the Origin of Species* was published, he had presented his theories about how a species evolves and adapts over time, the first theory of evolution. Historians suggest that due to the fervent religious atmosphere in France at the time and to Lamarck's own awkward disposition, he was never taken seriously. In the end, his sole professional distinction was to have coined the word "biology." Today, in Paris's Natural History Museum, his old seashell specimens sit in a small glass case in a dim corner next to an emergency exit.

Meanwhile, Luke Howard's cumulonimbus set the world to dreaming of Cloud Nine, and his cloud drawings directly inspired Romantic painters Joseph Turner and John Constable. Johann

Wolfgang von Goethe (1749–1832) dedicated four poems to Howard's honor and credited him with "bestowing form on the formless and a system of ordered change on a boundless world."

DAHLIAS AND GLADIOLI

Two of the showiest blooms in the average garden

Two celebrated and serious-minded women of letters from either side of the Atlantic, Bloomsbury stalwart Vita Sackville-West (1892–1962) and *New Yorker* editor Katharine S. White (1892–1977), took on the topic of gardening during the twentieth century, each working in a breezy style that brought the arcane poetics of soil and seed to a broad new audience. They besieged their readers with tips—what to plant, when, and how, down to the Epsom salts Sackville-West used to keep rabbits from eating her pinks. And they waxed romantic. White rhapsodized over the colonial-era apple trees and the wildflowers of her girlhood, while Sackville-West suggested her *Observer* readers resurrect the old English word "garth," for a small piece of enclosed ground, and use *floraison*, French for "in full bloom." But both writers were at their best when debating gaudiness in the garden, and what to do with razzle-dazzle flowers such as dahlias and gladioli.

DAHLIA
varieties

White, a true-blue New Englander who worked at *The New Yorker* for more than thirty years, despised ostentation, though she was plenty stylish. She refused, as her husband writer E. B. White (1899–1985) explained, "to dress down to a garden," and dug up plant beds on their thirty-six-acre Maine farm in a tailored tweed skirt and her Ferragamo shoes. But her experiment with a big, bright dahlia crossed the line. "The dahlia is a flower I have never been able to make up my mind about," she admitted. The results were simply "embarrassing." "The flowers were so enormous, one was bright red and the other bronze, and both were as big as dinner plates," she reported. "The only word for them was vulgar."

Sackville-West, who wrote about her gardening triumphs and travails at Sissinghurst Castle in Kent, loved a flourish. "I believe in exaggeration," she declared in 1938. "I believe in big groups, big masses." She stalked weeds while wearing a loosely tailored jacket, jodhpurs, high-laced boots, and her signature strand of pearls. Sackville-West's aristocratic lineage and androgynous allure inspired her lover Virginia Woolf's *Orlando*. She was, as one wit put it, "Lady Chatterley and her lover rolled into one."

But even for the bold Sackville-West, the brazen gladiola was "problematic." Despite its good points (it was "as showy as the dahlia and far less of a nuisance," invaluable for keeping the garden going into fall, and "supreme in the late summer flower shows, yes, in those great peacock-tail displays like swords dipped in all the hues of sunrise, sunset and storm"), the gladiola was top-heavy and suffered a "florist-shop look." Try as she might to romance them, recalling Pliny's thoughts on the flower and remembering the wild gladioli she picked once "at sunset off a mountain in Persia," they never fit the fantasy of her celebrated gardens.

At the start of World War II, as Sackville-West converted the ruined Tudor castle she shared with her husband, writer Harold Nicholson, into a bunker (stashing away a suicide pill in case of German invasion), she became mesmerized by the idea of an all-white garden—the ultimate chic—dreaming of the white magnolias, white tulips, white roses, and white lilies she'd plant there. "Let us plant and be merry," she wrote to Nicholson, "for next autumn we may all be ruined."

It wasn't until the winter of 1949 that she got her plans under way. "It may be a terrible failure," she demurred, describing her all-white strategy in her column. "All the same, I cannot help hoping that the great ghostly barn-owl will sweep silently across a pale garden, next summer, in the twilight—the pale garden that I am now planting under the first flakes of snow." The white garden at Sissinghurst, one of the most elegant gardens in the world, is now open to the public and hits its *floraison* in June.

DARK TOWER

A swank literary salon-cum-nightclub in 1920s Harlem

Manhattanites, intrigued by reports of the exotic nightlife, flocked to Harlem by the droves in the late 1920s, looking for a good time.

The lucky ones made it to A'Lelia Walker's town house on 136th Street. Walker (1885–1931), Harlem's hostess supreme—its "joy goddess," according to Langston Hughes—knew how to throw a party, and her reputation lured luminaries of the Harlem Renaissance, like Hughes and W. E. B. Du Bois, as well as royalty from Europe and the princes of Park Avenue. The thrill was in the mix, rich and poor, black and white.

But "unless you were there early there was no possible way of getting in," Hughes (1902–1967) wrote in his autobiography. "Her parties were as crowded as the New York subway at the rush hour." And her open-door policy meant no preferential treatment for the glitterati. When the crown prince of Sweden couldn't push his way through the throngs one night, he sent word up to Walker, who shrugged and sent a bottle of champagne back down to his car. At another party, she supposedly served chitterlings and bathtub gin to her white guests while her black guests dined on champagne and caviar.

Heiress to her mother's vast hair-care fortune, Walker dressed in turbans and jewels, carried a riding crop, and presided over the family business. Decor in the Dark Tower, the literary nightclub she opened in one wing of her mansion, was just as stunning—a blue Victrola, rosewood chairs, and the walls painted with poems by Hughes and by Countee Cullen. But the club never took off like Walker's house parties. Following the stock market crash of 1929, the white gawkers from downtown were the only patrons willing to pay her steep prices. After several failed attempts, Walker closed the Tower down. "Non-theatrical, non-intellectual Harlem was an unwilling victim of its own vogue," Hughes explained. "It didn't like to be stared at by white folks." The real Saturday-night fun was found at your average Harlem rent party, where you could "do the black-bottom with no stranger behind you trying to do it, too," Hughes remembered. Hosts served bootleg whiskey and fried fish in their small apartments, where the floor-shaking dancing went on till dawn.

Still, for the denizens of Harlem, the closing of the Dark Tower, and Walker's death shortly after, marked the end of an era. Unlike at her parties, mourners came to her funeral by invitation only. Walker was laid out in a silver casket, and a crooning quartet called the Four Bon Bons sang a swinging rendition of Noël Coward's "I'll See You Again." "That was really the end of the gay times," wrote Hughes.

DIVAN

A low, plump couch

The idea of the divan got its start in the East, with the Persian word traveling via Turkey to Europe, where, in the seventeenth century, a "divan" literally meant a sultan's council meeting in which all the attendants sat on cushioned benches. Those comfortable seating arrangements ignited the European imagination, and soon in the West the word "divan" indicated any plush sofa or Eastern-inspired chaise longue, of the sort where an odalisque might languish in her harem, drinking coffee and smoking the afternoon away.

In Western cultures, reclining is suspect. It isn't sitting, exactly, and it isn't lying down, either. There's something a little too suggestive in the pose. In Imperial Rome, men and women alike reclined during their banquets, but, as many of the era's writers pointed out, while the men lay back during meals in earlier times, proper, and more modest, Greek women sat.

In the eighteenth century, the divan promoted the illicit pleasure of reclining, while the provocative tingle of stretching out on a chaise longue burned through the popular psyche. "I then went down to the drawing-room and discovered my lovely one reclining delightfully relaxed on a *chaise longue*," the heavy-breathing narrator of Pierre Choderlos de Laclos's *Les Liaisons dangereuses* (1782) reported. "This excited me and brought a glint into my eyes which I realized would give them an urgent, loving look. I therefore took up a position to ensure that this would have its full effect."

Portrait painters from Manet to David to Sargent took advantage of the situation in the next century, depicting their subjects sprawled across divans, sofas, and chaises, and lending their pictures a whiff of the exotic Orient. Likewise, writers depicted their most glamorous characters lounging. The sultry pose perfectly suited romance writer Marie Corelli's heroine in *Ziska* (1897). "In a half-reclining attitude of indolently graceful ease, the Princess Ziska watched from beneath the slumberous shadow of her long-fringed eyelids," Corelli (1855–1924) wrote.

Not surprisingly, as the cult of reclining spread, it met with disapproval. In 1842 the outspoken etiquette writer Captain Orlando Sabertash advised his male readers to lounge only when in private, railing against "the practice of lounging in graceless attitudes." "All these vile and distorted postures must be reserved for the library-couch, or arm-chair, and should never be displayed in the society of gentlemen, and still less in that of ladies," he wrote, further instructing any lady who found herself face-to-face with a flagrant gentleman lounger to "give the lounger the cut—direct, and go to some other part of the room."

Still, as a piece of furniture, the decorous divan made perfect sense among the exotic knick-knacks and

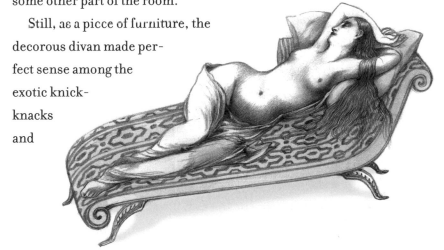

Oriental rugs filling bourgeois living rooms of the era. Getting comfortable on the divan took practice, but it was worth it, as an American writer explained in an 1891 article titled "How to Sit on a Divan." She learned to lounge while in Constantinople, when a Greek man saw her sitting on a Turkish divan, "gingerly upon the very edge, with two neat little toes carefully balanced to touch the floor." "Sit on your foot," he commanded. "Curl it comfortably under you, so. Now be seated, far back, build a wall of cushions about your shoulders, and know true happiness."

ELEPHANTINE COLOSSUS

One of several elephant-shaped buildings erected during the late nineteenth century

American real-estate speculator James V. Lafferty (1856–1898) registered U.S. patent number 268,503 with the central office in 1882, certifying his invention "of a building in the form of an animal, the body of which is floored and divided into rooms." But while Lafferty reserved the legal right to construct buildings of any animal shape, he stuck with that of the elephant, erecting a trio of mammoth structures on the East Coast.

There was the Elephantine Colossus on Coney Island, a hotel

offering a fifty-mile view from its top, high above the seaside lanes where crowds took in boxing matches, slunk into brothels, twirled in the dance halls, and indulged in after-hours "electric bathing" on the artificially lit beach. On Cape May, New Jersey, a smaller, forty-foot elephant building named Light of Asia went up. And just south of Atlantic City, a sixty-five-foot elephant building, called Lucy, offered views over the tidal creeks near the bustling new

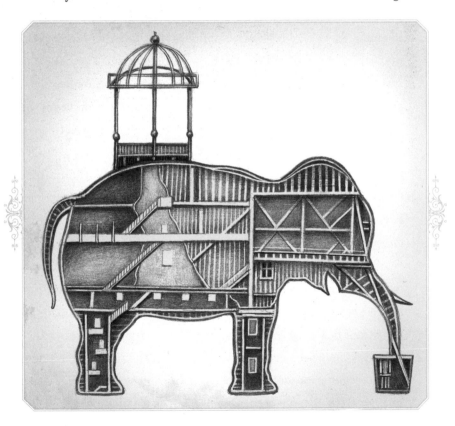

boardwalk, populated with snake charmers and tourists looking for a good pie-eating contest.

Beyond elephantine architecture, the animal enjoyed a cultural moment in mid-nineteenth century America. Gold rushers returning east worked the phrase "seen the elephant" into the vernacular. The term's origins are vague, linked to an apocryphal story about a farmer who crossed paths with a circus elephant when driving his mare to town. The elephant knocked him over, spilled his milk, and broke his eggs, but the wry farmer made the best of his lot, saying at least he had "seen the elephant." Pioneers who had toughed it out traveling west proudly painted elephants on the sides of their covered wagons as a symbol of their triumph over the odds.

In Paris, however, curiosity seekers saw the elephant and then some. Just across from an entrance to the 1899 World's Fair, a temporary amusement park with an *Arabian Nights* theme—the Pays des Fées, or Land of the Fairies—boasted a blue elephant-shaped building whose belly housed an exotic dancer called La Belle Féridjée. When the Pays des Fées shut down, the elephant migrated to the garden behind the Moulin Rouge nightclub, and for a while the vice squad officers who watched over the pleasure spot made its belly their headquarters. Otherwise, for one franc, bellydance aficionados could see performers like La Belle Zhora wriggle inside.

Sometime after the turn of the century, the Moulin Rouge's elephant quietly disappeared. Coney Island's Elephantine Colossus burned to the ground in 1896, and four years later the Light of Asia was razed. The only elephant building left standing is Lafferty's Lucy, just off Route 152 in Margate, New Jersey. Lucy was restored in the 1970s and made a National Historic Landmark.

ENTHUSIASM

"Passionate eagerness," according to The Oxford English Dictionary

In its current watered-down state, the word "enthusiasm," from the ancient Greek *enthousiasmos*—literally "having God in us"— means something like "peppy approval." But during the Enlightenment, when rationality trumped all, enthusiasm was a slur, and understanding its nature preoccupied the era's intellectuals.

Enthusiasm smacked of otherworldly possession, and after the religious wars of the late Renaissance, that notion was dangerous. Early on, poets, who admittedly received their personal lyrical communiqués directly from pagan muses, were accused of being enthusiasts. Like "inspiration," enthusiasm was suspect. A poet, though able to speak wisely, "loves rather to be thought to speak by inspiration, like a bagpipe," snapped English philosopher Thomas Hobbes (1588–1679). Enthusiasm was sneeringly used to describe nonconformists like the Quakers, who trembled and quaked when overcome by the divine. The Quaker "thinks that to be religious one is obliged to be uncivil, and flings his Wits overboard to make room for Inspiration," one pamphleteer stated in 1671. In heavily Protestant Germany, these enthusiasts were known as *Schwärmers*, or swarmers, zealots liable to congregate and to get fired up by a honey-tongued preacher. Enthusiasm was contagious, and implied a lack of self-control that led to ruin.

All that changed over the course of the eighteenth century. The word "fanaticism" replaced "enthusiasm" when describing religious zealotry. And the poet's inspiration was deemed sane. The thinkers of the day argued that the poets, through their art, demonstrated "rational enthusiasm," which, though extreme, was still governed by reason. "It begins as a trembling in his chest and passes in a wonderful and rapid way to the extremes of the body," wrote Denis Diderot (1713–1784), describing the poet's experience. "Not only a trembling, but a strong permanent heat which embraces him, excites him, kills him, but gives spirit and life to all that he touches." It might sound like the Quakers' shaking, but it was acceptable. Soon William Wordsworth (1770–1850) admitted that he succumbed to a "spontaneous overflow of powerful feeling" when he worked. So did Blake. So did Percy Shelley (1792–1822), who wrote, "We are aware of evanescent visitations of thought and feeling sometimes associated with place or person, sometimes regarding our own mind alone, and always arising unforeseen and departing unbidden, but elevating and delightful beyond all expression."

None of the era's writers, however, was more enthusiastic about enthusiasm than authoress Germaine de Staël (1766–1817), who described enthusiasm as the love of beauty. It was of a higher moral stuff than lowly passion, goading on the thinkers, the sensitive types, and the warriors alike. "Enthusiasm is the emotion that offers us the greatest happiness, the only one that offers it to us," she proclaimed, "the only one able to sustain human destiny in whatever situation destiny places us."

FANFARE

A flourish sounded by horns, often accompanied by timpani

Court musicians led the merrymaking for centuries by sounding the fanfare, a trilling flourish of trumpets joined by a big rumble of kettledrums louder than the roar of a runaway Mack truck. The rousing sound was first heard in the mid-thirteenth century by European Crusaders positioned across the battlefield from their Moorish opponents, who unleashed a symphonic uproar made "as if with glittering thunderbolts." A big-time sultan might travel with as many as sixty-eight musicians, including some twenty trumpeters and forty kettledrummers, joined by those on the oboelike shawm, and soon every European princeling had to have his own trumpet-and-kettledrum troupe, too.

In 1457 a squad of timpanists played Turkish cauldron drums on horseback while leading a massive embassy representing King Ladislas V of Hungary in his proposal of marriage to the French king's daughter, and including over five hundred courtiers, seven hundred plumed horses, and twenty-six baggage wagons weighed down with gifts. In the next century, at Queen Elizabeth I's court twelve trumpets and two timpanists "made the hall ring." Meanwhile, her contemporary Maximilian the Great of Bavaria traveled with twenty imperial trumpeters and four timpanists, announcing him wherever he went. The effect was majestic—and loud.

Fanfares were never sounded once, but three times, resounding with long trilling chords, fanciful arpeggios, and a drawn-out drumroll. Court composers wrote special fanfares for pageants, and before any fancy meal, a fanfare called the *corner l'eau* let guests know it was time to wash their hands. Another outburst accompanied the presentation of the first course. A trill punctuated every toast. A fanfare announced the host's entrances and exits. Another came at the end of the meal. Another kicked off the dancing. And a final fanfare told guests it was time to go home.

From the fifteenth century through the eighteenth century in Germany, only nobles above a certain rank were allowed to employ trumpeters and timpanists, provoking competition among aristocrats to see who could hire the most. Occasionally, a city magistrate might convince—or bribe—a local sovereign to issue a *Trompeter-freibrief* permit, allowing trumpeters and drummers to play at some civic ceremony. But for the most part members of the trumpeters' guild, which included timpanists, were forbidden to perform at lowbrow weddings or public dances. They ranked as officers in the military, since they led the troops to battle. They were allowed to wear ostrich feathers in their hats, as nobles did, and were prohibited from fraternizing with musicians outside the guild, like the lowly lute players and side drummers, who were considered mere servants. Conversely, nonguild musicians weren't allowed to play—or to even own—a kettledrum or a trumpet. When word spread that a nonguild musician in Hanover kept a trumpet in the late 1600s, wild-eyed guild members broke into his house, snatched his contraband horn, and knocked his teeth out with it.

Eventually, the old European courts disbanded. The trumpeters' guild dissolved, and its members finally joined their peers in the regular orchestra. But not before the fanfare returned to its roots. Inspired by Ottoman military marches, composers such as Mozart and Beethoven wrote exotic music *alla Turca* in the late eighteenth century, evocative pieces so popular that manufacturers built "Turkish" pedals into pianos, one of which simply thumped the wooden frame, simulating the timpani.

Drummers in military bands of that era wore turbans, while King Augustus II of Poland hired his own twelve-man Ottoman band, one that came recommended by a friendly sultan. Empress Anne of Russia sent to Istanbul for her group, and the Viennese Hapsburgs and the Prussian king in Berlin followed. Out on the march, the Ottoman bandleaders beat time, pounding the ground with long poles topped with jangles at every step they took. The tradition left its mark on the American drum major, leading a parade with his staff, and on the football game's drum majorettes, twirling their ceremonial batons during the halftime show.

FAR NIENTE

Sweet idleness

The languorous sweetness of doing nothing at all—*far niente* in Italian—is one of life's great pleasures. Few know it better than the strolling French flaneur, "that passionate spectator," who is a connoisseur of doing nothing, as Charles Baudelaire (1821–1867) noted. But decorous loungers throughout history have sung idleness's praises. The great woman of letters Madame de Sévigné (1626–1696), for one, wrote to her daughter about a motto she'd carved into one of the trees at her country estate. "Only yesterday I had inscribed in honor of lazy people: *bella cosa far niente.*" It's beautiful to do nothing.

While the French found lackadaisical bliss at home, others went straight to the source—Italy, where the easygoing ways and the sunny climate lulled visitors into a stupor. "All my activity of mind, all my faculties of thought and feeling and suffering, seemed lost and swallowed up in an indolent delicious reverie, a sort of vague and languid enjoyment, the true '*dolce far niente*,'" swooned Irish travel writer Anna Jameson (1794–1860), pondering the sweetness of idling in Naples. "I stood so long leaning on my elbow without moving, that my arm has been stiff all day in consequence."

The trouble was, too much idleness, however sweet, led to ennui. Lord Byron (1788–1824) noted that his English peers had "form'd of two mighty tribes, the Bores and Bored." The eponymous hero of Henry James's "Benvolio" suffered from the fashionable malaise. "Idleness, everyone admitted, was the greatest of follies," James (1843–1916) wrote, "but idleness was subtle, and exacted tribute under a hundred plausible disguises . . . Ennui was at the end of everything that did not multiply our relations with life." As Benvolio well knew, there was no better antidote to ennui than a torrid love affair.

Naughtiness born of leisure enraged sixteenth-century Protestant John Northbrooke, who denounced idleness as "the fountayne and well spring whereout is drawne a thousande mischiefes," including "whoredome, theft, murder, breaking of wedlocke, perjurie, idolatrie, poperie, &c.vaine playes, filthy pastimes, and drunkeness." Colonial Connecticut law demanded, "No person,

Householder or other, shall spend their time idly or unprofitably." (In a twist of logic, during the Great Depression civic authorities encouraged hobbies—like stamp collecting and woodworking—as a moral way to keep the unemployed occupied.)

Of course, the puritanical have opposed idleness since biblical times. Spiritual sloth was the "noonday demon" that distracted a monk from his prayers, a dreamy listlessness that "forces him to step out of his cell and to gaze at the sun to see how far it still is from the night hour, and to look around, here and there, whether any of his brethren is near," wrote the acclaimed preacher Evagrius Ponticus (349–399), describing the ancient equivalent of Facebook addiction.

History's most persuasive defender of the right to *far niente* was Robert Louis Stevenson (1850–1894), who diagnosed extreme busyness as "a symptom of deficient vitality." "There is a sort of dead-alive, hackneyed people about, who are scarcely conscious of living except in the exercise of some conventional occupation," he explained in his 1876 screed, "An Apology for Idlers." "They have no curiosity; they can not give themselves over to random provocations; they do not take pleasure in the exercise of their faculties for its own sake; and unless Necessity lays about them with a stick, they will even stand still. It is no good speaking to such folk: they can not be idle, their nature is not generous enough; and they pass those hours in a sort of coma, which are not dedicated to furious moiling in the goldmill."

Cleopatra knew the power of glimmering gems and big pearls, like the one she famously dropped into a glass of vinegar and drank in order to impress Mark Antony. For those with Cleopatra's taste, if not her budget, Egypt's faux pearls and perfect glass emerald and amethyst beads were plenty opulent. They were worn by rich and poor alike.

Faux jewels have enchanted the most discerning trendsetters for centuries. In Europe, formulas for concocting faux pearls have circulated since the third century. Leonardo da Vinci (1452–1519) recommended dissolving small pearls in lemon juice, then reconstituting the resulting paste with egg whites to "make pearls as large as you wish." Others called for baking powdered-glass mixtures bound with gum arabic or the "slime of snails." (No word on whether these recipes actually work.)

Queen Elizabeth I got a good deal in 1566, scooping up 520 tantalizing faux pearls manufactured by Venetian glassblowers at a penny apiece to trim her fluffy ruffs. In the next century, the Parisian rosary maker Monsieur Jacquin improved on the Venetian technique. He accidentally left a package of bleak fish—a small fish from the Seine—in a tub of water and later found they gave off a pearly substance. After cleverly concentrating this fishy liquor, with a tiny straw he blew a single drop into a hollow glass bead, shaking it around until the liquid coated the inside, then filled the bead with wax. Jacquin's pearly syrup, which became popular worldwide, was called *essence d'Orient*, a "pompous name invented for the sole purpose of concealing the true nature of the material from which it was prepared," one nineteenth-century science writer huffed. The scales of four thousand fish yielded four ounces of *essence*, but all in all those beads were a bargain when compared with genuine pearls.

Similarly, faux faceted jewelry developed over time. "Take the comb of a cock," begins a sixteenth-century recipe for diamonds, which goes on to describe the lengthy method of cooking it down into a gem. Some counterfeiters took an easier route, crafting doublets, made from two pieces of glass glued on either side of a piece of colored foil.

For the hypervirtuous, the false flash of faux pearls and paste jewels, as mock diamonds were called, was problematic. In her essay *Illustrations of Lying*, English author Amelia Opie (1769–1853) took on the topic, categorizing the wearing of paste as a "practical lie." "But on these occasions, the motive is not always the mean and contemptible wish of imposing on the credulity of others," Opie reasoned. Rather, wearing paste indicated a fair dose of devious ambition. "The lady who purchases and wears paste which she hopes will pass for diamonds is usually one who has no right to wear jewels at all," she hissed.

Opie's snobbery aside, leaded-glass diamonds had come into their own during the rococo era with plenty of glittering support.

Not only were they less expensive than the real thing, they were more versatile. While frugality didn't save Marie Antoinette in the end, the French queen glistened with imitation diamonds. Today, the modern diamond alternative, cubic zirconia, sparkles far and wide. And in 1996 a three-strand faux-pearl necklace worn by America's own fashion queen, Jackie Kennedy Onassis, was sold at auction for $211,500.

FELINES

Members of the cat family

The cat was one of the last wild species to turn domestic, after dogs, sheep, goats, cows, pigs, horses, chickens, and even water buffalo. Ancient Egyptians tamed the first house cats, revering them as representatives of the cat-headed sun goddess, Bastet. When a pet cat died, the entire family went into mourning, shaving their eyebrows as a sign of respect and burying the animal in vast underground vaults. Anyone who killed a cat paid with his life. It's understandable. If ever an animal acted goddesslike, it's the imperious, gluttonous, graceful cat.

The idea of keeping a cat as a pet didn't catch on quickly in the West. Exporting precious Egyptian cats was illegal, and the Greeks and Romans kept ferrets instead. In medieval Europe, cats were accused of being in cahoots with the devil. As late as the eighteenth century, the French scientist Georges-Louis Leclerc, the Count de Buffon (1707–1788), described cats with disgust. Kittens were cute, but "they have an innate malice, a falseness of character, a perverse nature, which age augments and education can only mask." Worse, the female cat was overtly sexual, the count claimed. She announced "her desires by her piercing cries, or rather, the excess of her needs."

Conversely, by the twentieth century the cat's sexy, slinky reputation was appreciated by bohemians, intellectuals, and some extremely glamorous women, who upped the ante by taking in leopards as pets, including Josephine Baker (1906–1975) and Hollywood vamp Pola Negri (1897–1987). As they proved, no animal makes a more stunning sidekick than a glowering great cat.

At age fourteen, Baker, born in the slums of East St. Louis and already separated from her first of five husbands, had struck out on her own to join a vaudeville troupe. She was deemed too dark and too skinny to join Broadway's chorus line, but eventually landed a role clowning across the stage as the "end girl," the one who couldn't quite keep up with the rest and crossed her eyes and goofed around instead. By 1925, Baker had polished her act. Performing the Charleston wearing nothing but a few pink flamingo feathers, she thrilled Paris with her shimmying audacity. Offstage, she was just as flamboyant, walking her leopard, Chiquita, down

the Champs-Élysées as people sitting in the outdoor cafés gasped. Fashion queen Diana Vreeland (1903–1989) saw the pair at a movie theater in Montmartre and after the show watched admiringly as Baker's cat pulled its mistress to an enormous white Rolls-Royce at the curb, then "whooped" into the backseat in a single bound. "Ah! What a gesture!" Vreeland wrote. "I've never seen anything like it. It was speed at its best, and style."

Baker's bravado was matched in Hollywood by Pola Negri, born in Poland and imported to the United States to play the exotic, kohl-eyed vamp in dozens of silent films. Negri, who ordered the floor of her dressing room strewn with orchid petals, lived in a Hollywood Hills replica of Mount Vernon, drove a Rolls, and paraded her pet leopard along Sunset Boulevard. She is best remembered, however, for throwing herself onto the casket of her lover Rudolph Valentino and fainting during his funeral. "I am a Slav. I cannot help that I have not the restraint of the Anglo-Saxon," she told skeptics. The scene turned her into something of a joke.

Redemption came in Negri's last picture, Disney's *Moon-Spinners* (1963), in which she played a sinister Egyptian millionairess, Madame Habib, an eccentric dripping with jewels. The part "was really rather autobiographical," Negri wrote in her memoirs. So, Negri suggested to the producers, why not exchange Madame's Siamese cat for something a little more appropriate—like a cheetah? Together she and the cat, Kima, wowed fans waiting at the door of her London hotel during the filming. "Miss Negri swept in with a friend. Friend being a three-year-old cheetah straining at its steel chain," one newspaper reported. An old hand with the big cats, Negri didn't flinch when Kima lashed out at a man in the crowd. "Stop that, darling," she coolly scolded the feline, "you will frighten the gentleman."

FIREWORKS

Explosive devices set off to generate colored flares and lots of noise

Built to delight, the earliest fireworks were made with potent, sulfurous gunpowder, long before gunpowder was used as a weapon. "Flames of fire move round the wheel. Peach blossoms spring forth from the falling branches. Clouds of smoke move round the house, and the fairy lake reflects the floating lights," wrote one seventh-century Chinese courtier, rhapsodizing over fireworks, or, as they were more dramatically known then, "fire drug plays."

During the sixteenth and seventeenth centuries, Europe erupted in a flurry of sparks with fireworks set off for almost any good reason—coronations, religious festivals, military victories, noble weddings, or royal births. Safety standards were loose. "Men masked as wild giants who by means of fireballs and wheels hurled sparks in the faces of the mob," was how the Venetian ambassador described London's professional "green men," who hid under hideous masks and a layer of lush green leaves to protect themselves as they spewed crackling flames to clear the way for Anne Boleyn's 1533 coronation pageant.

Over the next century, two distinct European pyrotechnic traditions developed: that of the north, favored by the experts from Nuremberg and typified by more stately, straightforward displays, and that of the south, defined by Italy's narrative shows, where allegorical drama fueled the action. In the northern tradition, the 1749 marriage of King Louis XV's twelve-year-old daughter to Philip V's eighteen-year-old son was celebrated with a slew of rockets that formed an exploding sun against the night sky, and, in flaming blue, the young couple's initials. By contrast, in the south, Italian pyrotechnicians once staged a mock naval battle that erupted in a rain of rockets. They also rigged up a mechanical Jupiter who hurled thunderbolts, sent Saint George after a faux fire-breathing dragon, and prompted Love to face off against Evil in an allegorical blaze of glory.

Most famous of all were Rome's ground-shaking displays, put on at the Castel Sant'Angelo every Easter from the fifteenth through the nineteenth centuries (by which time officials realized that the yearly explosions had damaged the ancient castle's foundation). "It seems as if the sky has opened, and that all the stars are falling to Earth," wrote the Italian metallurgist Vannoccio Biringuccio (1480–1537), describing the sight in his book *Pirotechnia*.

Biringuccio wrote about artillery design and casting metal bells, but reserved his zeal for gunpowder's stunning effects. "From these fires composed of forceful and horrible materials bringing harm and terror to men, a happy and pleasing effect is also produced," he marveled, "and, instead of fleeing from it, the people willingly go to see it."

"Fireworks," Biringuccio concluded, "had no other purpose than amusement, and endured no longer than the kiss of a lover for his lady, if as long." The exhilaration was fleeting—and eternal.

FOLLY

Any costly structure demonstrating the foolhardiness of its builder

Architectural fascination gave rise to plenty of lofty landmarks in the late nineteenth century, but those erected by two particularly obsessed builders stand out: King Ludwig of Bavaria's neo-Gothic castle Neuschwanstein, and Spanish architect Antoni Gaudí's extravagant Church of the Sagrada Família in Barcelona.

King Ludwig (1845–1886), a grandiose, melancholy aesthete, took the throne at eighteen, but was never quite comfortable there. At the outbreak of war with Prussia, he ran away and was later found in a dark room reading poetry aloud and dressed as the hero of an old fairy tale. But his dreamworld spilled over into reality most spectacularly through the building projects he initiated during his reign.

Of his three castles, Neuschwanstein—literally translated as "new-swan-stone"—was his favorite, styled as a turreted thirteenth-century palace like those in the story of Lohengrin, a folktale about a German prince who morphed into a swan, which Wagner made into an opera. Nothing about the project was easy. Workers built a steep road up to the site, a precipitous rock outcropping which offered vast views across the Tyrol in 1869. Once the castle itself was under way, unreasonable deadlines and Ludwig's obsession for detail often pushed work through the night. It took fourteen carpenters more than four years to complete the carving in his bedroom alone. A trapdoor in the dining room allowed the table to be lowered into the kitchen and set while the servants remained out of sight. The throne room was decorated in fantasy Byzantine style. A stalactite grotto off of Ludwig's study came complete with a waterfall and an electric "moon" moving through its phases. (Neuschwanstein's staggering exterior, with its spindly towers, served as a model for Sleeping Beauty's castle at Disneyland.)

When his construction expenses outstripped his resources, Ludwig wrote to neighboring rulers, asking for loans. Architecture was his vice. "I do not go in for ordinary amusements of men because they disgust me and are fatally against my nature," he explained. Accused of insanity in 1886, the king called the district medical officer to the castle, demanding a second opinion. "I have been in practice for many years and have rarely come across anyone completely normal," the doctor concluded, hedging his bets. Regardless, Ludwig was deposed and mysteriously died two days later, drowned in a lake. After seventeen years of construction, Neuschwanstein was still unfinished. Ludwig had lived there for only 172 days.

Another mystical-minded brooder of the same era, Gaudí (1852–1926) worked on the Sagrada Família church in Barcelona over a period of thirty-one years, and never finished it. It should have been a routine assignment, as another architect had already designed the church when Gaudí stepped in. But under his command, the bold basilica bloomed into a massive molten sculpture of undulating foliage, vegetables and fruits, birds, insects and animals, and spiky stalactite spires. The interior was designed to seat thirteen thousand. The towers grew to three hundred feet tall. Gaudí's vision was, as Salvador Dalí (1904–1989) put it, of a "terrifying and edible beauty."

Gaudí dedicated the last twelve years of his life to the project, hitting up wealthy patrons for money directly, and, as legend has it, begging for funds on the street. Though once a dandy, he became increasingly religious and austere, living inside the church as a celibate vegetarian isolated from any distractions. His approach became more and more fantastical. He "tried to put into effect each day what the Virgin Mary had revealed to him the night before," one of his supporters explained.

In 1926 Gaudí was run over by a trolley while on his way to mass and died, having lived to see only a fraction of his church completed. His funeral procession stretched for half a mile, from the hospital to Sagrada's crypt, where he was buried. Though history brands Ludwig a madman, the Vatican initiated the beatification process of Gaudí in 2003. His church is scheduled for completion in the first half of the twenty-first century.

FRILLY LINGERIE

Women's lacy undergarments and nightclothes

Underwear has existed in one form or another for centuries. Frilly lingerie, on the other hand, exploded in an exuberant froth of hidden lace flounces, secreted ribbons, and saucy bows at the turn of the nineteenth century, when the Victorians' stately white drawers and chaste chemises made way for something prettier.

"A virtuous woman has a repugnance to excessive luxury in her underclothing," the prim Baroness Staffa declared in 1892. Thankfully, while the baroness could condemn lingerie, she couldn't stem the tide of frills. As the new century opened, suddenly, no woman could "produce the effect of true chic," the Marquise de Panhael explained to American *Vogue* readers, without employing the new "marvels of lingerie adopted by all sincerely elegant women."

Their frills were stacked high: first a woman slipped into her featherweight chemise, tied with bows at the shoulders; next came a satin corset, more lax than the midcentury model; this she topped with the corset cover, a fluttery camisole in embroidered thin silk. Flouncy knee length knickers went on over embroidered silk stockings and under two petticoats—the lower, in muslin with ruffles in *broderie anglaise*, and the outer in satin or taffeta, and decorated with rosettes, lover's knots, or chiffon ruching. Considering the sensual froth of such froufrou, the tradition of showing the bridal trousseau to wedding guests became indecent.

Beyond the Parisian cabarets, where you could see it all, lingerie was a private indulgence. English authoress Marian Pritchard, aka Mrs. Eric Pritchard, proffered a link between "daintily perfumed lingerie, and a love of art and poetry" in her book *The Cult of Chiffon* (1902). Pritchard's pampered woman was well stocked with "much befrilled" underskirts, alluring Japanese kimonos, and diaphanous peignoirs. She knew how to tie a tulle bow, and displayed "that delicious coquetry which no woman can afford to disdain." After all, Pritchard reasoned, why should the courtesans and cancan girls have all the fun? "And why in the name of the sister-hood of women should we leave all the pretty arts and subtleties of everyday life to a class of women less favoured than ourselves?" she demanded. "Can one wonder that marriage is so often a failure, and that the English husband of such a class of woman goes where he can admire the petticoat of aspirations?"

Like Mrs. Pritchard, Lucile—aka the provocative British couturiere Lady Duff-Gordon (1863–1935)—made it her mission to banish ugly, puritanical underwear. "I started making underclothes as delicate as cobwebs and as beautifully tinted as flowers, and half the women in London flocked to see them, though they had not the courage to buy them at first," she remembered in her memoirs. They came around, sidling into Lucile's notorious Rose Room in Mayfair and leaving with inconspicuous packages full of illicit frills.

Her collection of evening gowns, worn by stars like Anna Held, Lily Langtry, and Irene Castle, was just as provocative. Lucile's dresses boasted names like "Passion's thrall," "Do you love me?," and even "Red Mouth of a Venomous Flower," titles thought up by her novelist sister, Elinor Glyn (1864–1943), the first writer to use the term " 'It' girl" to mean a woman with sex appeal. Together, the two sisters ushered in a glamorous, sensuous new era full of pleasure and lingerie.

The young heroine in Elinor's novel *The Visits of Elizabeth* pondered these new freedoms in 1900. "The Rooses told me it wasn't 'quite nice' for girls to loll in hammocks (and they sat on chairs)—that you could only do it when you are married," she wrote, "but I believe it is because they don't have pretty enough petticoats. Anyway . . . as I knew my 'frillies' were all right, I hammocked too, and it was lovely."

GIOCHI D'ACQUA

Whimsical waterworks and trick fountains of the Renaissance garden

Garden designers of the Italian Renaissance scoured ancient sources for witty, watery ways to keep their wealthy patrons laughing with *giochi d'acqua*, or "water jokes." In the era's formal gardens, that meant hydraulically powered statues suddenly came to life, shimmering rainbows appeared in the sky seemingly from nowhere, and hidden jets left unsuspecting visitors soaked to the bone.

At Villa Pratolino, one of the most impressive of such sites, a massive rushing aqueduct powered the garden's waterworks, designed for Francesco de' Medici by architect-engineer Bernando Buontalenti (1531–1608). There, a mechanical swan dipped its head into a garden pool, an automated nymph rose from a reed bed, the Greek god Pan piped a watery tune, and a gigantic washerwoman wrung out her cloth. In a dining-room grotto, an automatic hydro-servant greeted guests while an intricate wheel system delivered meals from the kitchen. "Slender pissings of water" overarched a long pathway so that "a man on horseback may ride under it and not be wet one drop," as visitor John Evelyn (1620–1706) noted, while in another grotto French writer Michel de Montaigne (1533–1592) discovered "seats [that] squirt up water to your backside." One last *gioco d'acqua* ensnared anyone left dry and running for cover up a flight of stairs, spraying the fugitive with "a thousand jets of water" that sprang from every second step. Medici's guests were "at the same time both tricked and astonished," as one noted.

In the gardens of another grand palace, the Villa d'Este in Tivoli, an automated owl menaced a musical, water-powered aviary, silencing all the other mechanical birds when he swooped into sight, a nifty sequence borrowed from the Greek mathematician Hero of Alexandria, who wrote about pneumatics in the first century. Meanwhile, the Florentine Francini brothers exported their classically rigged magic to Henri IV's gardens at Saint-Germain-en-Laye in 1589, installing Orpheus in a fountain flanked by automated animals. Bacchus sat drinking on a barrel while a mechanical organ player filled the garden with music and Perseus plunged his sword into a dragon rising from a great pool.

The trend continued in the 1630s, when, with an arsenal of pumps, waterwheels, and valves, Salomon de Caus and his brother Isaac filled the garden at England's Wilton House with "toys" and "freak jets," as one visitor recalled. The garden was chockablock with devious inventions. *Giochi* included a tabletop pierced by a hidden jet that could toss heavy objects up into the air, a mechanical sea monster, and statues that sprinkled tears on any passersby. Hydraulic birds sang the "melody of Nightingerlls," drawing the curious into a grotto, which triggered devices "to wett the Strangers," as guest Celia Fiennes (1662–1741) noted.

By the end of the eighteenth century, however, such waterlogged amusements were thought passé. The ninth Earl of Pembroke destroyed "the old ridiculous water works and whims" at Wilton House, while the grounds at Villa Pratolino were transformed in 1819 into a more stately—and definitely more boring—English garden.

GLOVES

Hand coverings made with a separate sheath for each finger and for the thumb

Gloves boast an obvious utility, but when exaggerated—say, delicately embroidered or done up with gems—they're just as likely to get in the way. Yet, over the centuries, gloves became both a part of daily life and a symbol of seduction.

While the sensible Greeks and Romans only wore gloves to protect their hands when gardening, after the sixth century Christian bishops put them on to say mass, keeping their Bibles extra tidy and lending gloves a new cachet. They ascended quickly from there, and by the Middle Ages a king's glove served as a proxy for the king himself, whether entrusted to a messenger as a sign of his good faith or guaranteeing safe passage to a traveler carrying the five-fingered talisman. French kings gave their gloves to their sons on their deathbeds. At any English king's coronation a friend to the monarch-to-be dashed his glove to the ground—"throwing down the gauntlet"—as a challenge to anyone opposing the proceedings. Gloves also symbolized honor. Striking a medieval knight with a glove was an invitation to brawl. Once the time and place were set, the duelists exchanged gloves as a promise to return for the fight.

But as an item of feminine fashion—and of fetish—gloves signified fidelity of a different sort. A medieval lover gave gloves to his mistress during a formal betrothal ceremony, and when a lady gave up a glove, it was proof of her favor. Shakespeare's Cressida dreamed of Troilus covering a glove she'd left him with "memorial dainty kisses." Queen Elizabeth's favorite, George Clifford, third Earl of Cumberland, wore her bejeweled glove folded and set on his helmet just above his forehead, while another devotee, Robert Devereux, tied one of the queen's gloves to his arm, over his armor, with a silver ribbon.

In those days, European royals and aristocrats hoarded and traded gloves with a frenzy. Universities gave gloves to visiting dignitaries. The rich gave their servants gloves with money inside. Pardoned criminals presented gloves to their judges, a custom later outlawed. As a prewedding gift in 1599, Philip II of Spain gave his bride, the Archduchess Margaret, two hundred pairs of gloves.

There were as many customs surrounding glove wearing as there were styles of gloves to choose from. Women's gloves were perfumed with musk and ambergris, rampantly embroidered with flowers, butterflies, and birds, and decorated with jeweled buttons, though some had slits at the knuckles to show off the rings worn underneath. Soft chicken-skin gloves came into fashion in the seventeenth century, as did "limericks," made in Limerick, Ireland, from the skin of unborn calves. Others were pieced together from rat skin, mouse skin, dog skin, or kid. (An eighteenth-century French naturalist managed to succeed in making a pair from woven spider's silk.) The finest could be packed into a nutshell, and many were valuable enough to be willed to the next generation.

Fads in length and color came and went, but long or short, trimmed or plain, well into the twentieth century no lady would venture out into public without them. Fashion-conscious women of the rococo era changed their gloves five times a day and left them on while eating meals and when playing the harp or clavier. Conversely, a noble with gloved hands could touch nothing of value. Friends were always offered a bare handshake, a custom that continues to this day.

Pulling gloves on and off again was a ceremonial nuisance. But occasionally, for men, the rules were warped for practicality's sake. On a hot day a gentleman should leave his gloves on to shake hands with a lady rather than offer her a sweaty palm, one nineteenth-century etiquette writer explained. "If it be off, why, all very well," he concluded, "but it is better to run the risk of being considered ungallant than to present a clammy, ungloved hand."

HEELS

Shoes built up at the sole to make the wearer taller

Since the seventeenth century, when high heels appeared in Venice, they've given fashion lovers a saucy boost. "This place is much frequented by the walking May-poles," wrote a visitor to Venice in 1648. "I mean the women . . . they walke betweene two handmaids, majestically deliberating of every step they take." Stylish Venetian women of the era wore *chopines*, sculpted platform shoes modeled after those that Turkish women wore to the baths, and decorated with stamped leather, inlaid with silver foil, painted with lacquer, tufted in silk, or studded with jewels. The shoes reached staggering heights, with some built to over twelve inches, which left the Venetians teetering, clinging to their servants below or to long walking sticks. Still, despite their peril, high heels became fashionable across Europe. When Charles I met his future queen, Henrietta Maria (1609–1669), she seemed taller than reported, and he suspected she was wearing *chopines*. "Sir, I stand upon mine own feet," she said, lifting her hem an inch to prove it. "I have no help of art; thus high I am, and am neither higher nor lower."

Over the years, as trends changed, high heels were alternately reviled as an emblem of evil vanity or celebrated for their pretty artistry. Yet no woman down through the ages has stirred up as much fuss with her footwear as Marilyn Monroe (1926–1962), whose signature stilettoed stride was purring provocation. Even before she was famous, her heel-enhanced walk got her noticed. Groucho Marx (1890–1977) remembered sitting with a film producer to audition three young actresses for a bit part in *Love Happy* (1949). Each woman walked across the room, then the producer asked Marx to choose one of them. "How can you take anybody except that last girl?" Marx told him. "The whole room revolved when she walked." Marilyn got the part—one of her first film roles.

Sure, other actresses wore heels. In fact, most of them did. But Marilyn knew how to use hers to sex up her stride and further her career. She was, as one wit put it, "Jell-O on springs," her spike heels providing a sexy contrast to her baby-doll whisper. Working her heels overtime at the beginning of her fame, she played a curvaceous secretary with a slinky walk in *As Young as You Feel*. For her role in *The Asphalt Jungle*, she performed what she called "a rather self-conscious slither." But her walk in *Niagara* (1953) gave Monroe her star turn and caused a furor. Wearing strappy black stilet-tos, she took a languorous, 116-foot stroll toward the falls while the camera tracked behind her, steamy innuendo in every sway of her hips. Newspaper columnists claimed to be scandalized. Monroe shot back, "I learned to walk as a baby and I haven't had a lesson since." One of her husbands, Arthur Miller (1915–2005), vouched for the unadulterated sexiness and authenticity of her strut. "It was, in fact, her natural walk," he wrote in his autobiography. "Her foot-prints on a beach would be in a straight line, the heel descending exactly before the last toeprint, throwing her pelvis into motion."

Gossip columnist Jimmy Starr (1904–1990) offered a less inno-cent explanation, claiming that Monroe's dizzying gait was artifice after all: "She learned a trick of cutting a quarter of an inch off one heel so that when she walked, that little fanny would wiggle."

 ## HELLO

A word used in greeting, especially over the telephone

In one guise or another, "hallo," "halloo," and "hullo" have been used to solicit attention and signal surprise since the Middle Ages. Hunters urged on their dogs with "halloo," and the word was also used to signal a ferryboat captain from across the water. (Some etymologists say it originated with the Old French *Ho là!*, meaning "stop" or "pay attention.") As a greeting, "hello" had a gutsy, modern air in the late nineteenth century. It was sleeker than "Do I get you?," another early option for those greeting each other over the telephone, and it was more suave than England's awkward choice, "Are you there?" "Hello" was "a thorough-bred bulldog, ugly enough to be attractive," one journalist wrote in 1899. "It makes courtesy wait upon dispatch, and reminds us that we live in an age when it is necessary to be wide awake."

For those who normally spoke only with people to whom they'd been introduced, striking a balance between politesse and wasting time was tricky when greeting faceless strangers over the primitive, buzzing phone lines. Delays and disconnections exasperated early subscribers. In the beginning, tough young men working the switchboards in the din and clamor of the lawless central offices, like the Chicago exchange, known as "a howling madhouse," happily battled complainers. They were soon replaced by the less abrasive "Hello Girl," whom we now know as the operator. She flirted instead of fighting and quickly became a national archetype, known for her honeyed voice and her love of gossip. In a small town, she'd even tell you the train schedule.

In the name of efficiency, Hello Girls received elocution lessons after the turn of the century. Then, in a further attempt to improve service, they were instructed to answer all calls with a curt "Number?" Callers bristled and the Girls went back to "Hello." By the late 1920s, however, some company executives across the country banned the word again, with operators restricted to the phrases "Number, please?" and "Thank you." "Synthetic courtesy is not soft and sentimental," opined the *New York Times*. "It is hard and virile."

Something about "hello" just felt right. Nevertheless, as late as 1937 the New York telephone company tried to kill it once more, advising subscribers to answer their own phones with only their name, or company name, and recommending above all that callers "avoid such old-fashioned, indefinite and time-wasting words as 'hello.'"

ITALICS

A slanting font used in printing

Try as he might, Venetian publisher Aldus Manutius (1449–1515) couldn't keep printers across Europe from counterfeiting his new font, an elegantly slanting cursive he called Aldine. Books illegally using the typeface appeared almost as soon as he introduced it in 1501. Germans called it "Cursiv." The French called it "Italic." The Italians called it "Aldino." And, though Manutius's exclusive use of the font was protected by the Venetian Senate, everyone forged it.

Italics, with its informal, handwritten look, perfectly suited Aldine editions—mostly reedited books of poetry, and classical literature—which were affordable and portable, unlike the era's massive tomes. In turn, the spread of printed italics across Europe spurred a revolution in handwriting, which gradually lost its pointiness and took the more rounded look of today's cursive.

There was never a book more closely associated with Aldine's italics than the press's 1501 edition of Francesco Petrarch's (1304–1374) poetry, which was the first book printed in italics and, editors claimed, was "taken from the very handwriting of the poet." This rumor gave rise to the notion that the font was based on Petrarch's own hand. Ever since, paleographers have analyzed the poet's every pen stroke, comparing his handwriting to italics, with conflicting results.

Like a true proto-Renaissance man, Petrarch thrilled to the classics, collecting ancient Roman coins, visiting the ruins of antiquity, and writing letters to long-dead idols, such as Cicero and Seneca, when he wasn't crafting odes to Laura, a mysterious beauty whom he saw at Good Friday mass in 1327 and who haunted him for the rest of his life. But fine books equally roused his passion. "I am unable to satisfy my thirst for books," he wrote to a friend. "Gold, silver, precious stones, beautiful clothing, marbled homes, cultivated fields, painted canvases, decorated horses and other similar things, possess silent and superficial pleasure. Books please the core of one's mind."

That is, books pleased when one could read them. Petrarch detested the era's overly ornamental Gothic script, which scribes packed onto pages. It looked good from far away, but was "designed for something other than reading," he grumbled. His call for hand-writing reform later inspired a group of fifteenth-century Florentine intellectuals to develop a new, clearer style, which in turn inspired Aldine's italics one hundred years later. Petrarch's hand laid the foundation for the italic font.

Petrarch's own handsome penmanship, however, was not only supremely legible, it was so elegant that it impressed friends such as Francesco Nelli (d. 1363), who wrote to him: "Tell me, please, with what hammers or anvils you strike all your words, and even the forms of your letters, so that their fragrance, although filling most of the world, rightly deserves to reach all of it?"

JESTER

A jokester or fool employed to entertain

The European court jester is remembered as a clown who turned cartwheels for kings in a jingly bell-trimmed hat. But beyond his jolly capering the jester played a risky role as an adviser who spoke the truth when no one else dared in kingdoms from ancient India to medieval France to Montezuma's Mexico.

An unknown female jester galloped into King Edward II's banquet hall at Westminster in 1316, performed some riding tricks, and got the crowd laughing before she handed the king a letter that accused him of favoring unworthy people while neglecting his loyal knights and servants. Likewise, at a banquet given by the Chinese emperor Qin Shi Huangdi, the dwarf Twisty Pole (You Zhan), a court jester during the Qin dynasty (221–207 BC), noticed the palace guards freezing outside in the pouring rain. "Huh, look at you, great tall, lanky fellows!" he shouted over the railing. "There you are, left out in the rain. While I'm just a short-arsed runt, and here I am taking it easy indoors with the Emperor." Huangdi took the hint, and quickly decreed that guard duty be taken in shifts, as Beatrice K. Otto describes in her wonderful book *Fools Are Everywhere*.

Jesters were expected to say whatever came into their heads. Their truthfulness made them trustworthy—and appreciated. Patrons remembered their jesters in wills, and gave them aristocratic titles, land, and extravagant gifts. In return, they were responsible for keeping their betters from sulking. Richard Tarleson, Queen Elizabeth's jester, could always cheer her up, or, in other words, "undumpish her at his pleasure," just as the famous jester Will Somers (d. 1560) knew how to get a smile from Henry VIII.

Working his wit for amusement's sake, Somers played a raunchy rhyming game with his boss. The king offered up the opening line, "The bud is spread, the Rose is red, the leafe is green." Somers finished it off, "A wench 'tis sed, was found in your bed, besides the Queene." They weren't done yet. Henry started afresh with, "In yonder Tower, theres a flower, that hath my heart." Somers fired back, "Within this houre, she pist full sower, & let a fart."

But Somers was more than a ribald playmate. He called the king simply Harry, and was consulted on affairs of state. "For he was no carry-tale, nor whisperer, nor flattering insinuator, to breed discord and dissension," the jester's biographer explained, "but an honest plain down-right, that would speak home without halting, and tell the truth of purpose to shame the Devil." He slept "among the spaniels," the biographer noted, making Somers's lowly position plain, but historians say he was the person who was closest to the king.

Of course, sometimes a jester's jokes went too far. After one such incident in the mid-fifteenth century, Edward IV of England (1441–1483) exiled his jester John Scogin, warning him never to return to English ground. Banished, Scogin went to France, filled up his shoes with soil, and returned, claiming, once he was caught, that he wasn't standing on English ground, but on the dirt of Picardy.

A good jester took his antics right to the edge, but always found his way out of trouble. Ebn Oaz, clowning at the Baghdad court of Haroun-al-Raschid (763–809), went behind a curtain and gave the caliph a good pinch in the rear, one that sent him roaring from his chair. Haroun wasn't in the mood. He ordered his guards to kill the joker. "Hear my excuse," Oaz pleaded. "I declare by way of apology that when I pinched your Holiness behind, I thought I was pinching the Sultana, your wife." Oaz was forgiven—just.

KIMONO

A long Japanese robe with wide sleeves

The kimono is defined by its simplicity and a loose shape that hasn't changed much since the seventh century. Even its name is humble, meaning merely "a garment that hangs from the shoulders." But the kimono's pared-down chic makes it a potent cultural touchstone.

In 1868, under diplomatic pressure, Japan opened its borders for the first time in 250 years and was flooded with the corseted, flouncy dresses worn by Western women. Adopting the European style, Empress Haruko (1849–1914) gave Parisian bustles a try, as did her ladies-in-waiting and the era's fashion-forward geishas, but by the end of the century most had gone back to the kimono, which the majority of Japanese women continued to wear well into the 1930s.

Unlike curvy Western dresses, the kimono boasts *yugen*, the beauty of suggestion, a notion at the core of Japanese aesthetics. It's not an easy concept to grasp. "Yugen can be apprehended by the mind, but it cannot be expressed in words," explained the monk Shotetsu (1381–1459). "Its quality may be suggested by the sight of a thin cloud veiling the moon or by autumn mist swathing the scarlet leaves on a mountainside. If one is asked where in these sights lies the *yugen*, one cannot say, and it is not surprising that a man who fails to understand this truth is likely to prefer the sight of a perfectly clear, cloudless sky."

Demonstrating that mysterious ideal, during the Heian era (794–1185) the kimono was the innermost of twelve layered court robes. Custom dictated that a lady hide herself behind screens. The sight of her kimono's hem, or her colorful cuff, glimpsed below it, or as she rode past in a carriage, could turn her lover woozy. Flamboyance trumped subtlety briefly during the early Edo period (1603–1868), when women donned ponderously ornate kimonos woven with gold, embroidered, and decorated with semiprecious stones. In the mid-eighteenth century, the geisha of the pleasure district restored discretion with a subtle new style—*iki*. Unlike flashy courtesans, geisha were professional entertainers, skilled conversationalists, and musicians who could sing and play the three-stringed shamisen. A geisha with *iki* wore a subdued kimono in muted colors, but the way she wore it exuded restrained eroticism.

In English, *iki* means something like "cool" or "chic," though, like *yugen*, it's nearly impossible to translate. It encompasses the geisha's sly flirtatiousness, and her fiery pride, her sophistication, and her nonchalance. It's coquetry with an edge. In practice, it meant a geisha of the era wore a light layer of pale face powder when women from the provinces layered it on thick. A geisha styled her hair with water, not heavy oil. She walked lifting the hem of her kimono ever so slightly, revealing the occasional flash of leg, or her red underslip. And her footwear was pure *iki*—platform sandals worn sockless, even in the snow.

Most telling of all, however, was the way a chic geisha wore her kimono pulled back off of her neck, revealing a tantalizing sliver of bare nape. Her exposed neck "faintly suggesting to the other sex a pathway to the skin still concealed," as the philosopher Kuki Shuzo (1888–1941) described it, defined the kimono's subtle charge in contrast to "the boorish Western custom of exposing large areas of bosom, back and shoulder."

KUMARI

The living goddesses of Nepal

The Kumari, Nepal's living goddesses, are real little girls worshipped as deities. A child chosen to serve as the Royal Kumari of Kathmandu leaves her family to live in a palacelike temple at the heart of the city, dressed in regal red silk robes and mounds of gold jewelry. She rides through the streets in a golden litter, and everyone is required to bow to her holiness, even the king.

The history of Nepal's virgin cult is ancient, and the practice of revering little girls as goddesses there dates back to before the thirteenth century. Kathmandu's Royal Kumari is a manifestation of the deity Teleju, who, centuries ago, played dice with Nepal's king, until he offended her with his lust-filled glances, and she vowed never to return, except in the guise of a young girl.

The young Kumari is a well-known national icon, but her replacement is never easy to find. When the sitting Kumari gives evidence that the spirit of the goddess is deserting her (at the onset of puberty), temple priests launch a search for a new candidate. The ideal Kumari descends from a Buddhist caste of gold- and silversmiths and exhibits the required thirty-two perfections, including a neck like a conch shell, a chest like a lion's, and a voice as soft as a duck's. The final candidate must prove her supernatural courage by remaining calm while strolling through a dark courtyard full of gruesome slain animals.

Once installed in her pagoda-roofed temple, the Royal Kumari never sets foot on the ground outside it during her reign. She's carried to her carriage to make the rounds during festivals. Every morning she's dressed and painted by attendants and led to her throne to be worshipped. In the afternoon, she plays with visiting friends in her private quarters and occasionally greets curious foreign tourists lingering in the temple's courtyard, craning and hoping to catch sight of her in an open window. Call up to the Kumari and she might appear, suddenly leaning nonchalantly on her windowsill, dressed in fire red, her eyes ringed with heavy kohl, every inch the jaded, imperious princess. She is expected to indulge her whims like a goddess.

Yet the custom may not last. The unusual demands posed by

playing a goddess have come under scrutiny in the twenty-first century, with several legal cases arguing that the tradition amounts to child abuse. Until recently, the Kumari wasn't given a formal education, as goddesses were expected to be omniscient. (She now has a tutor.) And there is controversy over removing the young girl from her parents' care. With the Maoist ascendancy in Nepal, and King Gyanendra deposed, the goddess's earthly position seems particularly precarious. (Her blessing grants the king his authority to reign each year.)

While some Kumaris suffer a severe letdown once released from their duties to return home, often as spoiled, adolescent ex-deities, others cherish the experience of short-lived goddesshood. "It was fun," said Rashmila Shakya, a computer technician who served as Kumari from 1984 through 1992, and who left the temple at age twelve. "No one was mad at me. I didn't have to work either. I spent my days playing with dolls."

"Not everybody gets to be a goddess," she said. "In one life, I got to have two lives."

L'ART POUR L'ART

Art for art's sake

French writer Théophile Gautier (1811–1872) gave a name to the urge: *l'art pour l'art*, a mid-1800s notion that explained painter Claude Monet's radically hazy sunrise, and a concept which American painter John McNeill Whistler (1834–1903) exploited and exported from Paris to London.

Until then, good English painting took its cues from nature and from classical literature. It wasn't mottled or vague. But Whistler, a West Point dropout, had plunged deeply into the bohemian scene while in Paris, styling himself as a dandy, and a combative defender of the hazy aesthetic. The English weren't ready for the half-lit landscapes he showed in 1877—and no one less so than the august critic John Ruskin (1819–1900). Ruskin worked himself into a lather over Whistler's *Nocturne in Green and Gold*, a bleary night scene inspired by fireworks blazing across the dark London sky. "I have seen, and heard, much cockney impudence before now, but never expected to hear a coxcomb ask two hundred guineas for flinging a pot of paint in the public's face," he wrote. Provocative paintings like Whistler's "are almost always in some degree forced," he went on, "and their imperfections gratuitously, if not impertinently, indulged."

Instead of sulking, Whistler sued for libel, asking for damages of £1000. The resulting trial erupted in the headlines. Denizens of the art world were deeply divided. One witness for the defense described Whistler's paintings as "delicately tinted wallpaper." Artist Edward Burne-Jones, a Ruskin favorite, told the court that Whistler's *Nocturne* was nothing more than the start of a painting. Under oath, Whistler admitted that he'd spent only two days working on it. "The labor of two days is that for which you ask two hundred guineas?" the defense lawyer demanded. "No," said Whistler, "I ask it for the knowledge I have gained in the work of a lifetime." He was devoted to the ideals of *l'art pour l'art*. "Art should be independent of all claptrap," Whistler proclaimed, "should stand alone, and appeal to the artistic sense of eye or ear, without confounding this with emotions entirely foreign to it, as devotion, pity, love, patriotism, and the like." Whistler won the case. The jury awarded him damages of a farthing—a coin worth less than a penny—which he pierced and proudly wore on his watch chain, though the costs of the trial forced him into bankruptcy.

Such bravery paved the way for the extreme abstraction and monochromatic canvases of the next century's artists, like Robert Rauschenberg (1925–2008). Showing his all-white paintings in the early 1950s was "almost an emergency," he explained to his New York gallerist. Each was made with house paint and a roller. The effect was controversial, and stunning. "I always thought of the white paintings as being not passive but very—well—hypersensitive," he later told an interviewer. "So that people could look at them and almost see how many people were in the room by the shadows cast, or what time of day it was." Fifteen years after their creation, no one had yet bought one, though the white works influenced John Cage's silent compositions.

In fact, Cage (1912–1992) bought the only Rauschenberg sold during his 1951 exhibition—a pink-and-tan collage painting—and went to meet the artist at his downtown loft, where the two sat talking together on a mattress, the only piece of furniture. When Cage came away itching with bedbugs, he offered Rauschenberg his apartment while he was out of town so that the artist could escape his own loft's squalor. (Evidently, he was more concerned with high art than with the notion that the vermin might infest his home.) With Cage away, a thankful Rauschenberg decided to make over the piece Cage had bought, painting it entirely black. Cage, though he found the monochromes inspiring, wasn't thrilled to see his collage blacked over. Only after a thirty-year delay did Rauschenberg restore the piece to its original state. "Anything you do," he concluded, "will be an abuse of somebody else's aesthetics."

LAZZI

Comic gags used by actors during the Renaissance

When their audience drifted, Commedia dell'arte players on the Renaissance stage relied on *lazzi*, comic riffs that diverted from the plot, but kept things lively. These well-rehearsed bits of clowning looked spontaneous—take the perfectly timed pratfall, for example—and they worked like a charm, inspiring vaudevillians and slapstick stars centuries later. (Some scholars say the word *lazzi*, and the singular *lazzo*, come from the old Tuscan word *lacci*, or ribbon, the thing that knotted together the action.)

When a *lazzo* worked, actors guarded the bit as a trade secret. So while thousands were tried, few were recorded. Still, one manuscript kept in Perugia outlines the old tricks, like the *lazzo* of the ladder, instructing an agile Arlecchino to slip and cling to his ladder while the other actors try to shake him off, until a rival ladder is brought in and leaned against the first, so two characters can climb up and over each other at the top. In other *lazzi*, the players slurped each other's drinks through secreted straws. They picked each other's pockets and pulled chairs out from under one another. Tooth extraction was always good for laughs, as was pantomime— say, pretending to chase a flea. When a gentlemanly character in another classic *lazzo* complained that the robe he was wearing was dirty, his servant grabbed a bucket and a broom and scrubbed him down from head to toe.

Silent-film comics like Buster Keaton (1895–1966) worked all the tried-and-true *lazzi* in the early twentieth century, reestablishing the pie throw and the pratfall as an art form. For his part, Keaton did it all without ever smiling on camera, exuding a dark charm. Since his earliest days he'd been trained as a comic stoic. As a child, he performed with his parents' vaudeville act as "The Little Boy Who Can't Be Damaged," not that his father didn't try. The duo riled their audience by roughing each other up. Buster launched a basketball at his father's head while he shaved with a razor, and his father retaliated by heaving the boy into the orchestra pit. He learned early on that "the more serious I looked, the better laughs I got." The family stayed one step ahead of the child welfare officers, dodging charges of abuse until Keaton came of age.

Along the way, he became a master of the *lazzi*. In his first film in 1917, Keaton took a sack of flour to the face, did a headspin, and tumbled right out of a door and into the street, righting himself with a backward somersault. In his subsequent work, any filmic plot became a thin excuse for Keaton's endless capering and elegantly choreographed tricks. He was yanked from his bicycle by a clothesline. He sawed through a beam while sitting on it, plummeting off the side of a house. He somersaulted up and over a table and into a chair. He casually lifted his right leg onto a shop counter, followed by his left, and went crashing to the floor. His endless repertoire of stunts came out spontaneously once the camera was switched on. "We didn't stick to any format. We would just get an idea, and once you started on the idea it would lend itself to gags and natural trouble of any kind," Keaton said. He fell across a railroad track once while filming, but shook it off and went on with his work, only to discover years later that he'd broken his neck that day.

When Hollywood turned corporate, winging it went out. Budgets were bigger, and there was more to lose. Then silent films gave way to sound, and producers focused on funny scripts rather than on physical comedy. Centuries earlier, versatile Commedia players based witty *lazzi* on wordplay. Not Buster. "Don't give me puns. Don't give me jokes. No wisecracks," he said. "Give that to Abbott and Costello. Give that to the Marx Brothers." Though he had been a huge star in the 1920s, Keaton was washed up ten years later. Relegated to writing gags for other acts, he drank, and was buried with a rosary in one pocket and a deck of cards in the other.

According to Keaton, modern filmmaking killed comedy. "What we called a belly laugh is not what they call a belly laugh today," he told an interviewer in 1958. "Today they call just a substantial hearty laugh a 'belly laugh.' We didn't; that was just a laugh."

LIGHTNING

Visible electricity traveling across the sky or down to the ground

Each bolt of lightning is charged with upward of one million volts of electricity, making it harrowing and splendid. Despite the danger, its allure is strong. In fact, lightning left two inventors, Benjamin Franklin and Nikola Tesla, mesmerized. Benjamin Franklin (1706–1790) first attempted to steer the power of lightning with metal rods in 1752. "Would not these pointed rods probably draw the electrical fire silently out of a cloud before it came nigh enough to strike, and thereby secure us from that most sudden and terrible mischief?" he asked in a letter to a friend. But at Franklin's house the nine-foot rod mounted on his roof didn't secure the inhabitants as much as it provided him with lightning to experiment on in his at-home science lab. Bells attached to the contraption rang to let Franklin know when it was time. Yet one night it wasn't the sound of bells that woke him, but "loud cracks on the staircase." Electricity drawn in by the rod flew through the air, "whereby the whole staircase was inlightened as with sunshine, so that one might see to pick up a pin," he wrote.

Not even Franklin had the intrepid nerve of eccentric inventor Nikola Tesla (1856–1943), however. At age twenty-eight, Tesla left his native Yugoslavia for New York, briefly working with his rival Thomas Edison before setting out on his own to invent the first radio and to devise the alternating-current electrical system still used worldwide today. At his Houston Street laboratory, electric sparks ricocheted off of the walls, thanks to an oscillator that produced four million volts. But to test his theories about harnessing lightning, he needed to up the voltage—and to move out of Manhattan.

Arriving in rural Colorado in 1899, Tesla, backed by his friend John Jacob Astor, set up a barnlike structure topped with a pyramidal tower and a mast capped by a three-foot copper ball, all rigged to generate between 10 million and 12 million volts. Creating ever-mounting sources of electricity was his quest. "We are whirling through endless space with an inconceivable speed, all around us everything is spinning, everything is moving, everywhere is energy," he once told a *New York Times* reporter. "There must be some way of availing ourselves of this energy more directly."

No one knew what would happen once Tesla flipped the switch and started to fabricate his own highly charged—and highly dangerous—lightning. On the evening of his first experiment, dressed in a formal frock coat, white gloves, and a derby hat, as well as electrocution-proof shoes with four-inch cork soles, he looked, according to one of his assistants, like "a gaunt Mephistopheles." At his signal, the team fired up the giant electrical tower and sparkling, crackling masses of blue electricity formed an eerie aura around one of the tower's coils, arching and snaking their way up and down its center. Then, from the top of the mast, Tesla shot 135-foot bolts of artificial lightning flashing across the sky, causing a deafening racket that could be heard fifteen miles away. He was thrilled. The sight of his man-made lightning compared favorably with nature's own, which Tesla described as resembling "gigantic trees of fire with the trunks up or down." Though he never saw natural fireballs in Colorado's sky, "as a compensation for my disappointment I succeeded later in determining the mode of their formation and producing them artificially."

Tesla made attempts to commercialize his finds, burning through a half-million dollars until his funding ran out. He fell behind on his rent. He ventured into various lawsuits over patents he held or didn't. He turned down the Nobel Prize in 1912 because he wouldn't share it with Edison. And four years later he declared bankruptcy, admitting to the court that he'd been living on credit at his friend Astor's Waldorf Astoria for years.

He was a true New York eccentric. For most of his career, Tesla preferred working alone and late into the night, sometimes breaking for dinner at swanky Delmonico's. He arrived at his headquarters at the stroke of noon each day, handing off his hat, cane, and gloves to his secretary, and entering his office, where the shades were kept drawn tight. Only during lightning storms did Tesla allow the blinds to be raised. He would take a seat on his black mohair couch, watch the grand performance outside his window, and happily applaud.

LOVE NOTES

Written communications expressing affection

Love notes are breezier than formal love letters, but they're often more revealing. Take, for example, those that were passed between Russia's Catherine the Great (1729–1796) and the strategist by her side, Prince Grigory Potemkin (1739–1791). Whether flirting, flattering, scolding, or frothing over, each note in the collection shows the formidable lovers at his or her most vulnerable.

Public fascination with Catherine the Great's private life, and the legend of her many lovers, followed the empress beyond the grave. Early on in her relationship with Potemkin, she set the record straight, letting him know with a love note that she hadn't had *that* many affairs. "You'll be pleased to see that it wasn't fifteen, but a third as many . . ." she wrote. "The trouble is that my heart is loath to be without love even for a single hour."

Potemkin, who was ten years younger than Catherine, tall, handsome, and, luckily for her, an impassioned politician, became her lover in 1774 and was soon installed at the Winter Palace, with his rooms directly beneath hers and connected to them by a private staircase. In her notes to him, Catherine, who could be a ruthless ruler—and who many believe played a part in her husband's murder, before her affair with Potemkin began—revealed her human side. She called Potemkin her "tiger," her "hero," and her "little pussycat," morphing his name into Grishenka, Grishatka,

Grishootka, and Grishefishecka. He, in turn, called her *matrushka*, little mother. "If at all possible, I must not see you for three days or so for my mind to calm down and to regain my senses," she wrote when their affair was new, "otherwise you will soon tire of me, and rightly so." The breathless stage lasted a little more than a year, but the two were deeply bonded by then, and, some historians say, were probably secretly married. Catherine took new lovers during their relationship, mostly pretty-boy soldiers introduced to her by Potemkin, while he conducted a series of debauched affairs. Yet they ruled together until his death.

The Romanov czars who followed their reign, and later members of Stalin's regime, kept Catherine and Potemkin's letters suppressed for almost two hundred years. Though many of their missives were destroyed, some 1,162 survived. The small notes that a messenger carried back and forth down the palace halls are the most candid. "Come to me so that I might calm you with my infinite caress," Catherine wrote in a playful mood. Peeved, she scrawled, "Do you intend on leaving your things here with me for long? I humbly beseech you not to throw your kerchiefs all about . . ." She liked to scold. "My doll, either you're pig-headed or you're angry, and so I've not seen a single line from you," she wrote. "Fine, precious darling. I'll punish you, just you wait—I'll smother you with kisses."

Potemkin, trying to expand their empire in 1791, fell fatally ill while out on the front. "Beloved *matrushka*," he wrote in one of his last notes, "my not seeing you makes it even harder for me to live." He died holding Catherine's letters in his hand. She retreated from society and never recovered from the blow.

MARAVIGLIA

Marvels, in Italian

The artists serving Europe's princes during the sixteenth century were expected to provide *maraviglia*, or marvels, on a regular basis. These exotic novelties ranged from nature's most unusual specimens to rare artifacts, and from exceptionally rendered artworks to newfangled amusements and anything else that stoked curiosity. The artists' aim was to wow their patrons as often as possible.

The Milanese artist Arcimboldo (1530–1593) worked overtime, serving the Hapsburg emperor Ferdinand I in Prague. His projects ran the gamut. He titillated the court with his surrealistic portraits, depicting each sitter's face with clusters of various fruits, vegetables, and flowers. He tracked down stuffed birds from the New World, gigantic mussels, precious stones, demons imprisoned in blocks of glass, mummies, automata, and antiquities. He planned over-the-top parties, designing costumes and imaginative new games. And when he wasn't otherwise occupied, he took on engineering projects, sketching out new ways to ford rivers, inventing ciphers, and drawing up a set of illustrations to explain the silk-making process.

The Hapsburgs were happiest when they were amazed. "This noble mind found a great number of varied, ingenious, charming, and rare inventions, which left all the great Princes who were there universally filled with astonishment, and Maximilian his principal Lord most happy," one sixteenth-century historian wrote of Arcimboldo and his employers.

Not too far away, Arcimboldo's contemporary, engineer-architect Bernardo Buontalenti (1531–1608), rose to the difficult task of amusing the Medicis in Florence. Not only did Buontalenti design architectural additions to the Uffizi Gallery and a series of famous Medici villas, including Pratolino, considered his masterpiece, he made fountains flow from trees. He rigged up new weaponry, designed fireworks displays, engineered canals, and planned harbors. He played sidekick to Grand Duke Francesco de' Medici on nights when he wandered incognito through the city's streets. As the family's set designer, he planned the duke's solemn funeral rites. And at the elaborate festivities culminating in Ferdinando's 1589 wedding to the Valois princess Christine of Lorraine, Buontalenti awed the crowd with inventive *maraviglia*, including a mechanical cloud filled with musicians and singers that floated down from the upper reaches of a theater.

His most marvelous creation, however, is surely the frozen

zabaglione he made for a lavish Medicean banquet. In the family ice cave below the Boboli Palace in Florence, Buontalenti, who's often credited with inventing gelato, whipped up a boozy dessert of sweetened milk, eggs, and wine, churning it together in a bowl cooled over salted ice. Some of Northern Italy's *gelaterias* still serve a rich, eggy flavor named in honor of the artist and his tasty *maraviglia*. Though Buontalenti isn't mentioned by name on the menu at Grom, the amazingly good *gelateria* in Florence, there's a perfect homage in the old-fashioned flavor *crema come una volta* ("ice cream as it once was"): thick with cream, yolky yellow in color, and lightly perfumed with orange water.

Buontalenti Gelato

(Makes about 1 quart)

1½ cups half-and-half
⅔ cup, or a little less, sugar
a tiny pinch of salt
6 egg yolks
1½ cups heavy cream
½ tsp Di Saronno amaretto

1. In a heavy pot, warm the half-and-half, sugar, and tiny pinch of salt over medium heat until steaming, but never boiling, stirring occasionally to dissolve the sugar.

2. Temper the egg yolks by whisking in a bit of the warmed half-and-half, and then whisk the egg mixture back into the pot. Continue gently cooking, as you would custard, stirring constantly until the liquid thickens just slightly and coats the back of a wooden spoon. The temperature should be 170 degrees F. But beware—if you boil the custard, you'll have to start all over again.

3. Off the heat, pour the custard through a strainer into a metal bowl. Place the bowl in another bowl full of ice. Stir in the heavy cream and amaretto. Chill covered with plastic until cold, and up to 4 hours. Freeze the custard mixture in a gelato maker. Either serve it immediately—topped with crushed amaretti cookies, if you like, or sliced toasted almonds—or keep in a container in the freezer for several hours to harden it up.

MASQUERADES

Masked parties and disguised amusements

Masquerades have been popular the world over for centuries, but few cultures have gone in for masking as the Venetians did during the early 1700s, when nobles went out in disguise for more than half the year, from early October through Lent. Cloaked, hooded, and watching the world go by from behind their stern masks, their likenesses haunt eerie paintings by the city's masters—Tiepolo,

Guardi, and Longhi. By decree, the upper classes wore the *bauta*, a black capelet, white half mask, and black tricorn hat combination named, scholars say, for the cry "*bau, bau*," used to frighten children. Some aristocratic women chose the even more disturbing *moretta*, a black oval mask held in place by a button clenched between the wearer's teeth, leaving her speechless. During the long weeks of delirious public celebration, both disguises let the wealthy pass through the city unscathed.

The well-traveled English writer Lady Mary Wortley Montagu (1689–1762) thrilled to the freedom of walking through the Venetian streets under her *bauta*. With "every mortal going in a mask," not only didn't she worry about what to wear beneath it, but she learned that anonymity suited the city's laissez-faire outlook. "It is so much the established fashion for everybody to live their own way, that nothing is more ridiculous than censuring the actions of another," she wrote, describing sophisticated Venetian life to a friend at home in London. "I bless my destiny that has conducted me to a part where people are better employed than in talking of the affairs of their acquaintance."

While Venetians winnowed masquerading to its abstract essentials, in London the freewheeling Midnight Masquerades of the eighteenth century drew hundreds of eccentrically costumed partygoers each week. The ticket-buying public, done up as shepherdesses, Harlequins, demons, and witches, kicked up their heels with a masked George II and the Prince of Wales. Rowdy women went as pirates and as bishops, while daring men went as milkmaids and spinsters. Miss Chudleigh, maid of honor to the queen, shocked them all in 1794, appearing as a bare-breasted Iphigenia. One man dressed as Adam, wearing a flesh-colored body stocking and a scanty apron of fig leaves.

The ladylike courtesan Harriette Wilson (1786–1845) loved a masquerade "because a female can never enjoy the same liberty anywhere else," as she explained in her spicy memoirs. "It is delightful to me to be able to wander about in a crowd, making observations, and conversing with whomever I please, without being liable to be stared at or remarked upon, and to speak to whom I please, and run away from them the moment I have discovered their stupidity."

MILK BATHS

Bathing in a tub of milk

While scholars doubt that Emperor Nero actually fiddled as Rome burned—it seems more likely that he sang—few question the legend of his infamously licentious wife Poppaea's milk-based beauty regime. The mules pulling her carriage may have been decked with gold, but Poppaea (AD 30–65) is remembered for the herd of four hundred asses whose milk filled her daily bath.

Forever after, soaking in milk demonstrated a debauched sensuality. Following in Poppaea's footsteps, Napoleon's favorite sister, Princess Pauline Bonaparte Borghese (1780–1825), a notorious pleasure seeker who once asked a lady-in-waiting to lie on the floor and expose her bosom so that the princess could warm her feet there (or so the story goes), was carried by her servant Paul to and from her daily hot milk bath, which she followed with a cold milk shower.

Almost a century later, regal sizzle was just the tone showman Florenz Ziegfeld hoped to strike when importing Parisian chanteuse Anna Held (1872–1918) to Broadway. Held, a genuine tease, sang numbers such as "Come Play wiz Me," in Ziegfeld productions like *La Poupée*, *The French Maid*, and *Mam'selle*. But it was her milk baths that made Held a household name.

A month after her 1896 New York debut, newspapers reported that H. R. Wallace, a Long Island milkman, was suing Held for sixty-four dollars—the money she owed for the forty gallons of milk he delivered to her hotel every other day so she could bathe in it. The gist was that she refused to pay because the milk wasn't fresh, though her publicist told reporters the parties would settle out of court, as "milk baths were too peculiar to be discussed in public." The papers—and the public—went wild, and by the time the story was discovered to be a Ziegfeld-crafted hoax, Held was a star. She wore giant jewels and an impossibly cinched corset, doled out beauty tips to *Vogue*, and became Ziegfeld's common-law wife.

Claudette Colbert (1903–1996), another French-born siren, picked up where Held left off. At the beginning of her career, she came across as plucky, likable, and cute, jumping from Broadway to Hollywood during the Depression to star in a string of fluffy comedies—until 1932, when director Cecil B. DeMille asked if she'd like to play "the wickedest woman in the world" in *Sign of the Cross*, his over-the-top epic depicting the plight of pious Christians in Nero's ancient Rome. And her Poppaea was wicked. In the film's lustiest scene, Colbert, just millimeters shy of baring her bosom, lolled in a black marble tub of what's meant to be asses' milk, when one of the ladies of her imperial retinue dropped by with some gossip. "Take off your clothes, get in here and tell me about it," came Colbert's purring command.

No one could have guessed that Colbert's bath—full of Klim, a powdered milk solution (milk spelled backward)—had curdled, literally, under the set's big movie lights. It wasn't Colbert's last on-screen bath. The racy tub scene hastened enforcement of Hollywood's decency standards, the Production Code, cooling things off considerably for the next two decades, but DeMille's *Cleopatra* (1934) came in just under the legal wire, starring Colbert as another ancient diva who, in the name of pleasure and beauty, took yet another seminude, milky dip.

MIRACLES

Inexplicable events thought to be the work of divine intervention

Answering prayers and curing illnesses built a saint's posthumous reputation in the Middle Ages, when an impressive track record could draw pilgrims to a saint's shrine by the hundreds, which, in turn, led to yet more miracles. So many marvels were reported in the tenth century at St. Swithin's shrine at Winchester, England, that the monks there complained they were sick of it.

Yet no other deceased saint had a tally like that of Thomas Becket (1118–1170), the Archbishop of Canterbury who was killed inside Canterbury Cathedral by Henry II's henchmen. Becket's first miracle was recorded on the night of the murder, and within a month mysterious, marvelous acts attributed to the martyr spread, occurring as far away as Gloucestershire. He was canonized quickly, sainted in 1173, and within ten years he was revered in distant Sicily.

Two Canterbury monks—Benedict and William—vetted and recorded Becket's miracles, and his cult grew. As visitors poured in from all corners to touch Becket's coffin through a hole in his stone tomb, the two did their best to verify the accuracy of each miraculous claim. Those recently cured of blindness were asked to follow the light of a candle with their eyes. Those who suddenly overcame paralysis or other crippling injuries were asked to walk back and forth. Witnesses testified under oath. Villagers brought their priests to speak on their behalf. As Canterbury became Europe's most popular shrine, the stories grew more fantastic, and more vague. In the most flagrant cases, "We let their stories pass out of our ears as fast as we let them come in," one of the monks explained. Still, Benedict and William recorded 703 miracles during the first decade after Becket's death, the largest number attributed to any medieval saint.

One miracle is especially fascinating, a posthumous *jocular*, a whimsical miracle done just for fun, which, in this case, helped two children from the English village of Ramsholt locate a missing cheese. At the suggestion of her younger brother, a little girl prayed to Saint Thomas after misplacing the cheese. That night, the martyr appeared to both children in a dream, reminding them that the girl had forgotten the item in an old jar. And there it was.

The thankful children went to Canterbury with their priest, "where almost everyone to whom he told the story smiled at it."

MISERERE

A seventeenth-century choral composition

The English and American tourists who flocked to Rome during the nineteenth century hadn't really done the Grand Tour until they'd heard the haunting choral composition the *Miserere*, composed by Gregorio Allegri (1582–1652) and sung by the Papal Choir at the Sistine Chapel during Holy Week. Tickets were scarce. There was mayhem at the door. And inside, the scene was solemn and sensational. At twilight, the pope and a procession of the clergy dressed in their finest paraded past. Michelangelo's fearsome *Last Judgment* faded slowly into the perfumed gloom, and then, after two hours of droning chant, came the anticipated moment: the first sustained C-minor chord of the *Miserere*. With a dramatic flourish, the chapel's candles were extinguished one by one, dramatizing the darkness of the crucifixion. The haunting music was both mournful and angelic. The otherworldly voices of the a cappella choir rose and fell, intertwining in the ancient harmonics of the composition until, at last, the singers slowed their tempo and the chapel was left in silence.

In the seventeenth century, intricate new choral compositions such as the *Miserere* required powerful solo voices. Falsettos were too weak. Choirboys grew too fast, and women were banned from singing in the church altogether. Allegri's *Miserere* was written by a castrato for castrati, who had the pipes to sing the soprano parts in the Papal Choir, and who replaced falsettos in court chapels across Europe. In those days, Italian parents led their boys to the surgeon's door for an operation which slowed the growth of the larynx (generally kept secret, or attributed to a sham riding accident), hoping to ensure lifelong musical employment for their sons. Though the church launched the fashion for castrati, soon enough church choirmasters couldn't compete with the royal courts and opera houses paying castrati stars top salaries.

Yet while the Papal Choir had sung Allegri's *Miserere* for years at the time of Wolfgang Mozart's (1756–1791) visit to Rome in 1770, it was the fourteen-year-old prodigy who gave the composition cachet by writing it out after just one hearing. Only three copies of the *Miserere* score existed at the time: one owned by the King of Portugal, another by Holy Roman Emperor Leopold I, and a third by the Vatican. The pope forbade transcription of the composition on pain of excommunication. Rather than excommunicating young Mozart, however, the pope invited him to perform his transcription. The story gave fans proof of Mozart's genius and made the composition famous, which is how hearing the Papal Choir's *Miserere* became an essential stop on the Grand Tour.

The castrati fell out of vogue everywhere except the Vatican after a brief Napoleonic ban on castrati singers in 1796, which turned seeing them into a novelty for tourists in Rome during the next century. But once the Papal Choir and its renowned *Miserere* no longer drew the jostling foreign throngs at the end of the nineteenth century, Pope Leo XIII quietly pensioned off the choir's remaining castrati members.

Like those singers of the *Miserere*, artificially bound to their boyish voices, Mozart never escaped the mystique of his childhood. At twenty-two, he wrote to his father from Paris, complaining, "What annoys me most of all here is that these stupid Frenchmen seem to think I am still seven years old, because that was my age when they first saw me."

MORITSUKE

Traditional Japanese rules of food arrangement

"I will not praise Japanese food for it is not good, albeit it is pleasing to the eye," wrote one sixteenth-century European visitor, making an unknowing reference to the Japanese rules of *moritsuke*, which govern the topographical placement of every mound of rice and the angle of every strip of sashimi. Whether or not one likes the taste of Japanese food, its beauty is obvious.

Cooking schools of the Edo era established the foundation for the technique in secret, though some sixteenth- and seventeenth-century records survive, including one detailing the fifty-five ways of carving carp and serving it on an unvarnished board. Variations included the "Congratulatory Carp," appropriate to occasions when plum branches decorated the dining room. During maple leaf viewing season, the "Misty Morning Carp" was to be served. And the "Isle of Eternal Youth Carp" was just the thing when the white chrysanthemums bloomed. From these exacting banquet traditions rose the *moritsuke* rules still followed today in very formal restaurants in Japan.

First and foremost, the rules stipulate that the meal be made entirely from ingredients at the peak of freshness. Gourmets and poets of the Heian period (ninth–eleventh centuries) recognized twenty-four different seasons, which changed every two weeks. Additionally, to show off these prime ingredients at their best, each component should be perfectly contrasted with its vessel—round food in a square container, and square food in a round one, using a slew of porcelain, pottery, wood, and lacquer dishes, unlike the limited range of perfectly matched plates and bowls found in the West.

Mathematics supplies the visual effects. The five foody colors—green, yellow, red, white, and black—are included in each meal. In turn, giving each of the five flavors its due, the chef chooses foods that are spicy, tart, bitter, sweet, and salty, never neglecting any of the five culinary arts, with dishes done raw, boiled, grilled, steamed, and fried. Just to make things more complicated, and to create a pleasing asymmetry, each item is served in lucky multiples of three, five, or seven. (Sushi is an exception, and pieces are served in pairs.)

Overall, there are eight overarching styles that dictate arrangement of the carefully selected fare. One consists of sashimi mounded to suggest the shape of a cedar tree. Another is low and horizontal, and another involves piling food into a neat pyramid. Prescriptions for nestling some items behind others and rules about how high to fill a bowl follow, emphasizing the concept of *ma*, the use of empty space. A dish is never filled to the rim. A plate is never buried.

The *wanmori* style, the most complex *moritsuke* composition of all, is assembled inside a lacquered bowl politely brimming with ingredients, each prepared in its supreme and precise way. The whole is topped with strips of yuzu citrus fruit that scent the air when the bowl's lid is lifted. For the Japanese connoisseur, that moment is transcendent, and eating European soup served in a plain bowl is numbingly bland by comparison. "With lacquerware there is a beauty in that moment between removing the lid and lifting the bowl to the mouth when one gazes at the still, silent liquid in the dark depths of the bowl, its color hardly differing from that of the bowl itself," author Junichirō Tanizaki (1886–1965) wrote in 1933. "What a world of difference there is between this moment and the moment when soup is served Western style, in a pale, shallow bowl. A moment of mystery, it might almost be called, a moment of trance."

MOUCHES

Fake beauty marks

"Our ladies have lately entertained a vaine custom of spotting their faces out of an affectation of a mole," remarked one English style watcher in 1650, as the bubbly fad for wearing faux beauty marks broke out across Europe. Moles were considered a lucky sign of distinction, so women and men, young and old and of all classes, dabbed a bit of glue on their faces and applied their spots—made from black taffeta or red leather, and called "patches" in England and *mouches*, meaning "flies," in France. The simplest were shaped like moons, suns, stars, birds, beasts, and fish. Fancier options were cut in the shape of a coach and horses or like a tree with love-birds in its branches.

Members of the English Parliament were among the few who frowned on faux moles, introducing a bill calling for the suppression of the vice in 1650. (It never took off.) Likewise, the pious railed against *mouches*, likening them to plague spots. "If you are yet unmarried, but intendest it, get thee a wife Modest rather than Beautiful," advised the author of *Youth's Behaviour* (1706), "meddle not with those Ladies of the Game who make Pageants of their Cheeks and Shops of their shoulders and (contrary to all other Trades) keep open their Windows on the Sabbath Day . . . Black Patches are an abomination in the Sight of the Lord."

For her part, Madame de Montespan (1641–1707), King Louis XIV's fallen mistress, didn't think that the Lord would mind. She defended her right to wear faux moles even though she'd joined a convent, and insisted her *mouches* "meant no offense to God." In France, the position of each spot spurred intrigue: placed at the corner of the eye, it was called an *assassine* (for killer coquettes); on the forehead, it lent the wearer majesty (like the modern Indian *bindi*); at the corner of the mouth, it indicated playfulness. In England, rival political parties proclaimed their allegiances by wearing patches on different sides of their faces during the political upheaval of Queen Anne's reign (1702–1714)—Whigs on the right, Tories on the left.

Indian nobles visiting London found the trend confusing. "The women look like angels, and would be more beautiful than the sun were it not for little black spots that are apt to break out in their faces and sometimes rise in very odd figures," one was reported to have said. "I have observed that those little blemishes wear off very soon, but when they disappear in one part of the face, they are apt to break out in another, insomuch that I have seen a spot upon the forehead in the afternoon, which was upon the chin in the morning."

NEBULA, THE POWDERED SUGAR PRINCESS

A romantic ballet created by artist Joseph Cornell

Though artist Joseph Cornell (1903–1972) never staged a production of his sad, sweet ballet, *Nebula, the Powdered Sugar Princess*, it exemplifies the ethereal melancholy of his best work.

In the basement of a small house he shared with his mother on Utopia Parkway in Queens, Cornell combined unusual and mundane objects in an astounding series of collages. With a mountainous supply of antique doll parts, bird's nests, nineteenth-century sheet music, marbles, sequins, and silk flowers, he flaunted his obsessions and evoked an eerie, magical world in miniature, one where innocent yearning—as both dreamy nostalgia and as pie-eyed celebrity worship—bordered on eroticism.

One series of works made during the 1940s pays homage to featherlight ballerinas of the nineteenth century, when *en pointe* dancing came into vogue and when love stories concerning airy sprites and magical forests ousted classical themes. His favorite dancer was Marie Taglioni (1804–1884), who had been born into the most celebrated Italian dancing family of the era. Rigorous training made up for her hunched shoulders and less than stellar looks, and, despite these disadvantages, in 1832 Taglioni became an overnight star. Her hallmark was her fluid fragility. Her leaps looked effortless. Her landings were silent. Wearing roses in her hair and gossamer white layers—the first tutu—she created an ethereal new balletic image. The French bestowed high honors, adopting her name as a verb, *taglioniser*, "to refine."

Cornell harbored a lifelong obsession with the dancer. In her honor, he put together a handsome jewel case containing a few spare glass cubes, beads, and baubles, an abstract homage to the story that a Russian highwayman once stopped Taglioni's coach in the snowy woods and ordered her to dance. (The piece is now part of the Museum of Modern Art's collection in New York.)

When he died, his sister gave the artist's massive haul of files and collections—the largest amount of documentary material on any American artist—to the Smithsonian Archives of American Art. Besides boxes of gum balls, feathers, and Christmas angels, the lot contains Cornell's diaries, letters, and notes, some scrawled in pencil across the back of a receipt or a ravaged envelope. "Approach Taglioni," reads one slip of gray paper. "The absence of a jelly-roll—delectably pink icing-ed—in a baker's window from the lace doily framing it earlier in the day produced such an absurdly profound regret . . ." Another was just as enigmatic: "For Taglioni file," it read. "Taglioni + owls. Garage few yrs ago." Among the masses of papers, however, six intricately reworked pages describe *Nebula, the Powdered Sugar Princess*, the filmic ballet Cornell dreamed up, to be set to music by Claude Debussy and by Erik Satie, and shot in Technicolor.

In the blue-lit first act, called "Neigeux," Cornell's Taglioniesque princess "floats & dances in adoration to the falling snow as her arms continuously open in ecstasy to welcome its falling and drifting clouds of flakes," he wrote. "Include close-ups of the Princess' pantomime with the snow melting & glistening on her features . . ." On a green-lit stage in the second act, Nebula glided underwater wearing a phosphorescent tiara and swimming like a fairy in an aquarium. In the third act, "Aëréan," Cornell's weightless muse floated through the starry night sky.

Passages detailing the ballet's finale are minute, layered with cross-outs and rewrites. "The final tableau must be handled with extreme delicacy to prevent it from becoming over sentimental or ludicrous," Cornell explained. In the end, his Princess Nebula looked directly into the camera. She "solemnly blows a kiss to the audience & then presses her hands over her heart, gazing longingly & adoringly into the eyes of the audience," he wrote. "Only the deep blue of the skies remains as the stars also gradually fade out . . ."

NECTAR AND AMBROSIA

The mythological sweet drink and food of the gods

Infants are born with a natural love of sweetness, scientists say, so it's no wonder that when the ancient Greeks imagined what their gods might dine on, they dreamed of nectar and ambrosia, the former usually describing a divine drink and the latter the food of the gods. (The word "nectar" is a compound of the Greek *nek*, for "death," and *tar*, the verb "to overcome," signifying its immortal nature.) In the sixth century BC, the Greek poet Ibycus described ambrosia as nine times sweeter than honey, and some historians conclude that both nectar and ambrosia were actually forms of honey itself, as fermented in a mead liquor or eaten fresh and gooey off the comb.

Before the Crusades, cane sugar was an expensive luxury in Europe. Honey was the sweetest thing most people had ever tasted. Spanish rock paintings of stick-figure honey hunters dating from 4500 to 4000 BC demonstrate the enduring human love for the stuff. In many ancient cultures, ranging from Greece to Germany to India to Palestine, an infant's lips were smeared with honey before it had even tasted milk. Honey was offered to the gods. Ancient Greeks baked honey cakes for their dead to bribe Cerberus, the ferocious dog who guarded the gates to the underworld. And as part of ancient Egyptian wedding vows, a husband promised his wife he'd "deliver to thee yearly twelve jars of honey."

Doctors touted honey as a cure-all in those days, a balm for dressing wounds and for smoothing wrinkles. But philosophers, too, praised honey in their way, noting the bee's uncanny ability to extract something oozing and sweet from even the thorniest plants. (To make a single liter of bees' honey nectar takes between 20,000 and 100,000 flights to and from the hive. Five liters of bee's nectar makes one liter of honey.)

Honey's obvious appeal, however, was most succinctly stated in the Bible's Proverbs: "My son, eat thou honey, because it is good."

OBELISK

A monumental, monolithic column of stone

At the entrances to their majestic temples ancient Egyptians constructed mammoth hieroglyphic-covered stone monoliths, obelisks, honoring their gods and pharaohs. Each weighed hundreds of tons and stood as high as one hundred feet tall. But since the days of Augustus Caesar, their massive size never stopped foreign visitors from hauling them away like so many cumbersome souvenirs. Among the forty-eight obelisks the Roman emperors swiped, thirteen are still standing, including the red granite spike in front of St. Peter's basilica at the Vatican, imported by Caligula in the first century.

When Pope Sixtus V (1521–1590) decided to move the Vatican's obelisk to its present spot in 1586, five hundred engineers and architects competed for the honor of orchestrating the maneuver. Architect Domenico Fontana was awarded the job. He sent for rope, horses, buffalo, timber, and man power from across Italy, constructing an elaborate cranelike apparatus to coax the monument into place. On the big day, a silent crowd filled the surrounding streets and rooftops, waiting. The pope had issued an edict that anyone who spoke, or spat, during the proceedings would suffer severe consequences, as Fontana would use a trumpet and a bell to signal the scores of workers with coded commands.

Two masses were said in the cathedral before they began. Sixtus performed a benediction over Fontana, but also, for good measure, warned him that if anything went wrong he would lose his head. Obelisks were valuable and they broke all too easily, as evidenced by Rome's shattered mistakes, still lying where they landed. (The Egyptian ruler Ramesses let workers know the value of an obelisk by having his son tied to the pinnacle before they moved it.) Sixtus, however, was more lenient than he seemed. Secretly, he ordered a horse made ready so that Fontana could escape him—and the crowd—if things went wrong. But it was an unnecessary precaution. Fontana's scheme worked, and it made him rich, though he did set the obelisk just slightly off center, an awkward geometry that a later architect tried to correct by building St. Peter's slightly askew.

After Napoleon's campaign in Egypt, obelisk fever struck again in the nineteenth century. The French carried off one from the temple at Luxor in 1836, raising it in Paris's Place de la Concorde. The English snapped up a fallen Alexandrian obelisk in 1877, putting it up in London. The Americans set their sites on an obelisk originally erected by Thutmose III outside of Cairo, and which Augustus Caesar had floated down the Nile to Alexandria around 10 BC. The Egyptian government offered it to the United States as a diplomatic gesture. "It would be absurd for the people of any great city to be happy without an Egyptian Obelisk," commented the *New York Herald*. "If New York was without one, all those great sites might point the finger of scorn at us and intimate that we could never rise to any real moral grandeur until we had our obelisk."

While no one in Egypt seemed to mind when all the other obelisks left their shores, the American obelisk was one too many. The Egyptians protested its removal, and in the United States Americans petitioned against installing the thing, a strange object which newspapers depicted as an inexplicable extravagance. Outside the telegraph office in Alexandria, the American engineer in charge of transporting the monument faced "a storm of hisses and a succession of choice epithets," he wrote. He quickly draped an American flag around the stone, staking his claim, and set crews to work day and night to get it onto a steamer ship and out of Egypt, an expensive undertaking funded by William Vanderbilt.

On the other side of the water, the *New York Sun* called the obelisk "terrific humbug," and "only a broken, decaying and disfigured old block of stone." But finally, after a risky ocean crossing, as gangs of men and horses struggled and strained for weeks on end, inching the thing off the boat and down Manhattan's snowy streets, the American press and the public rallied around the pillar and its odyssey. "There is no longer any hope that we shall escape the Alexandria obelisk," the *New York Times* reported. It was erected in 1881 in Central Park next to the Metropolitan Museum of Art with great pomp and ceremony "as a monument to—nobody knows what."

OBSIDIAN

Black volcanic glass

Obsidian, buffed until it shines like a black mirror, is made from naturally occurring volcanic glass. But for those who gaze deep and long into its dark surface, its fascination is supernatural. Hallucinating Aztec priests slicked their bodies with black ointment and stared into black obsidian slabs, falling into trances they claimed revealed the future. With deadly obsidian blades, they performed human sacrifices, offering up the precious hearts to the supreme Aztec deity, Tezcatlipoca, or "Smoking Mirror," a fearsome warrior depicted with a black mirror hovering over his head. "May he desire the flowery death by the obsidian knife," went their prayer.

The Aztecs weren't the only ones to fall under obsidian's spell. Dr. John Dee (1527–1608), an English mathematician, astrologer, and one of the great scholars of the Elizabethan age, carefully guarded his own iridescent obsidian mirror, which he used as a divining "shew-stone," or show-stone. Dee rejected job offers from five emperors across Europe, preferring his life at Queen Elizabeth I's court, where he was in good favor. He calculated the most astrologically auspicious day for her coronation, and, after a comet flashed across the sky, spent three days at Windsor Castle conferring with the queen about its significance. He coined the term "British Empire" and hatched schemes to "discover and settle the northerly parts of Atlantis, called Novus Orbis"—in other words, to colonize North America. Twice, the queen herself dropped in on Dee at home. He entertained her on one occasion by bringing out his magic mirror, "to her Majestie's great contentment and delight."

For Dee, however, consulting the spirits in the stone was no parlor trick. Though his library was the biggest in England, boasting four thousand volumes and manuscripts, it didn't provide the insight he craved. He resorted to the occult to satisfy his curiosity, attempting to contact the angels and begging heaven to send Michael or Raphael. A charlatan called Edward Kelley answered the call instead, arriving in 1582 to serve as Dee's astral intermediary and to relate the prophecies and commandments revealed by the angels who appeared in Dee's wondrous mirror. Dee couldn't see them himself, but Kelley assured him that the specters in the mirror promised "all our mysteries shall be known unto you." Dee's young wife, Jane, immediately denounced Kelley's "wicked nature and abominable lies," but Dee was hooked. He recorded reams of Kelley's celestial pronouncements, including suggestions of the "new and strange doctrine" of wife swapping. At the end of their five-year friendship, the two men and their wives had joined in a "unity both spiritual and corporal," pledging "all things between us to be common, as God by sundry means willed us to do," Dee wrote.

The complex liaison didn't last. Dee died in obscurity, ridiculed and poor, but his diaries surfaced in the mid-seventeenth century, some found in a field where he had buried them, and others rescued from a maid who was using the pages to line pie tins. Meanwhile, Dee's magic mirror, snug in its leather-covered case, wound up at the British Museum, where it is displayed today.

Modern X-rays revealed that Dee's famous "Devil's Looking Glass" was probably an Aztec relic, sent to Europe at the time of Cortés's conquest of Mexico, where ferocious Tezcatlipoca's ancient obsidian mirrors can still occasionally be found in old chapels, intermingled with the sacrificial images of the Catholic Church, and usually shining out from the intersection of the two arms of the cross.

OGI

The Japanese folding fan

The world has known rigid palm-leaf fans since the days when average Romans and Egyptians cooled themselves with them, while their rulers luxuriated in the breezes that attendants stirred with choice bouquets of plumes. From Japan, however, came the cleverest device for fluttering and for flirting: the folding fan, or *ogi*.

In the seventh century, according to some scholars, a hermit called Toyomaru made the first *ogi* as a gift for the Japanese emperor Tenchi. By the ninth century, fanciful *ogi* were de rigueur at the imperial court, flaunted by top-tier aesthetes like Fujiwara Tadahira, who, with an extra-decorous flourish, never opened his cuckoo-painted fan without first doing his best bird cry. An *ogi* expressed its owner's taste, whether made in paper, leather, or silk, decorated with silk flowers and rainbow-colored ribbon tassels, or painted with misty blossoms wafting on the wind. By the sixteenth century, they were popular with men and women of every rank.

The folding fan reached Europe around the same time, thanks to the Portuguese traders who imported spices and silk from Asia. Every Spanish infanta kept one close at hand, and soon more than 150 fan dealers had opened shop in Paris. At the opera, the fluttering turned the theater into a field of busy butterflies. Even King Henry III of France (1551–1589) fell for the fan, though the affectation left him vulnerable to the satirists behind a lampoon called *The Island of Hermaphrodites*. What might they have made of the iron-stiffened fans carried by Japan's fierce warriors, like the nimble samurai Ganryu, who once defeated his opponent armed only with his deadly *ogi*?

Women wielded fans in prettier pursuits. "Women are armed with fans as men with swords," England's Joseph Addison (1672–1719) wrote in 1711, characterizing the various flutterings of the day—angry, modest, timid, confused, merry, or amorous—and noting that "if I only see the Fan of a disciplin'd Lady, I know very well whether she laughs, frowns or blushes." Bucolic scenery à la Watteau made a popular fan motif. Others came gussied up with lace, fitted with a peephole magnifying lens, or tricked out with a watch in the handle. They flapped through summer and winter, too, though one German doctor warned against the fevers, headaches, and colds that afflicted those who fanned themselves too much, instructing women to "leave these deleterious instruments at home, or at least to make more sparing use of them for the future."

No one was more likely to catch a chill than the flirt. Before the eighteenth century, "to flirt" meant to move with a sudden, brisk motion, similar to flitting or flicking. "Flirting a fan" described the coquette's pastime, and later a new fan-related word, "flirtation," was used to describe her aim, too—playing at love, without serious intentions. In ancient Japan, lovers gave each other *ogi*, pledging devotion as they did in Europe by exchanging gloves. In both the East and the West, however, lovers arranged their liaisons and conveyed intimate messages via fan signals. A spate of nineteenth-century handbooks decoded the various international languages. In Spain, for example, covering the left ear with an open fan meant "Do not betray our secret." Snapping it open, then shut, in England translated as "You are cruel," while holding a half-opened fan to the lips proclaimed, "You may kiss me."

No doubt, it made for an extremely subtle conversation, but over the years women had become fluent in speaking fan. "The woman of breeding differs from others in her use of the fan," declared the authoress Germaine de Staël (1766–1816). "Even the most charming and elegant woman, if she cannot manage her fan, appears ridiculous."

OMELET

A dish made from beaten eggs cooked in a frying pan

The perfect omelet is an exacting work of simplicity: delicate, but not puffy; golden, but not burned; firm enough to fold, but not so stiff it breaks; creamy, but cooked through. Ancient Romans ate omelets. Chefs in the seventeenth century cooked them on both sides. Jean-Jacques Rousseau was known for his perfect flip. France's hallowed gourmand Jean-Anthelme Brillat-Savarin (1755–1826) wrote an entire essay on an omelet Madame Recamier's priest ate for supper, which was served on a hot platter oozing with melted parsley butter. "This dish is to be reserved for special breakfasts, gatherings of connoisseurs who know what they are about and eat deliberately," he stipulated. "If it is washed down with good old wine, wonders will be seen."

Chefs and gourmets went to great lengths to describe the art of omelet making over the centuries, though they rarely agreed on the essentials—how long to whisk the eggs and how to heat the butter.

Culinary pilgrims at Normandy's Mont-Saint-Michel swore by the "omelet of omelets" made by innkeeper Annette Poulard at the turn of the nineteenth century. As her devotees watched, Poulard stood smiling next to a yawning fireplace, working a long-handled pan over the flame and rolling her omelet with a quick flip of the wrist. Omelet worship all but eclipsed interest in the mountain's holy shrine. "The pilgrims come from darkest Africa and the sunlit

Yosemite, but they remain to pray at the Inn of the Omelette," one traveler reported. While Poulard's efforts inspired fanciful recipes and theories, she never admitted to a technique beyond the ordinary.

There were plenty of others willing to advise. "Omelette is exacting, will have attention, must not be neglected for an instant, and, to crown all, wants a delicate hand and a quick eye at the critical moment," one journalist wrote in 1874. "For any one calling himself, or herself, a cook, to fail in turning out a perfect omelette, would be utter disgrace."

Two writers addressed the topic in the next century, England's French-cooking expert Elizabeth David (1913–1992), and America's expert, Julia Child (1912–2004). David's instructions were reassuringly simple. "An omelette is nothing to make a fuss about," she wrote. Melt butter in any old pan. Don't let the pan get too hot. Don't overstuff with fillings. But most important, she pointed out, "the eggs are very often beaten too savagely. In fact, they should not really be beaten at all, but stirred." Just a turn or two with the fork will do.

And yet, David took a realist's perspective of the situation. "As everybody knows, there is only one infallible recipe for the perfect omelette: your own," she concluded. "Argument has never been known to convert anybody to a different method, so if you have your own, stick to it and let the others go their cranky ways, mistaken, stubborn and ignorant to the end."

To her credit, Child, who offered up numerous instructive diagram-covered pages dedicated to omelet making in her famous cookbooks, was one of the few willing to be converted. While writing the foreword to one of David's cookbooks, she decided to follow David's omelet recipe instead of her own. They differed over beating the eggs. "I have always beaten them vigorously, but certainly not savagely, to mix whites and yolks thoroughly," Child reported in 1998. "Today, I just stirred, leaving patches of white mid patches of yolk, and—she's right! I made an unusually delicious and tender omelet. I shall try it again tomorrow, stirring even less."

ORIGAMI

The Japanese art of folding paper

Harry Houdini (1874–1926) liked his magic big, escaping from heavily secured jail cells, the sealed hull of a Steinway piano, or tricky handcuffs, often working a telescopic lock pick with his teeth (though sometimes Mrs. Houdini slipped him a key). But in 1922 Houdini championed the most modest illusions with his book *Houdini's Paper Magic*, which was full of origami's folding and tearing tricks.

Houdini learned to transform a sheet of paper into an elaborately detailed bird by watching an Americanized Japanese diner in a New York club refashion his menu card. "Gradually all those within seeing distance became interested," he wrote, "and before he finished he was quite surrounded by spectators who applauded him roundly when, from that scrap of pasteboard, he at last produced a little paper bird that flapped its wings quite naturally."

Origami, the art of paper folding, is known as a Japanese invention. But while paper folding plays a ceremonial role in both Shintoism and Buddhism, the first evidence of recreational folding doesn't appear in Japan until the seventeenth century. Some experts believe an independent tradition evolved in Europe, where for centuries baptismal certificates were folded into little paper windmills, and where children twisted paper scraps into flytraps.

German educator Friedrich Fröbel included paper folding in the curriculum of his kindergarten concept, giving the craft a boost in the mid-1800s, though origami has always lured the geometrically minded, such as Leonardo da Vinci and British mathematician Charles Dodgson, aka writer Lewis Carroll, who folded paper fishing boats and popped paper pistols to amuse the little girls he knew.

Few, however, took paper folding as seriously as Count Leo Tolstoy (1828–1910). Near the end of Tolstoy's life, the czar's government kept close tabs on the aristocratic author, who'd grown increasingly radical, having taken up humble hobbies like boot making and railing against imperial repression. His relatives at court begged Alexander III to spare Tolstoy from being tried or exiled, and the ruler agreed, if only to avoid creating a martyr.

Responding to a world he saw as tawdry, Tolstoy lashed out in 1898 with "What Is Art?," an essay concluding that great art is easy to understand, and that all art should benefit humankind. He targeted ballet (lewd), Kipling (unintelligible), Wagner (incomprehensible), Baudelaire (decadent), Beethoven's late works (meaningless), Manet's paintings (gratuitous nudity), and novels (lust kindling). Critics, in turn, denounced Tolstoy's theories as moral propaganda, finding it absurd to judge art "by the interest it excited in the healthy peasant," as one put it.

Like Houdini, a flapping paper bird left Tolstoy spellbound. In an early draft of his essay, he weighed a flapping paper bird, which he identified as a rooster, or cockerel, against all of Western culture. "It is much easier to write a poem, paint a picture, or compose a symphony than to invent a new cockerel," he wrote. "And, though strange to say, the production of a cockerel like this is not only art, but good art . . . the state in which people sit on their little settees in front of the 'Sistine Madonna,' straining to recollect other people's recollections about the picture, has nothing whatsoever to do with the aesthetic feeling."

A tiny paper bird that Tolstoy folded to entertain the children of a local painter during a train trip now sits behind glass in a provincial museum near his family estate.

PAINTED LADIES

Made-up muses who sat for prominent artists of the 1920s

Two of the wildest model-muses of the Jazz Age, Alice Prin, known as Kiki de Montparnasse, and Greenwich Village eccentric Baroness Elsa von Freytag-Loringhoven, played their over-the-top roles with guts, gusto, and striking originality, never forgetting the powerful effect of their unusual makeup.

Prin (1901–1953), a cabaret singer who danced across the tables at Le Jockey Bar in Montparnasse, got her bohemian start at fourteen modeling nude for an elderly sculptor. "All I need is an onion, a bit of bread, and a bottle of red. And I will always find somebody to offer me that," she wrote in her steamy memoirs. Soon she had befriended everyone from Ernest Hemingway to Chaïm Soutine, always dressed "in all the glad-rags of the Quarter," favoring a man's hat worn with a dramatic cape, or a hat trimmed with chenille "like you find on Christmas trees" paired with a jacket she decorated herself with lace samples snatched from a trash can.

In her early days, Kiki used a petal plucked from the artificial geranium plant on her mother's mantelpiece to rouge her cheeks and redden her lips, and burned matches to blacken her brows. But after she moved in with the radical American photographer Man Ray, and became famous for starring nude in his voluptuous work, Man Ray took over Kiki's beauty regime. "Her maquillage was a work of art in itself," one memoirist explained. Before they went out for the night, Man Ray shaved Kiki's eyebrows, then replaced them with glued-on designs—sometimes cut like the accent over the Spanish ñ. Her eyelids might be cobalt blue one day and copper the next, while her searing red lips "blazed against the plaster-white of her cheeks on which a single beauty spot was placed, with consummate art, just under one eye."

In New York, the Baroness Elsa von Freytag-Loringhoven (1874–1927) took her own avant-garde look even further—to the brink. "With a royal gesture she swept apart the folds of a scarlet raincoat. She stood before me quite naked—or nearly so," wrote artist George Biddle (1885–1973), remembering the day he met the baroness, as she was known, in 1917. "Over the nipples of her breasts were two tin tomato cans fastened with a green string around her back. Between the tomato cans hung a very small bird cage and within it a crestfallen canary. One arm was covered from wrist to shoulder with celluloid curtain rings, pilfered from a furniture display in Wanamaker's. She removed her hat, trimmed with gilded carrots, beets, and other vegetables. Her hair was close cropped and dyed vermillion."

Born Else Hildegard Ploetz, the baroness left her tiny German village for Berlin at eighteen, posing as a marble figurine with a traveling vaudeville troupe. Before long, she made her way to New York, where she married a baron who promptly left to fight in World War I. Tall, handsome, and broke, the baroness entrenched herself in the city's avant-garde scene, creating art, posing for painters, and inspiring artists like Marcel Duchamp and Man Ray, who teamed up in 1921 to direct a film that consisted solely of footage of the baroness shaving her pubic hair. Ezra Pound and William Carlos Williams wrote poems in her honor. Peggy Guggenheim and Djuna Barnes lent her cash. Hemingway, working as a literary editor, published her poetry. As photographer Berenice Abbott (1898–1991) explained, "The Baroness was like Jesus Christ and Shakespeare all rolled into one."

She also produced witty found-object sculptures, but her manic wardrobe was her real medium. She wore a coal scuttle or a peach basket as a hat, tea balls and spoons as jewelry, and a dress she designed with a battery-powered taillight in its bustle. Sometimes she powdered her face with yellow paint, did her lips in black, or stuck postage stamps on her cheeks. She "is not a futurist," said Duchamp (1887–1968). "She is the future." At her most audacious, for an appointment at the French consulate in Berlin she wore a birthday cake strapped to her head, hoping to prove to the visa-issuing bureaucrats that she was an artist. She is now considered by some to be the embodiment of the Dada movement and the first performance artist. "I am keenly conscious of [my] own self, as if I were both theater and spectator in one," the baroness wrote in her memoirs, "not only the author."

PELL-MELL

A term meaning without order or discrimination

Since medieval times, rules of precedence governed how one approached the European banquet table and where one sat, a system that carefully weighed the social standing of viscounts, barons, marquises, dukes, earls, and their wives. Ladies were escorted from the drawing room according to rank, Dr. Trusler of Bath (1735–1820) explained in an early-nineteenth-century etiquette guide. "That gentleman who has the first rank, or the elder man of the company, is first to hand the lady of the house to the dining-room, the gentleman next in rank conducts the woman of highest rank present, following the lady of the house; and so on, the master of the house last, conducting the lady least in rank."

But the third American president, Thomas Jefferson (1743–1826), a lanky Virginia-born lawyer, couldn't be bothered with all that, and established instead at the White House a simple system of nonpreference he called "pell mell," or "pêle mêle," a term meaning without order or rank, though it also implies the chaos that erupts when the rules are lax.

Jefferson, who had served as a diplomat in France before becoming president, despised old-world ostentation. He liked laid-back dinner parties, where wine and conversation flowed freely, and no one stood on ceremony. He vowed to bring democracy to the dinner table. Guests to the White House were "perfectly equal, whether foreign or domestic, titled or untitled, in or out of office," according to Jefferson's own 1803 canon of etiquette. Europe's aristocratic titles wouldn't mean a thing. At official functions, foreign guests could take their seats on a first-come, first-served basis, he proposed, and when going in to dinner they would follow "the ancient usage of the country, of gentlemen in mass giving precedence to the ladies in mass."

"The principle with us, as well as our political constitution, is the equal rights of all," Jefferson wrote. "Nobody shall be above you, nor you above anybody, pêle mêle is our law."

Unfortunately, the new British ambassador, Anthony Merry (1756–1835), and his haughty wife were not pell-mell types. Merry turned up for his first appointment at the White House dressed in a navy coat decked with gold braid and wearing a fancy sword. Jefferson was nowhere to be found. So, trailing behind Secretary of State James Madison, Merry tracked him down, finally bumping into the president in a back corridor. Jefferson was "not merely in an undress, but actually standing in slippers down at the heels, and both pantaloons, coat, and under-clothes indicative of utter slovenliness and indifference to appearances, and in a state of negligence actually studied," Merry complained. He took Jefferson's sloppy clothes and ultrarelaxed manner as an intentional insult to the British Crown.

Then, at Merry's first Washington dinner, the unthinkable happened. Believing himself the guest of honor, Merry assumed the president would offer his arm to Mrs. Merry and guide her to the table. Instead, Jefferson escorted Madison's wife, Dolley, to the table, placing her in what Merry considered the seat of honor to the president's right. The Spanish minister's wife flanked his left, and Madison escorted a stunned Mrs. Merry to her place. Meanwhile, as her husband proceeded toward his chair, "a member of the House of Representatives passed quickly by me and took the seat without Mr. Jefferson's using any means to prevent it or taking care how I might be otherwise placed," he later reported to his Foreign Office. Worse, when the couple dined at the Madisons' days later, none of the gentlemen offered an arm to Mrs. Merry, and her fuming husband had to lead her to the table himself.

In their fashion, the Merrys waged social warfare against the offending Americans, disparaging their unspeakable manners and their impudent pell-mell. Merry wrote home, requesting permission to make a formal protest (which was denied). For her part, Mrs. Merry "established a degree of dislike among all classes which one would have thought impossible in so short a time," Jefferson noted. "If his wife perseveres she must eat her soup at home."

Everyone knew the Merrys were unhappy. For his part, Jefferson attempted reconciliation, but he refused to apologize. Consequently, on the other side of the Atlantic in London, U.S. special envoy James Monroe was seated last at diplomatic dinners, after representatives of small German states like Liechtenstein. The Merrys never accepted another invitation from Jefferson, or from

Madison, who later became president. Their pell-mell policy is said to have hastened the outbreak of the War of 1812.

PENTIMENTO

An underlying image in a painting

For the most part, pentimenti, the blotted-out scenes art historians find when X-raying old paintings, interest only the academics by revealing the innuendos of an Old Master's technique through the minute changes made to a canvas over time. The word comes from the Latin *paenitere*, "to regret." But one tender pentimento, hidden under a self-portrait by French painter Gustave Courbet (1828–1885), tells a deeper story of remorse.

"I want all or nothing," a teenage Courbet wrote from the French capital to his parents in the countryside. "Within five years I must have a reputation in Paris." And he did. In the big city, Courbet cultivated a country-boy persona, smoking a pipe, wearing wooden shoes stuffed with straw like a hick, and speaking in a drawling hayseed accent. But his work was savvy, confronting the art world with a jolt of realism and sensuality.

In an early series of self-portraits, he played a bright-eyed, cocksure young man with a smirking grin. But *The Wounded Man*

(1844–1854), his most striking, is different, full of veiled heart-break. Courbet lies slumped under a tree, a defeated duelist, his eyes half closed with his lips curled—in agony or in rapture?—making a pretty image of pain as a rosy bloodstain spreads over his heart.

At one point, the sad subject had been happy, as a 1973 X-ray of the painting reveals. Courbet's painful regret? In an earlier version of the work, his love of fourteen years, Virginie Binet, had been painted at his side, the two figures snoozing intertwined in the tree's shade, his arm around her shoulders, her face pressed to his chest. After Binet left him, taking their young son, Courbet painted her out of the picture, replacing her image with the duelist's bulky brown cloak. He aged his features, added his wounds. The pain is apparent. "I am in a sad state of mind," he wrote to a friend years later, "my soul drained, my heart and spirit filled with bitterness. In Ornans I frequent a cafe of poachers and outlaws. I screw a waitress. None of that cheers me up."

Still, even Courbet could see that the painting was all the better for his misery. "Real beauty can be found for us only in suffering and pain," he wrote, "that is why my Dying Duelist is beautiful." Courbet never put the painting up for sale, and instead carried it with him even as he left France for Switzerland, where he lived in self-imposed exile at the end of his life. It now hangs in Paris's Musée d'Orsay.

PERFUME

An aromatic liquid prized for its pleasant fragrance

Undoubtedly, great women since Cleopatra have spritzed and dabbed their way through an ocean of perfume. "For her actual beauty, it is said, was not in itself so remarkable that none could be compared with her or that no one could see her without being struck by it," Plutarch (AD 46–120) wrote of the Egyptian queen, "but the contact of her presence, if you lived with her, was irresistible." She was no great beauty evidently, but Cleopatra heightened her allure with cyprinum, made from henna flowers, though she also owned a grove of prized balsam of Judea plants, which produced an aroma so tantalizing that it was worth twice its weight in silver. Under her reign, perfume ruled Egypt. Banquet halls were perfumed. Sweets were perfumed. Baths were perfumed. Incense smoke filled the streets. And Cleopatra had the sails of her barge soaked with perfume when setting off to seduce Mark Antony.

Likewise, during the Italian Renaissance, everything—including mules and paper money—was doused. In 1533 Catherine de Médicis (1519–1589) arrived in France on a cloud of sophisticated Florentine scent, specifically *acqua della regina*, a green-smelling herbal concoction, sharp with lemon, bergamot, lavender, and rosemary, and still made by Officiana Profumo-Farmaceutica di Santa Maria Novella in her native city. (Some say Catherine's personal perfumers, who conducted her poisonings on the side, came to France as part of her entourage.) The queen's keen interest in perfumes of all sorts was key in establishing the French perfume center at Grasse, which soon overtook Florence's lead.

In the following years, Grasse cranked out pomades, powders, and perfumed gloves that kept every court in Europe reeling. Books scented in sixteenth-century England still smell today. But the Elizabethans were no match for Louis XV's mistress Madame de Pompadour, who, centuries later, frittered away half a million francs a year on perfume, including a favorite called *huile de Vénus*. For his part, Louis XV demanded his apartments be scented with a different fragrance every day. Not surprisingly, perfume was banned in France for ten years after the Revolution.

Following the heavy floral scents of the Victorian era, Guerlain's Jicky, considered the first modern perfume, was a revelation and a relief. Instead of imitating flowery smells found in nature, Aimé Guerlain (1834–1910) brewed a blend of synthetics into an original concoction in 1889 that smelled only like itself. His sophisticated Jicky is woodsy and spicy, dark and sultry, but a little lemony and sharp, too. Wearing it isn't easy—it smells complicated, androgynous—but it was quickly adopted by men, including Oscar Wilde, before women took to the scent around 1912.

One prominent, perfume-loving Jicky fan was novelist Sidonie-Gabrielle Colette, known as Colette (1873–1954). She was born during the perfume boom of the Belle Époque, but she was a modern *provocatrice*. Risqué, scent-infused scenes filled her stories of

Claudine, the naughty French every-girl, created when Colette's husband, Wily, the renegade son of France's foremost publisher, locked her in her room, thereby forcing her to write. "Don't be afraid of spicy details," he told her.

While Claudine's escapades titillated an adoring public, tales of Colette's own brow-raising seductions circulated among the literary crowd. Perfume fired her passion. "Know yourself, oh woman, madly overcome by so many perfumes . . . Know what happens to the precious drop when it touches you," she wrote, "when you moisten your earlobe or the shadowed valley between your breasts. Experiment! Watch, above all, the glance and the wrinkling of the nose of the one to whom you refuse nothing, nothing, that is, except the name of your perfume."

Turning her pungent poetics into action, the famous author opened a glass-and-chrome beauty shop, Société Colette, in Paris in 1932. "I see perfectly how to launch the thing," she said. "On the door of the boutique I would write, 'My name is Colette, and I sell perfumes.'" In a pristine white lab coat, she worked the floor, performing makeovers and hawking bottles of a scent brewed in her honor.

As for her own perfume, it's easy to imagine Colette ensconced in a particularly urbane, spicy-sweet aura. When Truman Capote conjured the legendary writer in his unfinished novel *Answered Prayers*, he didn't suppose that Colette would refuse to divulge the name of her scent, but instead would tell an admirer that—like

Empress Eugénie and like Marcel Proust—she wore Jicky. "I like it because it's an old-fashioned scent with an elegant history," Capote's coy Colette announced, "and because it's witty without being coarse—like the better conversationalists."

PILLOWBOOK

A diary, or book of musings, kept under the pillow

Reading *The Pillowbook of Sei Shōnagon*, full of moonlit verandas, scented robes, and wistful lovers who part at dawn, one inevitably wants to visit Japan. Sei Shōnagon (965–1020), the book's lyrical author and a lady-in-waiting to Japan's Empress Sadako, cataloged her years at court with casual immediacy, as if, just before falling asleep, she'd jotted a few lines in a bedside diary (or pillowbook). Scholars are grateful for the historical glimpse of the era. But while Shōnagon delivered plenty of stories, including a few about Emperor Ichijō's cat, Lady Myōbu, who ruled the palace, her proclivity for lists gave the book its sparkle.

More than half of Shōnagon's three hundred diary-like entries are lists, sure-footed catalogs of aesthetic miscellany that frame both her poetic nature and her prickling wit. A list of "Squalid Things" included the back side of a piece of embroidery and hairless baby mice. A list of "Vexing Things" singled out visitors who arrive when one is busy. A list of "Hateful Things" derided people who sneeze. Under "Embarrassing Things" she filed the memory of an oafish lover. "Lying awake at night, one says something to one's companion, who simply goes on sleeping."

Occasionally, Shōnagon exposed her own snobbery: sniffing at the sight of "snow on the houses of common people," for example, or that of a toothless old woman puckered up after a bite of sour plum. Ugly people taking naps worked her nerves, too, as did those who walked too fast, or nobles who didn't dress their ox-carriage drivers well.

More often than not, however, Shōnagon was distracted by beauty, turning her gaze to the cherry blossoms, the spring dawn, a note written on a purple lotus petal. The word she used most often to describe everything that's charming or amusing, in her slightly bemused way, was *okashi*.

The list of "Elegant Things" is one of her best:

A white coat worn over a violet waistcoat
Duck eggs

Shaved ice mixed with liana syrup and put in a new silver bowl
A rosary of rock crystal
Wisteria blossoms
Plum blossoms covered with snow
A pretty child eating strawberries

It has been suggested that Shōnagon played politics in her writing, glorifying the Sadako court even after a regime change reduced the empress's power to nearly nothing. But others say Shōnagon simply preferred to see the bright side, rather than dwelling on the tragedy of decline.

Little is known of Shōnagon's life beyond the intimacies found in her diary. She arrived at the court at around twenty-four years old and remained until the Empress died. A rumor circulated that Shōnagon herself died poor and alone in the countryside, a story that was publicized by a thirteenth-century literary critic who heard the tale from a traveler who saw Shōnagon in her later years collecting greens in her front yard: "She was overheard mumbling to herself, 'I cannot forget the court robes I saw in the days of old.' She was wearing a lowly robe and a hat of patched cloth—how very sad. Indeed, how she must have longed for the past." But Shōnagon's alleged destitution was probably wishful thinking on the part of moralists offended by her high living. (The era's other three famous female writers all were rumored to share that fate.)

Of course, if Shōnagon did wind up living alone and on the

cheap, she'd already voiced an opinion on that scenario long before, declaring that when a woman lives alone, her garden should look unkempt. "I greatly dislike a woman's house," she wrote, "when it is clear that she has scurried about with a knowing look on her face, arranging everything just as it should be . . ."

POUF

An extravagant eighteenth-century hairstyle

Besides the Mohawk, no other hairstyle has gone to the aesthetic extremes of the late-eighteenth-century *pouf*, when stylists built up women's tresses into towers and decorated them with baubles and figurines like hair-framed dioramas. Rose Bertin (1747–1813), who designed gowns and bonnets for a ritzy clientele, and who wore a parasol in her hair, introduced the *pouf* after opening her shop, the Grand Mogul, on Paris's rue Saint-Honoré. Collaborating with the hairdresser Léonard Autier, known as *"le grand Léonard,"* Bertin's extra-grand creations rose to a height of two and a half feet, all constructed over a stiff scaffolding of wire and gauze, which was covered with fake and real hair, lacquered with flour and lard, and heavily powdered. (Léonard once worked eighteen meters of fabric into a single hairdo.) *Poufs* could express a feeling (a *pouf au sentiment*) or mark an event (a *pouf à la circonstance*). The Duchesse de Chartres, one of the early adopters, commissioned a *pouf* to celebrate the birth of her son and ended up with her hair coaxed high to frame a figurine of a nursemaid and a suckling infant. Before long, Bertin and Léonard were on the royal payroll, and serving Marie Antoinette (1755–1793).

The young dauphine didn't start small. One of Marie Antoinette's first major coifs commemorated the king's vaccination with the *pouf d'inoculation*, incorporating a rising sun and a serpent holding a club as he shimmied up an olive tree nestled into her hair. The sun symbolized the king. The olive tree stood for peace. The slinky serpent represented medicine, with its club to clobber disease. Later, while in mourning for her father-in-law, Louis XV, the new queen wore a *pouf* garnished with a tiny cypress tree rooted by a black tangle of ribbons, as well as a sheaf of wheat and a fruit-filled cornucopia, promising a bountiful new reign. Topping all previous efforts, in 1778 she wore an exact replica of *La Belle Poule*, a French battleship that had just sunk an English frigate, riding the swelling sea of her hair. "Behold the coiffure of our Queen, whose perfect taste is therein seen," began one poem of the day.

Whether the look demonstrated good taste is debatable, but the queen had plenty of over-the-top competition. The Duchesse de Choiseul wore an entire rural landscape perched in her hair, complete with flowers, grass, a bubbling stream, and a mini windup windmill. The Duchesse de Lauzun sported a scene in which a hunter shot at ducks and the miller's wife was seduced by a priest. Needless to say, the *pouf* wasn't easy to manage. It was a fire hazard. It made sleeping tough, as the hairdo was worn overnight. And it turned climbing into a carriage, dancing, or simply passing through a doorway into a seriously inelegant maneuver. Worst of all, the *pouf* housed vermin, a nuisance that gave rise to ivory scratching sticks designed to plunge into the hair-covered hives.

Still, when worn with restraint there was something charming about the look. The most demure *pouf* on record was one worn by the Baronne d'Oberkirch (1754–1803), who had herself coiffed before a visit to Versailles. "I wore in my hair little flat bottles shaped to the curvature of my head," she wrote in her memoirs, describing how her hair hid the tiny vases filled with flowers. "Nothing could be more lovely than the floral wreath crowning the snowy pyramid of powdered hair."

PULU AND POONA

Pulu is the ancient game of horse hockey. Poona is an Indian badminton-like game.

Like the Victorians, members of the ancient Chinese Tang court were mad for games. "When we heard that Western tribesmen like to hit the ball, we ordered our followers to learn and practice it," said Emperor Tai Tsung, who, according to a visitor, ignited China's horse-hockey craze in the seventh century. Club-wielding riders (both male and female) dressed in embroidered jackets drove their decorated ponies across the field in hot pursuit of the ball, and the game's popularity soared—until it turned deadly. One Tang dynasty emperor, jealous of his best player's skills, ordered the man executed. Generals lured onto the field for a good time wound up "accidentally" trampled by galloping horses. The game was played rough all across central Asia, and the surrounding ambience was one of danger. Horsemen in ancient Afghanistan used animal skulls as balls, while in Tibet the uncombed manes of the horses and the long, loose black hair of their riders made for a sight "most wild and picturesque," as a British traveler noted in 1842.

British soldiers posted in the Indian Himalayas discovered the sport and tamed it over the next ten years, developing their own extensive rules and renaming the game polo, after the Tibetans' willow-wood ball, a *pulu*. In 1871, when they returned to England, where rugby, cricket, tennis, and golf dominated the Victorians' social scene, polo became all the rage.

In the same way, British soldiers popularized the more subdued Indian game of *poona*, a racquet game they'd picked up while stationed in Pune, India. One rainy afternoon, a group of British officers staying at the Duke of Beaufort's Gloucestershire home, Badminton House, improvised a *poona* match. Since the twelfth century, the English had played "battledore and shuttlecock," a game where players cooperated in batting a "shuttlecock," a ball stuck with goose feathers, with their "battledores," otherwise known as paddles, to keep the "birdie" airborne as long as possible. By contrast, in India's *poona*, played with racquets and balls of wool, the idea was to hit the ball so that the other player would miss it. Employing an old English shuttlecock, and *poona*'s competitive rules, Beaufort's guests strung up a net and played to win.

A pamphlet elaborating and standardizing the rules in 1876 officially dubbed *poona* "The Anglo-India Game of Badminton," after Beaufort's house. Like polo, badminton acquired an upscale air, especially as swatting a shuttlecock was one of the few sports that rule-bound Victorians deemed delicate enough to be a proper amusement for ladies. An hourglass-shaped indoor court accommodated the sweep of stately drawing-room doors, and men playing at the first badminton clubs wore silk top hats, formal frock coats, and buttoned shoes on the court. Any mutineer who dared to remove his coat, no matter how vigorous the match, could expect to be expelled from the premises.

But while the English discovered badminton in India, like polo, the game had its roots in China. Preceding the Victorians, the Chinese Tang court played *ti-jian-zi*, a first-century proto-badminton game in which players kicked a shuttlecock over a net.

PUNTO IN ARIA

A Venetian guipure lace

A bouquet of seaweed given to a nimble-fingered young Venetian lacemaker by her sailor boyfriend inspired the first distinctive *punto in aria*—or "stitches in air"—a dainty guipure lace from Venice that drove Europeans to distraction in the sixteenth and seventeenth centuries. Other laces were stitched onto a cloth backing.

Venetian Point, as *punto in aria* was also known, was made without a foundation by tracing an intricate design luxuriant with scrolls, blooms, and tendrils across a piece of parchment paper with thousands of tiny stitches, often as many as six thousand to the square inch. It was wearable Baroque sculpture in bas-relief.

Before the Venetians invented *punto in aria*, lace was used as an ecclesiastic trimming for the altar cloth. Later, in the early sixteenth century, lace edging became a decoration for bed linen and lingerie. Then came the lace boom of the early seventeenth century, when not even vast quantities of convent-made Venetian Point—the frill of fashion—could satisfy the demands of courtiers in England and in France who wore flat lace collars against austere black. In that era, the English peddlers went door-to-door, singing:

We travail all day through dirt and through mire
to fetch you fine laces and bring what you desire:
no pains we do spare, to bring you choice ware,
as gloves and perfumes, and sweet powder for hair.

Ladies wore lace collars, cuffs, aprons, and caps. Lace ruffles spilled out of the tops of French gentlemen's riding boots. Men tied lace garters around their knees and wore lace rosettes on the tops of their shoes. Charles I of England (1600–1649) ordered one thousand yards of lace to trim the collars and cuffs of his shirts one year, and six hundred yards more to prettify his nightshirts. Those who could afford it indulged heavily in Venice's *punto in aria*.

In fact, Venetian lace was emptying the royal coffers across Europe. Charles II of England (1630–1685) issued a proclamation banning the import of foreign lace in 1661, though he discreetly licensed a lone importer to bring in lace for "our dear mother, the Queen, our dear brother James, Duke of York, and the rest of the royal family." A similar French *déclaration* banned not only the sale of imported lace, but even that of inferior French lace more than an inch wide, further condemning the knee-ruffle fad as "*un excès de dépense insupportable*," an indefensible excess. With the royal debt mounting, Louis XIV desperately tried to cure the court's lace addiction—whether for foreign or for domestic frills. Both countries' laws failed miserably.

Nothing could lure the French courtiers away from lace, especially not the Venetians' lovely *punto in aria*—that is, until Louis XIV installed Jean-Baptiste Colbert (1619–1683) as his minister of commerce. Working in cahoots with the ambassador to Venice, Colbert managed to entice more than twenty Venetian lacemakers to come away to France in 1664, smuggling the women over the border and installing them at his château near Alençon so that they could teach the local women the secrets of their prized *punto in aria*. The Venetian Senate angrily summoned the errant workers home. Their departure was treasonous. When the women didn't come back, the doge threatened to imprison their relatives, and then to execute them.

But by then the French had learned all they needed to know about *punto in aria*. Madame Gilbert, who was in charge of Colbert's atelier, delivered the first imitation Venetian Point samples to Versailles, where they were hung up for inspection on the walls of a room done in red damask. They passed muster with the king, who ordered that no other lace should be worn at court, naming the new homespun lace *point de France*. With that, the French began exporting *punto in aria* instead of importing it. As Colbert assured the king, "there will always be found fools enough to purchase the manufactures of France . . ."

QABUS NAMA

An eleventh-century Islamic etiquette guide

Before chivalry brought them to their senses, Europe's knights didn't impress anyone. The twelfth-century Arab chronicler Ousâma watched horrified as Christian knights amused themselves by greasing an old woman's pig and sending her to chase after it. But then, for generations the polite and cultured young men of Arabia had benefited from etiquette books that gathered together the wisdom of the ages, offering smart maxims and instruction on good manners. These helpful tomes, generally known as "Mirrors for Princes," and including the celebrated eleventh-century manual *Qabus Nama*, or "Book of Good Counsel," compiled everything a young noble would need to know in order to rule one day.

Early examples of the style emphasized old Bedouin virtues: bravery, honor, and jaw-dropping generosity. One popular anecdote told the story of the young poet Hatim al-Ta'i (d. 578), who slaughtered his family's whole herd of camels in order to feed a party of strangers. When his father returned home, he anxiously asked his son what he'd done with the family fortune—the camels. "With them I have given you immortal glory," Hatim replied coolly, "and honor that men will forever carry in verses in praise of us, in return for your camels." Usually, however, such guides urged readers to decorous, moderate behavior, and instructed would-be rulers in remaining respectful and respectable. "Do not walk along showing an unseemly hilarity," the Persian governor Tahir ibn al-Husain wrote in one ninth-century book. "Do not send away empty-handed a destitute beggar."

The most famous and wide-ranging of such works was the *Qabus Nama*, written around 1082 by Kai Ka'us ibn Iskandar ibn Qabus ibn Washmgir for his favorite son and destined successor, Gilanshah. Kai Ka'us was an endearingly meticulous adviser whose counsel ranges from the parental to the strategic. Descended from a long line of dauntless warriors, he imparted down-to-earth advice informed by experience. His *Qabus Nama* included practical tips on buying real estate and on waging battle, but also offered a chapter on romantic love and another on sex, as well as those on table manners and on drinking wine. "I neither urge you to drink wine nor can I tell you not to drink, since young men never refrain from action at anyone's bidding. Many persons spoke to me but I did not listen, until, when I was past fifty years of age," Kai Ka'us wrote. Still, he told his son to open fine wines for his guests and hire "sweet-voiced and expert minstrels" to play at his banquets.

"If you drink wine, let it be the finest," Kai Ka'us reasoned, "if you listen to music let it be the sweetest and if you commit a forbidden act, let it be with a beautiful partner, so that even though you may be convicted of sin in the next world, you will at any rate not be branded a fool in this."

QUADRILLE NATURALISTE

A debauched nineteenth-century dance

At the end of a dark country lane, where the Arc de Triomphe now stands on the Champs-Élysées, gaslit lanterns once gave a cheery glow to the Parisian pleasure garden of the Bal Mabille. There, the city's young off-duty waiters, students, and cute shopgirls mingled with the most fashionable dandies of the mid-nineteenth century, including, when he was in town, the Prince of Wales, later King Edward VII. What lured them all there wasn't the unusual mix of people, though that was part of the draw, but the unhinged action on the Mabille dance floor, where the crowd let fly with a wild version of the quadrille, called the *quadrille naturaliste*, done as daringly as indecency laws would allow in the early 1840s.

Crowds thronged to watch as dancing partners faced off in a square, the men scrunching their top hats securely on the backs of their heads. The orchestra started in with Offenbach's jaunty "Galop Infernale," and *infernale* it was. Instead of prancing sedately in time to the music, as in the regular quadrille, the dancers cut loose, improvising and gyrating themselves into a mad frenzy. The Mabille's beloved dancing queens La Reine Pomaré and Céleste Mogador—Parisian every-girls who became famous for their audacious moves—frisked their long skirts and kicked up their boots, as young women in the countryside did when dancing the *chahut*. Their partners were just as fevered. The double-jointed Brididi spun his arms like a windmill. Eccentric Chicard did a convulsive parody of the ballet, leaping, screeching, and contorting across the hall. Each dancer moved "like a worm on a hook," one mesmerized English observer noted, "shaking so much that their clothes, if not their muscles would burst."

It was nothing like the apathetic dancing done in the city's fancier ballrooms, where the laconic dragged themselves through a sleepy quadrille. "What makes the balls of the fashionable worlds more wearisome than they have any right to be, according to the laws of God and man, is the prevalent mode of only seeming to dance," German writer Heinrich Heine (1797–1856) moaned in 1842, "so that the figures are only executed while walking, and the feet are only moved in an indifferent and almost dull or sulk manner."

In 1844 the polka reinvigorated both the gritty dance hall and the bourgeois ballroom alike. The Mabille dancers polkaed in their galloping way, integrating the wildness of the *quadrille naturaliste*, which was popular at the same time but never done in proper ballrooms. Overworked dancing masters taught the fundamental polka steps to the upper class. (It's said that the all-but-unknown Tennessee governor James Polk won the U.S. presidency thanks to the polka's popularity.)

In the meantime, the Mabille's *quadrille naturaliste*—or cancan, as it is now more popularly known—became an outright scandal. "The cancan ignores, disdains and eliminates all that recalls rules, regulations and method . . . it is above all a dance of liberty," proclaimed Rigolboche, one of the Mabille's next generation of stars, whirling across the dance floor in "a mass of limbs and lingerie," as one observer put it. She and her competitors, Rose Pompon and Nini-la-Belle-en-Cuisse ("Nini with the Beautiful Thighs"), kicked off gentlemen's hats. Police took up posts in the dance halls. Some places banned the cancan. Others thrived on the business it generated. By the 1860s, foreign tourists flocked to the notorious nightspots for a glimpse of the naughty dance. "I have been in Hell," Brooklyn preacher Henry Ward Beecher (1813–1887) told his congregation after a visit to the Mabille.

The Franco-German War put an end to it all in 1870, when many dance halls shut their doors, though the cancan made a comeback twenty years later with the opening of nightclubs like the Moulin Rouge. By then, transported from the dance floor to the stage, the cancan was no longer the spontaneous couple's dance of Mabille's *quadrille naturaliste* or its rough and frisky country cousin the *chahut*, but a burlesque performed by saucy professionals—commercialized, eroticized, and tapped of its innocent fun. In fact, the new cancan was too vulgar even for the old Mabille crowd. As Clodoche, one of the original *cancaneurs*, said, "The *chahut* of today is filthy!"

 QUINTESSENCE

The fifth element, thought to be the living substance
latent in all things

The alchemists' quest wasn't a hungry hunt for gold, as it's commonly understood. They were after quintessence, the fifth element, one beyond air, water, earth, and fire, an elusive link betwccn spirit and matter that permeated all life. Some believed that stars were made of quintessence, as was the human soul. It was luminous, but invisible.

Drawing on the ancient Egyptian and Hellenistic tradition, the alchemists' search played out in the chemistry lab, where, beginning in the first century, the spiritual scientists conducted their metallurgical experiments like a series of religious rites. They believed that matter and spirit passed into each other, that everything was subject to transformation, and, to take the idea a step further, that all metals were simply imperfect gold. By the seventeenth century, alchemy had become a philosophical system for observing nature, and one that promised spiritual refinement to those who practiced in the laboratory.

Though Sir Isaac Newton's revolutionary ideas about gravity and optics transformed the way we see the world, understanding his dedication to the practice of alchemy suggests that these important contributions are mere byproducts of his all but forgotten alchemical work. As a boy, before he discovered alchemy, Newton (1642–1727) exhibited an interest in both mysticism and natural science, often copying out formulas from *John Bate's Mysteries of Nature and Art*, a popular encyclopedia of natural magic. He learned recipes for making dye out of privet berries and followed instructions for constructing a water clock and for building a kite hung with lanterns, terrorizing the neighbors one night. Later in life, while he was practicing as an alchemist and teaching at Trinity College at

Cambridge University, data on light, prisms, and pendulums filled his notebooks, but he never really separated the mystical from the scientific. At Cambridge, he could be found with his long hair hanging uncombed to his shoulders and conducting alchemical experiments all night long in a shed he built outside his rooms.

He described quintessence as a vital, magnetic force that could draw life out of chaos, and thought that perhaps it was made of light. "The Quintessence is a thing that is spiritual, penetrating, tingeing, and incorruptible, which emerges anew from the Four Elements when they are bound together," he wrote. "It is the condensed spirit of the world."

In fact, Newton wrote over a million words on the subject of alchemy, though after his death the Royal Society deemed much of it "not fit to be printed." Whether the authorities swept Newton's esoteric experimentation under the rug out of embarrassment, or whether his files disappeared as a result of his own secrecy, some Newton documents were lost until 2005. Of course, Newton, who often wrote in his notebooks in secret code, wasn't the first alchemist to cover his tracks. The Church had denounced alchemy since the Middle Ages, and making gold had been a felony since 1404, when Henry IV declared it illegal. Newton once wrote to a fellow alchemist, reminding him to maintain a "high silence" about their experiments. Maybe he was onto something, after all.

"The fact that Newton never published a work on alchemy cannot be taken to mean that he knew he had failed," one historian reasoned. "On the contrary, it probably means that he had enough success to think that he might be on the track of something of fundamental importance . . ."

RED LIPSTICK

Red paint for the lips

For millennia, red lipstick has been both treasured and forbidden. Its appeal is primal, offering a vivid shortcut to glamour. Ancient Romans painted their lips with vermillion, though their rulers tried to ban it. Elizabethans used tinted red alabaster, though an edict proclaimed that any woman found wearing it "shall be punished with the penalties of witchcraft." Strict Puritans and Victorians felt likewise. But few moments in history have united so many in favor of red lips as World War II, when in the Allied countries vanity stood defiant in the face of adversity.

Lipstick was rationed in England in order to conserve glycerin to make explosives, but in the United States lipstick production continued throughout the war, packaged in polished cardboard in order to save brass. As an American War Production Board spokesman explained, a woman's "resultant vivacious spirit, self-confidence and geniality" was infectious, "to be transmitted directly to the male members of the family." It was a question of morale. Psychiatrists called lipstick "an essential nonessential," and a pamphlet written for the Marine Corps told female recruits that their lipstick and nail polish should match "the scarlet hat cord" of their uniform.

On the other side, the Nazi Party banned lipstick as early as 1933, announcing that "women with painted faces" would not be admitted to party functions, according to the *New York Times*. "The German woman must revert to the type of the Germanic mother," a party official said. "The German girl must prepare herself for becoming worthy of this honor."

The German ban on lipstick was news in the United States, but the press was fixated on England's lack of the stuff. Americans sent lipstick supplies in care packages for women in the British armed forces. For their part, English women who stayed at home melted down the stubs of their lipsticks to make them last. In her diary, a fifty-year-old Cumbrian housewife named Nella Last (1889–1968) pondered the potency of lipstick and its role in her own transformation after her son left for the front. "I contrast the rather retiring woman who had such headaches, and used to lie down so many afternoons with the woman of today who can keep on and will not think; who coaxes pennies where she once would have died rather than ask favours," she wrote in 1939, "who uses too bright a lipstick and on dim days makes the corners turn up when lips will not keep smiling."

ROSARIAN

One who loves roses

Gertrude Jekyll's (1843–1932) passion for cottage gardening transformed England's landscape in the early 1900s, and her naturalistic approach—both dignified and wild—gave the rambling rose back its freedom. Jekyll's rose gardens were soft-hued, slightly overgrown, and sensuous. "It should be remembered that a Rose garden can never be called gorgeous; the term is quite unfitting," she wrote in 1902. "The gorgeousness of brilliant bloom, fitly arranged, is for other plants and other portions of the garden; here we do not want the mind disturbed or distracted from the beauty and delightfulness of the rose."

Jekyll studied painting and pursued silver engraving until, at around forty, her eyesight failed and she turned to garden design instead. "Planting ground is painting a landscape with living things," she wrote. Like William Morris and the founders of the Arts and Crafts movement whom she admired, Jekyll rejected the ostentatious geometry of the Victorian era. With architect Sir Edwin Lutyens at her side, she roamed the Surrey countryside in her dogcart, photographing the traditional country details that inspired her work—a clump of hollyhocks growing beside a weathered barn, a porch swathed in fluffy roses, a quaint, patterned brick chimney. She designed over 350 gardens for others, but the garden at her own house, Munstead Wood, was her masterpiece.

She could be found there during the last decades of her life wearing two pairs of eyeglasses and a battered straw hat and wandering the paths lined with scented sweetbriar.

The roses she liked best were demure, like Maiden's Blush, or Provence (the cabbage rose), "sweetest of all sweets," and the Garland, which fades over the course of the morning from faint blush to white by noon. "It is well worth getting up at 4:00 a.m. on a mid-June morning to see the tender loveliness of the newly opening buds," she proclaimed. Jekyll's roses sprang from patches of rosemary and lavender, or flung themselves freely around her garden, throwing blooming arcs into the air, climbing trees, and prettying everything around them. They were great for "screening ugliness," she pointed out. "What a splendid exercise it would be if people would only go round their places and look for all the ugly corners, and just think how they might be made beautiful by the use of free-growing roses," Jekyll suggested. "Is not a grand rose worth the trouble of taking up two squares of flagging or cemented surface?"

RUFF AND CRAVAT

The ruff is an exaggerated collar projecting from the neck in starched flutings. The cravat is a man's neck scarf.

Historically speaking, England's dandies are notable for their cheek and for their outrageous neckwear, and none more so than George Villiers, the first Duke of Buckingham (1592–1628), and Beau Brummell (1778–1840). Though generations apart, each boasted remarkable style, and each was ruined by it.

Villiers first came to court in "an old black suit, broken out in divers places," but his fortunes, and his wardrobe, shaped up considerably once King James I noticed the striking young man performing in *Twelfth Night*. He was, as one contemporary noted, "the handsomest-bodied man of England; his limbs so well compacted and his conversation so pleasing and so sweet a disposition." Several backers lent him money to keep him running in the right circles, with hopes he would oust the king's detested favorite, which, after a few strategic meetings, he did.

The king granted Villiers royal titles and showered him with gifts, including, it was rumored, jewelry that had belonged to Queen Anne. Soon Villiers was "imprisoned in jewels," as one courtier snipped, with diamonds in his hatband, and gems gleaming from his hat feather, sword, girdle, and spurs. Like Queen Anne, he was a fan of the starched ruff, dyed golden yellow with saffron, as was the vogue since the reign of Elizabeth I.

Villiers's vast ruff may not have been any bigger or fluffier than those of his peers, but his conspicuous taste and his status as the king's favorite made him an easy target for critics. "He intercepts, consumes and exhausts the revenues of the crown, not only to satisfy his own lustful desires, but the luxury of others," wrote one. It wasn't long before he was assassinated, remembered beyond the grave as "the most debauched, the most unable, and the most tyrannical there ever was," according to one historian.

Another dashing dandy with a penchant for starched accoutrements was George "Beau" Brummell, whose crisp muslin cravats buried his chin and were studied by all of Regency London, including his friend the Prince of Wales, later King George IV. Though the prince used to wear a pink silk coat and an embroidered waistcoat, Brummell's stark militaristic look—a brass-buttoned coat, buff breeches, and shiny boots—did away with all that. Legend has it that the prince once burst into tears when Brummell criticized the cut of his coat.

Brummell's cravats were his hallmark, and drew a crowd every morning to his dressing room, where the prince regent sat a little off to one side, quietly watching Beau perform his magic. "The collar, which was always fixed to his shirt, was so large that before being folded down it completely hid his head and face," wrote Brummell's biographer. He stood before the mirror, poked his chin toward the ceiling, then gradually eased the cravat into shape by working his lower jaw. He made plenty of mistakes, which meant

1657

GEORGE VILLIERS

starting over again afresh. His valet, Robinson, left the dressing room with the rumpled rejects on a tray; "our failures," he would tell the assembled crowd.

Brummell himself admitted "folly, that is the making of me," and it was his unmaking, too, as his friendship with the future king cooled. One night in 1814, the prince arrived at a ball with Lord Alvanley and chose to ignore his fashionable mentor. "Alvanley," Brummell called out, furious, "who is your fat friend?"

The prince never spoke to him again. Brummell's popularity

plummeted and his creditors rushed in, knowing that out of royal favor, he could never afford his lifestyle. He gave them the slip—for a while—running away to France, where he struggled on for years and was briefly imprisoned. Brummell died in a charity home. He'd lost all interest in fashion.

SAFFRON

A seasoning made from the Crocus sativus *flower*

Each violet-blue *Crocus sativus* bud produces three fragile red stamens—saffron threads—gathered by hand while the flower blooms. Its nutty-sweet aroma is delightful, and its legend is luxe, as it takes more than seventy thousand flowers to amass one pound of the precious spice. In Greek and Roman times, sweet-smelling saffron water was sprinkled in theaters, and crocus buds were strewn over banquet-hall floors. Romans burned saffron as a sacrifice to the gods; Homer sang of the "saffron morn," while Alexander the Great drank his wine mixed with saffron, and the occasional dash of myrrh. Zeus was said to sleep on a bed of feathery red saffron threads.

Saffron was also used as a medicine, especially for eye ailments. Persians believed that the crocus threads induced sleep, cured

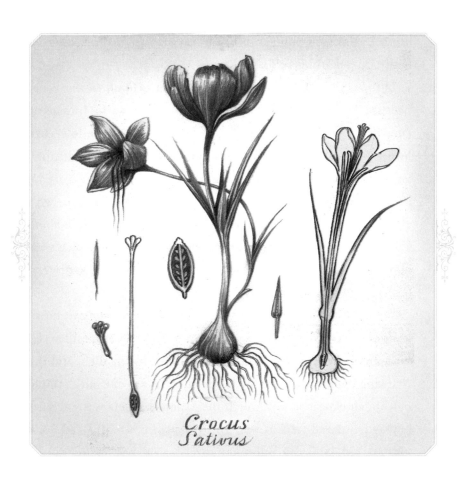

Crocus
Sativus

melancholy, and could be used as an aphrodisiac, which explains why they sprinkled saffron in the beds of newlyweds. Used as a dye, its deep golden color symbolized loftiness and illumination. Persian kings wore saffron-gold shoes, and ancient Irish chieftains wrapped themselves in saffron-hued cloaks. Buddhist monks dressed in saffron-tinted robes, and in the 1600s saffron was used to tint Queen Anne's ruffs.

European Crusaders introduced Persian *za'faran* to the West. Because it was outrageously expensive and easy to transport, enterprising medieval entrepreneurs also used saffron to secure business loans. Conversely, its value and portability aroused temptation to cheat the buyer. Inspectors in fifteenth-century Nuremberg ordered the execution of men selling tainted saffron, with offenders either buried alive or burned in the marketplace along with their wares. Modern charlatans weigh down the spice with moisture or with sugar, or adulterate it with marigold, safflower, turmeric, pomegranate, or even fibers of smoked beef.

Yet, while saffron is known as the world's most expensive spice, it often suffers from its flashy reputation. Since most recipes call for a mere pinch, saffron doesn't cost much by the dish, and the rich tang it lends a classic Milanese-style risotto or even a simple bowl of chickpeas is well worth the expense. Chefs warn against buying powdered saffron, which is usually impure. Instead, look for dark red, long, dry, unbroken threads. The best variety is Iranian Persian saffron, which is illegal to import to the United States, though with persistence it can be found.

Catalan Chickpeas with Tomatoes and Toasted Almonds
from Nancy Harmon Jenkins's *The New Mediterranean Diet Cookbook:*
A Delicious Alternative for Lifelong Health

(Makes 6 to 8 servings)

1½ cups chickpeas, soaked overnight
1 onion, finely chopped
¼ cup extra-virgin olive oil
2 ripe tomatoes, peeled and finely chopped
a big pinch of saffron threads, toasted
3 garlic cloves, coarsely chopped
⅓ cup toasted, chopped almonds
½ cup chopped flat-leaf parsley
sea salt and freshly ground black pepper
2 hard-boiled eggs for garnish (optional)

1. Drain the chickpeas and transfer to a saucepan with enough boil-
    ing water to cover to a depth of about 1 inch. Bring to a simmer
    and cook the chickpeas, partially covered, until they are tender,
    about 30 minutes to an hour, depending on the age of the chick-
    peas. Add a little boiling water from time to time as necessary.
2. While the chickpeas are cooking, combine the onion and olive
    oil in a skillet and set over medium-low heat. Sauté the onion,
    stirring, until it is soft, then stir in the tomatoes and cook for

about 20 minutes longer, cooking away all the liquid from the tomatoes so that they sizzle with the onions in the pan. Tip this mixture into the chickpeas and stir well.

3. To toast the saffron, fold it into a piece of clean white typing paper. Set the paper envelope in a pan over medium-low heat. Keep turning the paper until it starts to turn brown. Remove immediately and unwrap the saffron, which will have become crisp and darker.

4. Combine the toasted saffron, garlic, almonds, parsley, and a pinch of salt. Pound the mixture in a mortar or process it in a food processor until it's a coarse paste, thinning it with a little of the liquid from the chickpeas. Stir the paste into the chickpeas, tasting for salt and pepper.

5. Serve the chickpeas, if you wish, garnished with the eggs, peeled, chopped, and sprinkled over the top of the dish.

 **SEQUINS**

Small spangles used to decorate clothing

The word "sequin" is a Frenchified version of the Venetian *zecchino*, a pure gold coin the republic first issued in 1284. Some say that when the currency became obsolete, enterprising Venetian ladies pierced the old *zecchino* coins and embroidered their clothes with them, igniting the bedazzling fashion. How easily, then as now, a simple row of sequins turns the ordinary snazzy.

Though ancient Roman women didn't wear sequins stitched to their clothes, they did wear coin jewelry as early as the third century AD. The jingling tradition was carried on in the folk costumes of Turkey, Romania, Greece, and Syria, where glittering head scarves and bridal costumes flickered with coinlike discs. No mere display of wealth, the scintillation offered magical protection, confusing the evil eye. In the old days, the coins were thought even more potent when stamped with the image of a mighty ruler. Fake coins printed with images of ancient emperors, like Constantine or Alexander the Great, were made into amulets throughout Byzantium.

Later, sparkling sequins punched from fine sheets of brass, gold, or silver glimmered from the costumes of Henry VIII, Edward IV, and Queen Elizabeth I. They brightened the French court during the eighteenth century, and Parisian fashion in the next, when dressing up with spangles was expected of stage performers. "Sequins create a charming effect. They catch the light in sudden and unexpected flashes that shimmer brilliantly before the eyes," French critic Théophile Gautier (1811–1872) wrote in 1837, bored with the virginal white worn by the local ballerinas. "What a dancer really needs are feathers, tinsel, silver tassels, gilded bells, all the crazy, fantastic dress of the wandering player."

While the Gilded Age saw its share of sequins, as did the 1920s, when the flappers shone in dresses glazed with celluloid sequins, in the 1930s sequins went Hollywood. Gautier would have loved the brilliantly shimmering costumes created by the era's most powerful costume designer, Gilbert Adrian (1903–1959)—known simply as Adrian.

Adrian defined mid-twentieth-century American glamour, dressing stars such as Joan Crawford, Marlene Dietrich, Jean Harlow, and Greta Garbo over the course of 233 films during his long career. His MGM workshop swarmed with as many as 250 seamstresses, tailors, pattern makers, and embroiderers, making slinky gowns slathered with sequins. His dresses caught the light, livening up the on-screen black-and-white palette, but when movies went Technicolor, Adrian brought sequins into the future. He secured his legendary status in 1939 by creating Judy Garland's famous ruby-red sequined slippers for *The Wizard of Oz*.

SHABBY CHIC

Unassuming stylishness with a disheveled edge

The allure of artistic dishevelment is hardly a twentieth-century phenomenon. Back in 1772 Denis Diderot (1713–1784) bemoaned, with bohemian pride, the loss of his favorite, battered garment in his essay "Regrets on Parting with My Old Dressing Gown; or, a Warning to Those Who Have More Taste Than Money." "Why on earth did I ever part with it?" he crowed. "It was used to me and I was used to it." While the old dressing gown was agreeably covered in ink stains, the new one was anonymous. Worse, Diderot realized that the new dressing gown suddenly made the rest of his apartment look tired.

Similarly, the rebel poet Arthur Rimbaud (1854–1891) admitted a fierce attachment to his tattered overcoat. At sixteen, Rimbaud arrived on the doorstep of fellow poet Paul Verlaine, who became his lover, with his hair in a tangled whirlwind, wearing clothes he'd outgrown and a dirty string as a tie. He was eager to be corrupted, and he looked it. He wrote "Ma Bohème" around that time, describing his vagabond life, strolling under the open sky with holes in his pockets, his trousers torn, and sporting a battered overcoat that was just "becoming ideal." Over a hundred years later, Rimbaud's precocious thirst and ravaged looks inspired sensitive rock stars like grunge icon Kurt Cobain and the punk poetess Patti Smith, who came across one of the poet's books when she was also sixteen.

But during the early part of the twentieth century, the lesser-known poet Edna St. Vincent Millay (1892–1950) served as a model of lightly mussed, edgy chic. Just out of Vassar, she was already a budding celebrity in 1920 when she moved to Greenwich Village and a small book of her poetry, *A Few Figs from Thistles*, made Millay an icon of wild youth. Her most infamous quatrain reads:

My candle burns at both ends;
It will not last the night;
But ah, my foes, and oh, my friends—
It gives a lovely light!

Her shabby-chic attire was part of the mystique. A reporter at one poetry reading noted, "the reading of her verses was as quiet and simple as the blue dress," and "at times as flaming as the flame-colored scarf that clung about her." Formal portraits show Millay dressed in stark, slightly rumpled, serious clothes, looking grave, but she was known for her exotic bright batiks, Eastern European peasant blouses, and dresses that were far from new.

Men dropped at her feet, including Edmund Wilson (1895–1972), who fictionalized their young love in *I Thought of Daisy*, describing Millay's allure via his fictional character Rita Cavanagh. "She wore a shabby black dress," he wrote of Rita/Edna. "She was so small that I hadn't noticed her. But, as I shook hands with her, she gave me, from eyes of a greenish uncertain color, a curious alert intent look, as of a fox peering out from covert." Four men competed for her attention as she puffed a cigarette and recited a poem she'd written just that afternoon.

"All to me was a wonder then—" Wilson wrote, "her old dress, her mother's sewing machine, her wide gamine's grin . . ." He'd been struck by the glamour of her shabby chic.

SHOWSTOPPER

A performance during a show that brings the action to a stop

Choreographer Busby Berkeley (1895–1976) brightened the dreary Depression era with his flamboyant fascination for chorus girls, sending battalions of them swarming across the soundstages of Hollywood. His kaleidoscopic vision was unmistakable, with chorines forming a geometric glut of platinum curls and long legs moving in time. Sure, it was camp, but it was also hypnotic. "My philosophy was purely—call it gigantic entertainment," Berkeley told a *New York Times* reporter. "A lot of people used to say I was crazy. But I can truthfully say one thing: I gave 'em a show."

Berkeley's idea of a show was actually a showstopper, a song-and-dance number that interrupted a film's plot to bring in a bevy of beauties at the slightest excuse. In *Gold Diggers of 1933*, Ginger Rogers sang "We're in the Money" while Berkeley's showgirls, dressed in coin bikinis, waved platter-size dimes. In *The Gang's All Here*, they scampered around wielding enormous papier-mâché bananas as Carmen Miranda sang "The Lady in the Tutti Frutti Hat." In *42nd Street*, they high-kicked across town, then formed Manhattan's skyline with cutout skyscraper silhouettes. They splashed in a grotto, paddling their dancing slippers underwater, and smoked opium in a shady Shanghai nightspot in *Footlight Parade*, and they sprang from a sea of white ostrich feathers wearing wispy feathered bikinis in *Fashions of 1934*. Unconstrained by union rules, Berkeley filmed around the clock and followed the adage "the more the merrier." "Instead of using a dozen girls as others do, I prefer to use forty-eight or sixty," he said. His biggest numbers were rumored to cost $10,000 for each minute of screen time.

Berkeley, whose parents were touring actors, made his stage debut at five and performed and directed on Broadway before making it in Hollywood, though he couldn't dance. But then, his dancers didn't dance so much as maneuver, like the soldiers Berkeley herded around the parade grounds while serving as a lieutenant during World War I. Still, as famous as he became, he was put out of work once Hollywood's musicals took a turn for the sensical during the 1940s, when attempts at realism and a regard for the plot kept the showstoppers at bay.

Yet while Hollywood turned rational, the surrealistic song-and-dance tradition still reigns today in India. As in Berkeley's era, contemporary Bollywood film stars lip-synch song lyrics as troupes of chorus dancers rush in. Artsy Indian directors limit dance sequences to wedding scenes or religious festivals, but others don't mind making fantastical leaps, cutting from a group of actors talking quietly to a shimmying extravaganza.

Besides the old, Berkeley-esque numbers, Bollywood boasts a showstopping tradition all its own in Helen, the singularly named redheaded megastar who gyrated her way through hundreds of films during the sixties and seventies. Directors did whatever it took to work a "Helen song" into their films, diverting a film's action into a nightclub, where bad Helen, acting as a cabaret dancer, would do her thing. When she belly danced, spangles flew. Her Vegas-worthy tail feathers shook and trembled.

Born to a Spanish-Burmese mother and a French father, Helen Richardson Khan (1939–) joined the chorus at thirteen, performing her first solo number six years later. With her red hair, pale skin, and debauched dance moves, she was typecast as the quintessential Westernized vamp, a foil for Bollywood's innocent Indian heroines. At her most memorable, a tipsy and breathless Helen reeled across the dance floor in 1972's *Caravan*. She roiled on the ground and bopped in a go-go cage. Then, when her dress caught on a nail, she wriggled free and kept right on shimmying in a gold-spangled bra and miniskirt. Helen frolicked her way through the early 1980s, appearing in nearly five hundred films.

SILENCE

The absence of sound

Silence is expected in a library, customary in a museum, sacred in a monastery, but it's usually avoided onstage. Nevertheless, two avant-garde artists, composer John Cage (1912–1992) and playwright Samuel Beckett (1906–1989), each structured long, expressive stretches of silence into their performances, battling the onslaught of twentieth-century noise.

Cage, inspired by his Zen studies and by artist Robert Rauschenberg's all-white canvases, described silence as unintended sound, the quiet noises found outside of traditional music. When performing Cage's most famous silent piece, *4'33"*, a musician walks onstage, sits at a piano, and marks off time for four minutes and thirty-three seconds, without making any sound. Cage hoped the audience would sit patiently listening to the shuffles, creaking floorboards, and polite coughs in the auditorium as music. "I have spent many pleasant hours in the woods conducting performances of my silent piece," he said. Pianist David Tudor faced a less appreciative crowd while performing the work in a concert hall in 1954. "At the appropriate time, Mr. Tudor seated himself at the piano, placed a hand on the music rack—and waited," the critic from the *New York Times* reported, calling the evening's entertainment "hollow, sham, pretentious Greenwich Village exhibitionism."

Cage had a kindred spirit in Beckett, who admired the "great black pauses of Beethoven's Seventh Symphony," and who, with the tense silence of his scripts, tried to express "a whisper of that final music or that silence that underlies all," he explained. Like Cage, Beckett was known for the lengthy silences scripted into his plays, including *Waiting for Godot*, into which silence flooded "like water into a sinking ship," he pointed out.

One day, sitting in a café, Beckett honored that quiet abyss with

"Breath," a characterless, wordless thirty-five-second play that he scrawled across a paper tablecloth and called a "farce in five acts." It is birth, life, silence, and death, all rolled into one. The curtains open on a dim stage strewn with garbage. After five seconds comes the sharp sound of a baby's cry, followed by the sound of inhalation, synchronized with a brightening of the stage lights. Everything remains bright and silent for five seconds. Then comes the sound of exhalation accompanied by a dimming of the lights over a ten-second span. A cry, identical to the first, follows, this time representing a dying wail. And a final five seconds of dark silence concludes the show.

In 1969 Beckett offered the piece to theater producer Kenneth Tynan for his erotic revue *Oh! Calcutta!*, which included sexy, farcical fare by Sam Shepard, John Lennon, and Edna O'Brien. To spice up Beckett's part of the act, Tynan added naked bodies to the on-set rubbish, and instructed his actors to moan throughout the mini-play. So much for silence. Beckett was furious, but contractual legalities kept him from doing anything about it. During *Oh! Calcutta!*'s 1,314 performances, 85 million people saw "Breath," making it Beckett's most popular play.

SOTELTIE

A highly ornamented dish used as table decoration

For the fanciest medieval feasts, ambitious chefs sculpted pie-dough castles, served checkerboards of tinted jellies, and worked ground meat and bean paste into edible crowns, trees, and animals. These dishes of fantasy food, called "sotelties," or subtleties, at the English banquet table, and known as *entremets* in France, weren't served to satisfy hunger, but to amuse.

Some scholars say the tradition evolved while cooks searched out new ways to celebrate the drab, meatless days of Lent, disguising shish-kebabed dried fruit as roasted meat, or making faux veal from sturgeon. Sotelties, however, added a little sly wit. Dyed green fish eggs imitated peas. A cake could be decorated to look like baked fish. One inventive chef served a roasted cock wearing a paper helmet and holding a lance under its wing while riding astride a piglet. Others served peacock, skinned, roasted, and neatly sewn back together again, tail feathers spread and its bill covered in gilt. At an English feast, a stag formed from meat or vegetable paste was presented with an arrow stuck in its side. When the arrow was pulled out, claret poured from the wound.

The best-known soteltie is the "four and twenty blackbirds baked in a pie," of nursery-rhyme fame. Across Europe at the end of the fifteenth century, live birds were slipped into a baked pie shell through a hole cut in its bottom. Once an unsuspecting guest cut into the upper crust, they flapped out, free. "This is done," noted one Italian cookbook author of the era, "in order to create more gaiety and pleasure for the company." Varying the theme, Philip the Good feasted with his knights in 1454 at a table anchored by a huge pie shell containing twenty musicians. Nearly two centuries later, the Duke of Buckingham entertained Charles I and Queen Henrietta Maria by serving her a pie concealing the famous dwarf Jeffrey Hudson. Another popular tradition delivered an enormous bowl of quaking custard to the table. Inevitably, during the course of the meal, the town jester launched himself over the heads of the guests, plunging into the custard and splattering them with it.

By the mid-fifteenth century, however, sotelties took on a more serious, ceremonial tone, promoting allegorical and religious themes. Chiquart, chef to the Duke of Savoy, recorded his recipe for the allegorically charged Castle of Love, a foody diorama to be carried by four men into the dining hall on a platform. Fire-breathing beasts—a boar's head, a glazed piglet, and a re-dressed swan—roared from the castle's towers. A fountain in its courtyard gushed rose water and spiced wine. And across the castle grounds meat-paste riders set out on a hunt as a meat-paste army launched a futile attempt against the castle's tiny sculpted archers. Soon enough, the creativity of such sotelties outstripped the capabilities of the kitchen, and by the century's end inedible diversions made from wood and featuring living actors, dancers, and musicians replaced the edible amusements.

The soteltie's whimsy lived on in sweet marzipan figurines, as when the Earl of Hertford entertained Queen Elizabeth I in 1591, sending out a complete marzipan universe that was anything but subtle—full of sugary castles, forts, drummers, trumpeters, soldiers, lions, unicorns, camels, elephants, birds, snakes, mermaids, dolphins, and even conger eels—and ordering it delivered to the dining hall by two hundred servants carrying a thousand dishes, with a hundred torchbearers to light the way.

STRING

A cord, line, or thread

A bit of imagination and a length of string are all that's needed to enjoy one of the simplest, and most widespread, forms of entertainment known. Twisting and looping a series of string images, as one does when playing cat's cradle, illustrated folktales and provided a pleasant way to pass long nights for the Navahos and the Eskimos, Aboriginal Australians, African tribespeople, and those of New Guinea, to name just a few.

Most of what's known about the art of string stems from research done by A. C. Haddon (1855–1940), a charismatic Cambridge professor of anthropology who devised a notation method for recording hundreds of different string figures in the late nineteenth century, with the hopes of understanding the extent of contact between primitive tribes. (A shared battery of string figures indicated close relations.) String was his pet passion, one his students shared. "I can imagine that some people would think we are demented—or at least wasting our time," he noted. Haddon's followers fanned out, comparing Micronesian and Melanesian figures. They collected figures in India, and in the Anglo-Egyptian Sudan. They juxtaposed the Fijians' "Parakeet's Playground" with the Chama Indians' "Toad." The Navahos made the Pleiades in string, while the

Kiwai Papuans crafted crocodiles, crabs, and coconut palms. The most widespread figure was "The Mouse," in which a tiny looped mouse escapes a cat, slipping through a maze of fretwork. String figures done by Eskimos, however, were judged the most realistic, like one remarkable figure which, when manipulated quickly, looks like a river flowing between two mountains, down a range, and into a plain where a single mountain rises alongside a man in a boat catching salmon.

Only in Europe did the anthropologists come up empty-handed, or nearly so. Besides the cat's cradle, known in China, Korea, Japan, the Philippines, and Borneo, and introduced to England via the tea trade, there were few new figures to be found. "We may fairly safely venture the generalization that civilization kills cat's cradles," concluded Haddon's daughter, Kathleen.

Following in her father's footsteps, Kathleen Haddon Rishbeth (1888–1961) collected figures from all over the world and wrote several books on string. While other Western explorers traveled with hired riflemen to keep them safe, both Haddons relied on string games to win over the tribespeople they encountered in dangerous places like New Guinea or Borneo. "I once arrived alone at a village up the Fly river in Papua where no white woman had been before, and as I did not know the language I wondered at first what to do," Kathleen wrote. She took out her string and slowly the local villagers crowded around her, first the children, then their mothers, and then the men, all riveted by the new tricks she introduced and eager to show her theirs.

"There are few memories more delightful than those of chance encounters with parties of natives," she went on, "the squatting beside the track, the exchange of courtesies in string, the mutual delight in recognizing old favourites, the excitement and applause that greet new ones, the final regretful leave-taking—and all without one word being spoken on either side that was intelligible to the other."

SUBAQUATIC

Underwater

> *"There is, one knows not what sweet mystery about this sea, whose gently awful stirrings seem to speak of some hidden soul beneath," wrote Herman Melville (1819–1891), luring his readers into the subaquatic deep in 1851 with* Moby-Dick. *"For here, millions of mixed shades and shadows, drowned dreams, somnambulisms, reveries; all that we call lives and souls, lie dreaming, dreaming still . . ."*

The mysterious potential of the underwater world fascinated Victorians who, succumbing to aquarium mania, installed fish tanks in every mid-nineteenth-century bourgeois home on both sides of the Channel and on either side of the Atlantic. The urge to "possess such gorgeous living pictures" seized writers like England's

Charles Kingsley (1819–1875), the author of the children's underwater adventure *The Water-Babies*. "Those who have never seen one of them can never imagine the gorgeous colouring and grace and delicacy of form which these subaqueous landscapes exhibit," he wrote of the aquarium.

A goldfish circling in a glass bowl was all right—"few objects can be more ornamental or amusing," as one journalist noted—but an aquarium shaped like an ornate vase and decorated inside with tiny shipwrecks and grottoes was better. A flurry of handbooks instructed owners on tank cleaning, stocking starfish, periwinkles, and seaweed, and obtaining salt water, either by paying a friendly steamship steward to collect a cask en route, as one expert recommended, or by salinating water at home. But beyond its beauty, an aquarium provided a little daily drama, with the birth and growth of its inmates, but also "the freaks, pranks, and even crimes of its inhabitants—theft, murder, and cannibalism, contributing to the fun without any shock to our moral sensibilities," explained English author Shirley Hibberd (1825–1890). The depths were dangerous, and dark, even inside a pretty glass bowl.

If ever an underwater scene was designed to shock, however, it was the psychologically charged marine world Salvador Dalí (1904–

1989) installed at the New York World's Fair in 1939. Like Melville's depictions of the drowned and dreaming, Dalí's delightfully deranged *Dream of Venus* was a "panorama of the unconscious," he explained. Inside the central grotto, visitors found a hired actress, Dalí's "Venus," lying topless on a gigantic red satin bed strewn with lobsters and champagne bottles, while her "dream," visible through a window, was played out in a giant aquarium by women dressed as mermaids, the artist's "living liquid ladies," who wore nothing much beyond their rubber tail fins and spent their days playing a woman-shaped piano or tapping away at a floating rubber typewriter. (*Time* magazine called the performers "Lady Godivers.")

When Fair officials demanded that Dalí sanitize his subaquatic fantasy, and get rid of an image hung at the entrance of the performance space—Botticelli's Venus made over with a fish-head torso—he retaliated by hiring a plane to shower the city with copies of a ranting manifesto he called the "Declaration of the Independence of the Imagination and the Rights of Man to His Own Madness." "It is man's right to love women with ecstatic fish heads," Dalí declared. Though art historians now rue the day, his pavilion was demolished along with the rest at the end of the Fair.

SWING

A suspended seat that oscillates backward and forward

For all its charm and innocence, the swing's sensual rocking rhythm can't be denied. In the eighteenth century, artists tapped into both its bucolic and its more suggestive allure. "In this diversion there are very many pretty shrieks, not so much for fear of falling off as that their petticoats should untie," *The Spectator* noted in 1712. "The lover who swings his lady is to tie her clothes very close together with his hat band before she admits him to throw up her heels."

French painter Antoine Watteau (1684–1721) popularized the image of pastoral swinging with bright-eyed, rosy-cheeked maidens pushed by equally frolicsome lads. But a generation later, Jean-Honoré Fragonard (1732–1806) turned up the heat. Art critics of the nineteenth century, the Goncourt brothers, called Watteau's dignified young couples "listless, indifferent, morose, consumed by ennui." Fragonard, on the other hand, was the "cherub of erotic painting."

Fragonard studied under Chardin and Boucher and won the French Academy's first prize when he was starting out in 1752, but he soon abandoned serious historical subjects—and, Diderot would say, his self-respect—in favor of the libertine scenes of stolen kisses and bucolic romps that landed the big commissions. "Instead of working for glory and posterity he is content to shine in the boudoirs and dressing rooms," decried critic Louis Petit de Bachaumont (1690–1771).

But who else could have done *The Swing*? Fragonard's coy swinger, her pink slipper flying from her dainty foot, whisks through the air with her skirts mid-billow, offering a frilly, illicit peek beneath them to a young man lounging below in a tangle of bushes. The Baron de Saint-Julien is thought to have commissioned the painting, which became a symbol of those decadent times, in 1767, though he first approached another painter, Gabriel-François Doyen (1726–1806), for the job. "He was dying with a desire to have me make a picture, the idea of which he was going to outline," Doyen told a friend. De Saint-Julien proposed the subject of his mistress pushed on a swing by a bishop, with himself placed in the picture "in such a way that I would be able to see the legs of this lovely girl," he told Doyen, "and better still, if you want to enliven your picture a little more . . ."

"I was far from wanting to treat such a subject," Doyen snipped. "I referred this gentleman to M. Fragonat [*sic*] who has undertaken it and is at present making this singular work."

Engravings of Fragonard's resulting image circulated late in the century, printed with the caption "The Happy Hazards of the Swing." Because of its brow-raising subject matter, British customs agents destroyed the engraver's copperplate, and, initially, Fragonard's famous painting was refused admission to England, according to one art historian. It now hangs in the Wallace Collection in London.

TALK

To converse, exchanging ideas, thoughts, and information

The ancient Greeks said feeding the stomach wasn't enough—the mind needed nourishment, too. Good conversation was essential. With *The Sophists at Dinner*, Athenaeus compiled fifteen volumes of early-third-century table talk. The refined wits of the Italian Renaissance picked up the thread, touting polite conversation with etiquette guides like *Galateo* (1560), written by the Archbishop of Benevento, Giovanni della Casa (1503–1556), who reminded his young gentlemen readers that, when speaking with a "person of quality," they should not pummel his stomach or "pull him by the buttons, bandstrings or belt." One can only imagine the manners of young men who needed to be reminded not to punch a gentleman in the side, or to poke him with their elbows, repeating to him after each sentence "Did I not tell you so?"

Young women learned the art of conversation in the next century's literary salons, like those established by the Parisian elite.
Once or twice a week the typical *salonnière* gave an open house,
inviting authors, philosophers, dandies, and hangers-on, sometimes for dinner—but always for talk. For Germaine de Staël's
mother, Suzanne Necker (1739–1794), who held court on Fridays,
orchestrating the conversation in her salon was a near-religious
calling.

Necker, daughter of a Swiss evangelical minister and wife of
Louis XVI's minister of finance, encouraged high-minded ban-
ter in her salon, luring several greats of the day, including Buffon,
Gibbon, Baron Grimm, and d'Alembert—as well as Diderot, whom
she had subjected "to a regular persecution" until he turned up, as
he later told his mistress. Several volumes of epigrams and axioms
culled from Necker's private journals and published after her death
demonstrate the rigorous guidelines she followed in preparing for
her guests, researching potential topics in advance. "One is most
ready for conversation when one has written and thought about
things before going into society," she noted. A model *salonnière*
kept her guests' egos in check, and stopped them from droning on
or from losing their tempers. She offered her opinions sparingly,
not "like the sun that illuminates constantly, but like the stars that
pierce the darkness of the night from time to time, and which thus
make themselves more noticed."

However earnest Necker may have been, her constant striving
made her somewhat stiff. The Chevalier de Chastellux (1734–1788)

claimed to have found one of her little notebooks under an arm-chair when he'd arrived at her house early one Friday. He read in it about her plans to speak to an author about his latest novel, to talk with another guest about love, and everything else she recited "word for word" later that evening.

In that way, she didn't play by the rules. Then as now, etiquette dictated that conversation should be polished, but delivered with natural ease. On the receiving end, a good listener provided unwavering focus, even in a noisy room. "The great secret of conversation is continual attention," Necker confided.

Yet, besides interrupting, saying nothing might be the worst conversational crime of all. Etiquette maven Emily Post (1872–1960) wrote of a Mrs. Toplofty, who found herself at a dinner seated besides a man whom she openly despised. " 'I shall not talk to you—because I don't care to,' she told him, 'but for the sake of my hostess I shall say my multiplication tables. Twice one are two, twice two are four'—and she continued on through the tables, making him alternate them with her. As soon as she politely could she turned again to her other companion."

TASSEL

An ornamental tuft made from threads of the same length

Honorific tassels were an Etruscan status symbol in the fifth and fourth centuries BC, when high-ranking women wore them hanging from their shoulders in pairs. The look set them apart. Later, between the medieval era and the early nineteenth century, cardinals and archbishops wore as many as fifteen tassels dangling from their hats. In Japan, with a bit of pomp, samurais used them to decorate the hilts of their swords. In the nineteenth century, tassels were a favorite embellishment for European military uniforms. And today the tassel of distinction swings from the graduate's mortarboard cap.

Yet in many cultures this slightly absurd—but somehow pretty—item also served as an amulet. In the Old Testament, God ordered the Israelites to wear tassels or fringe as a mnemonic device to keep them from forgetting his commandments. The practice persists today in the tallith, or prayer shawl, which, some suggest, dates from the time when tassels were worn as charms against the evil eye. Tassels were protective talismans in Egypt, Mesopotamia, and across the Arab world, where children wore tassels on their hoods or caps in order to frighten away or to distract malevolent spirits. In the ancient Japanese Shinto religion, paper tassels safeguarded against trouble. In China, where tassels are still given as gifts in pairs, they're good-luck charms, often ornamented with bits of jade, glass beads, or complex knots.

But beyond the tassel's function as a status symbol or as a charm, it has been appreciated strictly for its ornamental value during many centuries. In the medieval era, tassels were used to tie capes and cloaks at the collar, while French couturiers of the eighteenth century took a less modest approach, wearing tassels all over. Mademoiselle Éloffe, a French couturiere favored by members of Marie Antoinette's court, supplied tassels to all the best-dressed women. She decorated a dress worn by Madame du Boscage with gold and silver embroidery, rhinestoned ribbons and lace, as well as silver-hued silk tassels and those in fine gold. For the Comtesse de Narbonne she made up a lacy gown embroidered with wreaths and silver spangles, sequined ribbons, rhinestones, and silver tassels, all finished off with a rhinestone-studded and tasseled belt.

At the same time, master trimmings makers, called *passementiers* in France, festooned the drawing rooms, salons, and bedrooms of the elite with yet more tassels. Zealous decorators hung long swags of tassels across window drapes, bed canopies, and sofas, or attached single tassels to the corners of cushions or to the ends of bell cords. Earlier, in the 1600s, uncomplicated, straightforward tassels livened up fine furniture. In the next century, even the trim was trimmed, and tassels themselves were often girdled with yet another ring of smaller tasselettes. The French Revolution put a damper on that sort of excess, but only for a short time.

With the emergence of the neoclassical style in the early nineteenth century, tassels were back, and interior trimmings became elaborate once again across the Western world. Window treatments especially were lush. Curtains came trimmed with trellised fringe, ribbons, pom-poms, and tassels galore, all held back with magnificently tasseled cords, in upper-class homes as well as in those of the middle class. While economy might make more basic curtains necessary, a simpler style "never can be introduced with a view of producing a better effect," stated the English author of *The Cabinetmaker and Upholsterer's Guide* in 1826. Those who couldn't afford real silk tassels went in for mock-tassel substitutes, such as those carved in wood and wrapped with an outer layer of silk fringe. That is, until at the turn of the century the naturalistic lines of Art Nouveau did away with the Victorians' glut of trimmings, ending the tassel's long reign.

TEA

A drink made from the leaves of the tea plant

Chinese texts of the first century BC described tea as the elixir of immortality, but no other cultures have celebrated the drink with the diligent fervor of Japan and England, where sipping tea is a matter of consequence.

Drinking powdered green tea developed into a poetic ritual in twelfth-century Japan when Zen monks cultivated Chinese tea plants to make the beverage that kept them awake during their long, moonlit meditation sessions. The tradition led to the formal tea ceremony, *chanoyu*, designed to encourage guests to savor the moment while sipping tea in a rustic retreat built like a lowly hermit's cabin. The mood is quiet, full of reverence. Every movement is prescribed, from palming the tea bowl just right to murmuring a few compliments on the decor as the tea master serves his guests.

To heighten the humble effect, the monk who founded the ceremony, Murata Shukō (1422–1502), built an ultramodest ten-foot-
square tea hut in Kyoto, promoting what was later recognized as the
rough-hewn *wabi* aesthetic—and what Shukō called "chilled and
dried up." His disciple Sen Rikyū (1521–1591) served tea elegantly
in shabby cracked peasant bowls, often with their rough repairs
left purposely visible. Another follower broke off one of the han-
dles from a vase he found too symmetrical. As Shukō explained, "A
prize horse looks best hitched to a thatched hut."

In England, tea was served with the same ceremonial gravity,
though the aesthetic emphasis was on delicacy, not destitution.
Anna Stanhope, seventh Duchess of Bedford (1783–1857), a lady-
in-waiting to Queen Victoria, formalized the tradition of afternoon tea, inviting the ladies to her boudoir for tea and thin toasts,
as by 5 P.M. each night—long before dinner—she suffered a "sinking feeling," as she wrote to a friend. The English tea was homey,
yet opulent. High taxes meant tea cost more per pound than a servant might make in a year during the 1600s. Moralists called tea a
frivolous luxury, though the taxes were reduced in 1834, around
the time India's more reasonably priced tea was discovered. Until
then, the mistress of the house kept the precious commodity
locked up in its caddy, and presented it in equally prized porcelain tea services, which she might wash herself in order to keep a
clumsy maid from breaking something irreplaceable. The china
of a true Victorian lady was "dainty," noted one etiquette guide,

"and the tea-cozy should be pretty and handsomely decorated with embroidery."

Performing her duties according to a precise set of rules, a hostess served the tea herself, aided by her staff. She always asked, "Do you take sugar?" There was a certain way to maneuver the lemon, and instructions on how long to brew and how to pour. Scones and finger sandwiches were obligatory.

Her overall demeanor was also carefully considered, as it was in ancient Japan. "During the whole process of making and pouring out of the tea, the conversation must not be allowed to flag for one instant," one English manual instructed, "and no guest must be permitted either to engross too much attention or to be neglected." Paradoxically, in both countries success in the elaborate art of serving tea lay in seeming artless.

Tea-making tips from *What Shall We Have for Breakfast? Or Everybody's Breakfast Book*, by Agnes Maitland (1901)

Fill the kettle with fresh cold water, and set it on to boil . . . Never make the tea with water that has been long on the fire simmering, or that has been twice boiled. The natural aeration of the water is drawn off by long-continued heating, and the "hardness" of the water, or the proportion of mineral matter contained in it, is increased by evaporation that takes place. The more rapidly the water is heated, the better the tea.

Warm the teapot. Put in the tea in the proportion of 1 oz to seven persons, or a teaspoonful for each person and a teaspoonful over. Pour on the boiling water, filling the teapot at once . . . Cover the teapot, and allow it to stand from five to seven minutes before pouring out . . .

If the tea is required in haste, while the water is coming to the boil put the tea into the teapot and stand it inside the oven until it is thoroughly hot through. Pour on the boiling water and in a minute it will be ready to pour out.

TEMPEST

A violent storm, usually accompanied by rain, snow, or thunder

While other sailors went out of their way to avoid tempests and raging thunderstorms at sea, two English poets, Lord Byron (1788–1824) and Percy Shelley (1792–1822), sailed toward danger—and excitement.

The two first met in the Swiss town of Sécheron on Lake Geneva in the summer of 1816, each drawn there by a love of Jean-Jacques Rousseau's breathless novel *Julie, ou la Nouvelle Héloïse* (1761), which was set in the heavenly spot. "I read *Julie* all day," Shelley wrote to a friend, "an overflowing, as it now seems, surrounded by the scenes which it has so wonderfully peopled, of sublimest genius, and more than human sensibility." Byron, who was so famous that other tourists watched him through their telescopes, met Shelley on the hotel's jetty and asked him to dinner. Soon, they had rented neighboring villas. And then the two poets went in on a sailboat together—because, as they discovered, if there was anything they both liked better than *Julie*, it was sailing, preferably on a dangerously rough sea. "Shelley was on the Lake much oftener than I, at all hours of the night and day," Byron remembered. "He almost lived on it; his great rage is a boat."

Accompanied by two boatmen, and their copy of Rousseau's book, they made a nine-day tour of the sites where Julie and her lover, named Saint-Preux, conducted their illicit affair, reading the appropriate passages aloud to each other. A near-fatal tempest, encountered in precisely the spot where Julie and her lover nearly capsize in a storm, only made their romantic hearts beat faster. Violent waves "added to the magnificence of all around," Byron wrote, "although occasionally accompanied by danger to the boat, which was small and overloaded." Of course, Byron was a champion swimmer. Shelley couldn't swim a stroke. With their boat filling fast, Byron pulled off his coat and told Shelley he would save him "unless we got smashed against the rocks which were high & sharp with an awkward Surf on them at the minute," Byron later wrote to a friend. "He answered me with the greatest coolness— 'that he had no notion of being saved—& that I would have enough to do to save myself and begged me not to trouble me.'" Their fictional counterparts went through a similar routine, watching each other with curiosity as death neared. Julie's lover, Saint-Preux, saw her fade as their frail boat broke into pieces, her "beauty struggling in the midst of the waves," Rousseau wrote, "the pallor of death dulling the roses on her cheeks." Like Byron and Shelley, however, Julie and her beau made the shore.

Tempests and high seas course throughout Byron's works, culminating in *Don Juan*'s stunning shipwreck. "If I must sail let it be on the ocean no matter how stormy—" he wrote in a letter, "anything but a dull cruise on a level lake without ever losing sight of the same insipid shores by which it is surrounded." He and Shelley set sail again together in the summer of 1822, renting a pair of villas in La Spezia, Italy, and buying themselves a grand pair of yachts to match: a lean racer for Shelley and a stately schooner—named *Bolivar*—for Byron, who ordered his friend's mainsail painted with "Don Juan," an homage to the disastrous poem of his imagination. Unamused, Shelley patched the sail, renamed his boat *Ariel*, loaded his library into its hull, and spent days cruising aimlessly, one hand on the tiller, one holding a book. *Ariel* sped past other boats "as a comet might pass the dullest planets of the Heavens," Shelley bragged. But it was rigged for speed, not safety, with enormous sails and hardly enough ballast to keep it steady. Gliding off under an ominous sky one July afternoon, Shelley, who still couldn't swim, was never seen alive again. His body washed up ten days later, identified by the copy of Keats's *Lamia* in his pocket. He was thirty.

As his body was cremated, burning slowly on the Italian beach, Byron swam three morose miles out to *Bolivar* and back. He later sold the boat, explaining that he'd "taken a disgust to sailing." Shelley's ashes were buried in Rome's Protestant cemetery, where his tombstone quotes Shakespeare's *The Tempest*:

> *Nothing of him that doth fade,*
> *But doth suffer a sea-change*
> *Into something rich and strange.*

THAUMATROPE

An optical toy made from a spinning disc

After dinner one night in 1824, the eminent English philosopher Sir John Herschel (1792–1871), amusing himself by spinning a pear on the table, offered a riddle to his guest, scientist Charles Babbage (1792–1871): Could Babbage show him two sides of a shilling at the same time? "I took out of my pocket a shilling, and holding it up before the looking-glass pointed out my method," Babbage wrote. " 'No,' said my friend, 'that won't do;' then spinning my shilling upon the table, he pointed out his method of seeing both sides at once."

The concept of persistent vision—that an impression made on the eye remains there for an eighth of a second—was proven long ago, but in the 1820s it provided new inspiration and entertainment with the Thaumatrope, or "Wonder-Turner," conceived of simultaneously by Babbage's friend Dr. Fritton and by Dr. John Ayrton Paris (1785–1856), who marketed and sold the toy.

Clever images printed on each side of a round paper disc merged into one when the disc was spun by twisting strings attached to its edges. Printed on the front of one disc was a parrot; on the back, a cage. As the Thaumatrope whirled, the bird landed behind bars. With another disc, a bald man got wigged. And with yet another, a rider mounted his horse. In his book *Philosophy in Sport made Science in Earnest*, Dr. Paris described the toy as a small machine "well calculated to furnish us with some capital puns."

For anyone desperately searching for an easy way to entertain a child, putting together a simple Thaumatrope is capital indeed. But the big payoff wouldn't come until 1895, when the optical games played by Paris and his peers helped give rise to the invention of the movie camera.

To Make a Thaumatrope

Take a circle of light cardboard. On one side draw the image of a birdcage. Flip the card upside down, and on the reverse draw a bird, measuring, then placing the animal so that he will sit in the center of the cage once the disc is set spinning. Pierce the disc at the right and the left sides with a needle, making a hole big enough to pass a piece of string through it. Thread each hole with a string (a length of rubber band also works well for this), knotted and neatly secured. When you twirl the string quickly through your fingers, rubbing thumb and index fingers together, the disc spins and the bird appears in the cage.

TOPPER

Otherwise called a top hat, a high-crowned, cylindrical man's hat in silk or beaver

London hatmaker John Hetherington incited a riot with his wondrous shellacked top hat in 1797, "a tall structure having a shiny lustre calculated to frighten timid people," according to one report. "Several women fainted at the unusual sight, children screamed, dogs yelled, and the younger son of a cordwinder, Thomas, who was returning from the chandler's shop, was thrown down by the crowd which was collected, and his right arm was broken." The authorities charged Hetherington with breach of the peace and he was fined £500.

Shocking as it once was, however, Hetherington's creation—called a stovepipe, high hat, or topper—became ubiquitous by the middle of the nineteenth century, worn by aristocrats, bourgeois strivers, and even stylish three-year-old boys. In fashionable Hyde Park, a long row of men in top hats and frock coats leaned on the railings of the bridle path each day, looking like "a flock of birds which had settled on a telegraph wire," as aesthete Ralph Nevill (1865–1930) put it. The topper was a mysterious, nearly surrealistic symbol of well-dressed anonymity.

At first, haberdashers made the top hat out of beaver skins, later substituting cheaper chopped silk plush, which, once petted into place, shone brighter than fur. Straight-sided, or curved like an hourglass, the most modest was five and three-quarter inches tall, though some, like the "Kite-High Dandy," climbed to nearly eight inches. Top hats were expensive. And hot. Charles Dickens (1812–1870) despised the "hermetically sealed black, stiff chimney-pot." But somehow they were indispensable. Working-class gents rented toppers, bought them used, or wore cheap imitations made out of papier-mâché.

Plenty of inventors suggested ways to ventilate the top hat or to make it lighter, but it remained a burden, prone to getting crushed in a crowd or blowing off in a big wind. When the Parisian hat-maker Gabriel Gibus and his brother Antoine introduced the collapsible top hat, which folded down into a slim flat disc that was easy to store under a seat at the opera, their achievement was glorified in verse:

I'm got up to perfection. In all that dandy place,
There's no cravat so faultless—no shirt so gay with lace;
My gibus hat—my shiny boots, there's none who see forget.
While words can't tell how tight my gloves, or huge my white
  lorgnette.

The top hat dominated men's fashion, lending wearers height and dignity, until the bowler overtook it. The Earl of Leicester commissioned the new hat for his gamekeepers around 1850, so they could avoid getting tangled in low branches. The sporty bowler was cheaper, easier to wear, and it stood out in a crowd—that is, until the end of the century, when the bowler had become just as ubiquitous as its magnificent predecessor.

TRAJE DE LUCES

The traditional bullfighter's costume

They don't call the matador's costume the "suit of lights" for nothing. The traditional *traje de luces* is dazzling and a little vulgar. The jacket hangs heavy, thick with gold embroidery and armored in beads. The knee-length pants are worn skintight, lest any wrinkle catch a pair of sharp horns. The sashed waist is dashing. The cape lends otherworldly panache. And as for the pink stockings—well, why not? No one is more glamorous than the Spanish matador.

Romantics have given the classic Spanish *traje* either an Andalusian or a Gypsy past over the years, but the costume probably owes more to fashion introduced by the Hapsburgs, who ruled Spain from 1516 to 1700, when bullfighting was an aristocratic privilege. After Philip V, a French, Versailles-raised melancholic, took the crown, courtiers dropped the sport, leaving it to a new group of nonnoble matadors. Philip despised barbaric bullfighting.

Beyond the bullring, however, the look was echoed by the *majos* and *majas*, fierce working-class Spaniards who dressed with flair. True *majos*, including bullfighters, were elegant toughs, swaggering in their capes under broad-brimmed hats, their jackets over-decorated just like those of the modern *traje de luces*. Their female counterparts, the brazen *majas*, wore black lace mantillas and a heavily embroidered overskirt, called the *basquiña*, cut short to reveal a little ankle. The *majas* were sassy. Their tempers flared. They flirted. And for the sheltered women of the Spanish aristocracy, the idea of being momentarily mistaken for a *maja* was a thrill.

But it was also an act of defiance. King Charles III's chief minister banned the fashion by decree in 1766, triggering riots in Madrid. A crowd shouting *"Viva España!"* sacked his house and the right to wear the costume was restored the next day. Still, nearly twenty years later Charles III persisted, threatening to arrest nobles who dressed in "startling colors" and "ridiculous" embroideries, looking like "gypsies, smugglers and bullfighters."

As the royal portraitist, painter Francisco Goya y Lucientes (1746–1828) played to both sides, but he was a *majo* at heart. He caroused in working-class bars and was rumored to have performed as a matador. And he wasn't the type to back down from a knife fight. His romantic paintings of the era's famous matadors, dressed in their lush *trajes de luces*, are iconic, and his portraits of the Duchess of Alba in her *maja* gear were as provocative as his steamy *maja* nudes.

Second in rank only to the queen, María del Pilar Teresa Cayetana de Silva, the thirteenth Duchess of Alba (1762–1802), was a rebel who went to bullfights instead of visiting salons. The year after her duke died, she was painted by Goya—who was said to have been her lover—with her chin in the air, dressed as a *maja* in a lace mantilla and a *basquiña* trimmed with black silk flowers. She points to her feet, where "Only Goya" is written in the sand. "The duchess of Alba has not a single hair that does not inspire desire," wrote one French traveler. "When she goes through the streets, everyone comes to the windows, and even the children stop playing to look at her." The duchess's rival, Queen María Luisa, gave in two years later, putting on a rich mantilla and *basquiña* to pose for Goya. And with that, *majismo* lost its edge, becoming the court fashion and Spain's national costume.

Of course, the Bourbon queen María Luisa was only a *maja*-of-convenience. Under her influence, Charles IV banned bullfighting altogether in 1805, a decree that wasn't repealed until three years later by Napoleon's brother Joseph Bonaparte, who then ruled Spain.

TRAPEZE

An apparatus made from a crossbar hung between two ropes

Talented tightrope dancers and agile acrobats have demonstrated their daring prowess for thousands of years, but when young Jules Léotard (1830–1870) performed the first trapeze act at the Cirque Napoléon in 1859, Paris had never seen anything like it. Swinging from one trapeze to another, he was, as one observer noted, "a tropical bird leaping from branch to branch and leaving in the dazzled eyes of the spectators a brilliant but confused impression of its bright plumage." The son of a gymnastics instructor, Léotard walked away from a law career to become a circus star, thrilling the audience with his midair somersault and his skintight suit, the first leotard. His popularity in London inspired the song "Daring Young Man on the Flying Trapeze":

He'd fly through the air with the greatest of ease—
A daring young man on the flying trapeze
His movements were graceful, all the girls he could please
And my love he purloined away . . .

By the late 1860s, women were swinging alongside their male counterparts. There was England's Madame Sanyeah, who was so nonchalant it was frightening, swooping through the theater "as calmly and self-possessed as if being rocked to sleep." Zuleila, another English performer, leaped from on high, flying toward her partner, Ventini, "causing a thrill of terror among the audience." But the infamous Louisiana native Leona Dare (1855–1922), who often hung her trapeze beneath a hot-air balloon, was the one the French called the "*reine du trapèze,*" the queen of the trapeze. "There is nothing better than seeing a young girl in a sequined skirt . . . leaping from the friezes of the theater, like a birdie hit by a racket," wrote critic Théophile Gautier (1811–1872). "Nothing is more airy, more light, and of a more graceful peril." Dare, whose real name was Susan Adeline Stewart, and who was also known as the "Queen of the Antilles" and the "Pride of Madrid," titillated the crowds with her stunts as well as with her steamy love life and legal disputes. Dangling under the basket of a hot-air balloon, she lifted her husband off the ground with a device clenched in her teeth. In Spain, she dropped and killed another performer, the unfortunate Monsieur George, when she was overcome with what the papers called "a nervous fit."

The breathtaking possibility of disaster was part of the act's draw. Nineteenth-century Parisian critics the Goncourt brothers claimed to go to no other theater besides the circus, because there a performer's talent was "incontestable, absolute, like mathematics or rather like a somersault," they explained. "Either they fall or they don't fall. Their talent is a fact."

As the Goncourts saw it, the danger of the trapeze turned the audience especially sympathetic. "We see them, those men and women risking their bones in the air to snatch some applause, with a stirring in the bowels, with a fiercely strange, and, at the same time, warmly commiserating *je ne sais quoi*," they went on, "as if these people were of our race and as if all of us, mugs, historians, philosophers, stooges, and poets, were leaping heroically for that imbecilic audience."

TRUFFLE

An edible fungus

"Whosoever pronounces the word 'truffle' gives voice to one which awakens erotic and gastronomical dreams equally in the sex that wears skirts and the one that sprouts a beard," declared France's great gourmand Jean-Anthelme Brillat-Savarin (1755–1826). After giving the matter careful consideration, and discreetly polling his fancy friends, Brillat-Savarin classified the truffle as rousing "certain powers whose tests of strength are accompanied by the deepest pleasure." One lady confessed that after a truffled supper she reached the brink of indiscretion with one of her husband's most dull friends. Afterward, she renounced truffles forever.

Since ancient times, the pungent, aphrodisiacal tuber has mystified scholars like Imperial Rome's well-respected doctor Claudius Galen (AD 129–216), who prescribed truffles to his patients, noting that they caused "general excitation, conductive to sensual pleasure." For just that reason, truffles, with their earthy, dark flavor, had a resurgence among the cognoscenti in Brillat-Savarin's day, when dining in an intimate boudoir was more chic than a banquet in a mammoth hall. An intimate supper called for elegant, voluptuous dishes.

The era's most notorious lover, Giacomo Casanova (1725–1798), began his seductions with oysters and champagne, and he never said no to a pleasure-filled truffled dinner, though then, as now, truffles were a pricey delicacy. "Cultivating whatever gave pleasure to my senses was always the chief business of my life," he wrote, prefacing his multivolumed autobiography. "I have never found any occupation more important." His tastes in women and in food were equally rarefied. He craved "sticky cod from Newfoundland" and a spicy stew called olla podrida, and "cheeses whose perfection is reached when the little creatures which inhabit them become visible," he explained. "As for women, I have always found that the one I was in love with smelled good, and the more copious her sweat, the sweeter I found it." And as for truffles, he loved them all—the white variety from Piedmont in Italy, and the black from Périgord in France. Truffles topped the menu when Casanova trysted with a debauched Venetian nun, known in his memoirs only as M.M., who served him luscious dinners in her mirrored love lair.

Another woman who knew the way to a man's heart was the Edwardian-era chef Rosa Lewis (1867–1952). Born in London's East End, Lewis started out at age twelve as a housemaid, but rapidly rose through the ranks of several aristocratic households, serving as a chef to Lady Randolph Churchill and later becoming the greatest English cook of her day.

A knockout beauty, Lewis wore all white in the kitchen, from her chef's hat to her high-laced boots, and was known for the extravagant, multicourse French meals she served as a caterer for hire and as the proprietress of the Cavendish Hotel. Rumors swirled that she'd had an affair with the gourmand Prince of Wales, later King Edward VII, who kept a suite at the Cavendish, but it's more likely that she satisfied his culinary drive. Because of his great appetite, Edward was nicknamed "Prince Tum-Tum." Early on, Lewis introduced him to an especially decadent dish, one that became his favorite: *truffes à la serviette*, boiled truffles, wrapped snugly in a white linen napkin and served in a silver dish with a little butter.

Truffes à la serviette, done in the eighteenth-century style

After soaking and cleaning the truffles, boil them in a mixture of half champagne, half water, with some minced shallots, thyme, salt, and pepper. Simmer covered for 40 minutes. Then drain and pat the truffles dry, sliding them into a heated, folded napkin on a warm plate. Serve in the old manner, alongside a small dish of cold butter.

TURBAN

A headdress made from a long, wound piece of cloth

Turbans—intricately wrapped, folded, and tucked—are worn by men and women throughout Asia and Africa. In India, a huge array of styles suits every caste and occasion, some popular since at least the fourth century. Each knot and tuck informs those fluent in turbanry about the wearer's status, profession, and hometown. A maharajah's turban takes an hour to tie. A wedding turban sprouts tinsel. Kalbi farmers wear enormous hot-pink bulbs, and nomadic cattle traders wear a copper skullcap under their rainbowed wraps, to protect themselves from blows to the head.

But it's the Turkish turban that made the biggest impact on the

European imagination. Western travelers in the sixteenth century marveled at what they called "tolipanes," "turbants," "turribants," or "turbands." It all translated into some creative interpretations. English, French, and American ladies had their portraits painted wearing turbans during the 1700s, guided by the published letters of the glitzy Lady Mary Wortley Montagu, who moved to Turkey when her husband was posted at the embassy there. Turbans hinted at artistic pretensions, and were favored by high society's grande dames, including the vivacious American first lady Dolley Madison (1768–1849).

Madison turned the turban into a nationwide trend. She was a "fine, portly, buxom dame," according to writer Washington Irving (1783–1859). She was known as the "Queen of Washington City." And she looked it. Shaking off her pious Quaker past, she wore low-cut dresses, and was known to have snuff-stained fingers and a flamboyant collection of turbans, which were coiled high and usually topped with a pair of towering ostrich plumes. To her husband's inauguration in 1809, she wore a purple velvet turban sent from Paris (somehow her hat made it from France despite a British naval blockade). At an assembly ball some years later, guests stood on benches in order to catch a glimpse of her outlandish headgear.

The look came into Western fashion again when Napoleon's Egyptian adventures sparked new interest in the Orient in the nineteenth century, and again in the 1920s, when Parisian fashion designer Paul Poiret looked east. Strong women like Simone de Beauvoir and the eccentric stars of Federico Fellini's films gave the look a midcentury boost, as did writer Isak Dinesen, photographed beturbaned in an elegant gray suit and a big fur alongside Marilyn Monroe.

But the turban's finest hour came in November 1944 when American *Vogue* reported on the first hats out of free Paris. That first season, Schiaparelli showed a turban striped in shocking pink, and the city's other top milliners followed, presenting fanciful turbans done up with feathers and pert rosettes. It was fashion born out of necessity. The hats "show how we had to make do, tell how we sharpened our wits," explained Paris correspondent Carmel Benito. "Felt gave out, so we made hats from chiffon. No more chiffon—all right, take straw. No more straw—very well, braided paper."

Naturally, hats weren't Benito's sole concern during the war. She told of hunting for food, dodging police, drinking hot water instead of tea, and playing bridge in the bomb shelters during the occupation years. Yet Parisian women demonstrated their proud savvy by the hats they wore. "Hats rose to bewildering heights," she reported. "When hungry, we made pastry-coloured hats covered with birds, fruits, berries. You see, hats have been a sort of contest between French imagination and German regulation." The imaginative power invested in the turban kept European and American women wrapped up in its exotic glamour well into the 1960s.

TWILIGHT

The period after sunset, between daylight and darkness

Any true poet can spare a few lines for twilight, waxing lyrical over the most beautiful time of day and working those transitory, moody metaphors for all they're worth. As Oscar Wilde (1854–1900) pointed out, twilight "is not without loveliness, though perhaps its chief use is to illustrate quotations from the poets." Then again, maybe poetry's chief use is to inspire us to watch the sun go down.

In the lengthening shadows, Virgil sang of the shepherds of Hesperus in the first century BC. William Blake (1757–1827) wrote a sonnet to the "Evening Star." Percy Shelley (1792–1822) brooded over the "Splendours, and Glooms, and glimmering incarnations/ Of Hopes and Fears, and twilight Phantasies." In the silvery light, William Wordsworth (1770–1850) took "An Evening Walk," and later penned "Beauteous Evening," when "The holy time is quiet as a Nun/Breathless with adoration . . ." Even Wilde succumbed, once chasing his faun "out of the mid-wood's twilight/Into the meadow's dawn."

John Keats (1795–1821) used twilight as a metaphor for poetry itself, explaining that for the reader a good poem should "like the Sun come natural to him—shine over him and set soberly although in magnificence leaving him in the Luxury of twilight."

With the weight of all that history on his shoulders, Wallace Stevens (1879–1955) picked up the theme in the mid-twentieth century, in his poem "Delightful Evening," calling "twilight overfull/ Of wormy metaphors." For Stevens, addressing the close of day demonstrated his dual urge to describe things as they are and as he imagined them. He was happy to find himself pulled between the two poles, vacillating between skepticism and longing. "Sometimes I believe most in the imagination for a long time and then, without reasoning about it, turn to reality and believe in that and that alone," he wrote to a friend. "But both of these things project themselves endlessly and I want them to do just that."

Stevens, an insurance executive who published his first collection of poetry at age forty-four, escaped through his imagination both the corporate world and his home in Connecticut. "Spring in Connecticut is just as wild as spring in Persia," he wrote to a friend. He crafted short poems during his walk to the office, and longer odes on thirty-mile rambles, all of which showed off everyday life as its fantastical best.

His twilight was a suburban affair turned almost mystical with poems like *An Ordinary Evening in New Haven* and "The Man on the Dump," in which the moon rises brightly over a glimmering mountain of garbage, a stark reality check that shimmered at the edges. For Stevens, everything—including everyday wormy twilight—was spectacular. As he admitted in "Evening without Angels," he could not resist the

> *Desire for rest, in that descending sea*
> *Of dark, which in its very darkening*
> *Is rest and silence spreading into sleep.*

UMBRELLA

A portable shade, usually circular and supported by spokes

Around the fourth century, the Chinese crafted early umbrella prototypes out of oiled paper stretched over bamboo spokes. Ancient Egyptians made umbrellas from palm leaves or feathers, while in ancient Rome they were fashioned out of leather. In India, where a traditional thirteen umbrellas distinguished a king's entourage, the umbrella was an early Buddhist symbol, representing the Buddha himself as the one who offers protection, or a refuge from suffering. From Asia, the curious device traveled west via

Venice. "Things that minister shadow unto them, for shelter against the scorching heate of the sun," was how the irrepressible English traveler Thomas Coryat (1577–1617) described the strange umbrellas he saw while on his way to Venice in 1608. Though they were unknown in England or France at the time, the Venetian doge had walked in the shade of an umbrella borne by attendants since the medieval era. (The word "umbrella" comes from the Italian *umbra*, or "shade.")

Naturally, umbrellas have always come in handy on a sunny day or during a rainstorm, but the most creative use for the device—one maximizing the umbrella's potential to lift, not shade—came from Thailand. The French ambassador Simon de la Loubère (1642–1729), visiting in 1687, saw a Thai acrobat entertain the king by attaching two big umbrellas to his belt and leaping from high up in the bamboo trees to float down, like a real-life Mary Poppins. Most of the time, the umbrellas broke his fall, though occasionally he was carried away by the wind, or drifted into the trees, or wound up in the river.

A century later, the clockmaker-physicist Louis-Sébastien Lenormand (1757–1839) read Loubère's account back in Montpellier, France. Inspired, just months after the launch of the first hot-air balloon in 1783, Lenormand rigged himself up with two thirty-inch umbrellas like the Thai performer of yore, his idea being that the apparatus might be useful to help people escaping fire. Equipped, he leaped from an elm tree, then from the high window of a house by way of demonstration. The French word for "umbrella" is *parapluie* (the prefix *para* means "guard" and *pluie* "rain"). Lenormand named his crafty umbrella creation the *para-chute*—this time, protection against *chute*, "falling."

UNICORN

A legendary one-horned beast

One of the first scholars to go on the record with his scientific observations of the unicorn was the fifth-century BC Greek physician Ctesias. "They fight with thrusts of horn; they kick, bite and strike with wounding force both horses and hunters," he wrote of the fearsome beast. The unicorn was as fast as a stag, with a snowy-white body and a dark red head, he reported, referring to the animal as the "wild ass of India."

Ctesias wasn't the only one who believed in the animal, which

cropped up in a variety of cultures. An ancient Egyptian papyrus depicted a lion sitting across a gaming board from a unicorn. In old Chinese folktales, the unicorn was described as so gentle that it wouldn't walk on grass, as it might accidentally crush a bug. The unicorn appeared in Indian fables, and the elusive creature is mentioned seven times in the Old Testament. Over the centuries, various authorities repeated and warped these accounts. Pliny claimed the animal had the head of a stag, the body of a horse, feet like an elephant, and a tail like a boar. Others described the unicorn as white with a purple head, or explained how to catch one by using a human virgin as bait.

Few neglected to mention the incredible magic of the unicorn's horn, which was generally thought to neutralize poison. In the Middle Ages, princes bought unicorn horn at exorbitant prices, counting on it to protect them from their enemies. They wore horn necklaces and horn rings, and they drank from goblets of carved horn, under the assumption that the vessels would sweat or steam when reacting against poison. (Only a handful of these cups still exist, as most were ground up and eaten over the years.)

Several European pilgrims visiting Jerusalem in the fifteenth and sixteenth centuries claimed to have seen the unicorn— almost. While traveling near Mount Sinai in 1483, Friar Felix Fabri glimpsed an animal standing on a nearby hill, which, though Fabri couldn't identify it, his guide insisted was a unicorn. Another friar, visiting in Abyssinia, reported a unicorn sighting there. "The prodigious Swiftness with which this Creature runs from one Wood into another has given me no Opportunity of examining it particularly," he admitted, going on to describe the unicorn as a beautiful, timorous, horned horse. Only the French adventurer Vincent Le Blanc (1554–1640) seemed sure, having run across several unicorns while traipsing through Asia in 1567. "I have seen a unicorn in the seraglio of the Sultan, others in India, and still others at the Escurial," he wrote. "That there are some persons who doubt whether this animal is to be found anywhere in the world I am well aware, but in addition to my own observation there are several serious writers who bear witness to its existence."

Skeptics and believers—French doctors, Italian courtiers, and Danish scientists—battled over the nature of the animal during the sixteenth and early seventeenth centuries, publishing dozens of tracts and pamphlets promoting or attacking tales of the unicorn and its magic horn. The hallowed ranks of believers included German philosopher Gottfried Leibniz, who climbed into the Harz Mountains to inspect the ancient remains of a unicorn skeleton found there.

Leibniz's unicorn was only a mammoth, but rhinos and antelope fooled many others. Walrus tusks, rhino horns, and those of rare mountain goats were passed off as unicorn horns, as were the narwhal whale's spiraling tusks, which grow from the jaw and can reach a length of nine feet. The narwhal rarely ventures south of Greenland and was all but unknown in Europe until a mid-seventeenth century surge in whale hunting flooded the market with narwhal-cum-unicorn horn. Prices for the coveted substance plummeted once the general public learned " 'twas nothing but the tooth of a fish." Still, until 1741 every apothecary in London carried unicorn horn on its list of available medicines, just in case.

VELOCITY

Rapidity of motion

When cars were doing 30 mph on the racetrack, Marcel Proust (1871–1922) swooned over the automobile's intoxicating velocity. There were fewer than fifty thousand cars yet on the road in France during the summer of 1907 when Proust rented one, leaving Paris for the coast of Normandy, following in the footsteps of one of his heroes, the English art critic John Ruskin, who had chronicled his visit to France's monumental Gothic churches years before.

Proust was ill so often that he'd hardly left his room for the previous six years, easing himself out of bed only once a week. But he planned to take full advantage of his road trip, writing to a friend of "what may well be the last journey to be granted me," and asking for recommendations of quaint towns "or some old port or whatever that you knew," which "would provide more food for my imagination than a cathedral that wasn't very special—or really sublime."

Seated next to a dashing young driver, Proust rocketed along the coast from one monument to the next, taking notes. The car's closed windows minimized his hay fever, while he counted on "a deadly dose of caffeine"—as many as seventeen cups of coffee—to combat his asthma.

And suddenly, there on the open road, Proust was living life "shot out of a cannon," as he wrote to a friend. As he followed Ruskin's progression down narrow country lanes, the landscape lurched to life. "Old lopsided houses ran nimbly toward us, offering us fresh roses or proudly showing us the young hollyhock they had grown and which already had outgrown them," he wrote, sharing his impressions of automobile travel in *Le Figaro*. The car tore toward the next ancient church, which Proust described as a giant throwing itself "rudely before us so that we had just enough time to stop before hurling ourselves against the porch."

Not only did renting a car save Proust from boredom and seclusion for the rest of his life, the impressions he gathered on that first excursion directly informed the novel he was working on, *Remembrance of Things Past*. A hotel where he stayed worked its way into the manuscript, and a passage from Proust's own article was recycled as his narrator's article for *Le Figaro*, reprinted nearly word for word.

Equally inspiring was Proust's velocity-loving, nineteen-year-old chauffeur, Alfred Agostinelli, whom scholars believe served as Proust's model for the novel's Albertine. Dressed in his long, hooded coat and goggles, Agostinelli was a "nun of speed," as Proust described him. "May the steering wheel of the young chauffeur who is driving me remain always the symbol of his talent rather than the augury of his martyrdom!" he wrote. Six years later, Agostinelli became the author's live-in secretary, and his unrequited love. How quickly his fortunes changed. Proust paid for the daredevil's flying lessons, but it was an ill-fated undertaking. Agostinelli died during his second solo flight, crashing off the Côte d'Azur in 1914. He was, "with my mother, my father," Proust said, "the person I loved most."

VIRIDITAS

Blooming life force

For the Christian mystic Hildegard of Bingen (1098–1179), green wasn't merely a color. Her blazing celestial visions burst with *viriditas*, translated loosely from Latin as "greenness" or "greening," a word she used eccentrically to represent all of life's goodness. *Viriditas* was fresh, budding, and vital. It was springtime and the Garden of Eden.

Hildegard, the abbess of a Rhineland convent, wrote books about her visions and the jagged migraines accompanying them. The strength of her convictions and the persuasiveness of her poetry drew pilgrims to her, and, though it was highly unusual at the time, the Church allowed her to preach, which she did in market squares and cathedrals throughout Germany. By mail, she advised popes, emperors, and the likes of Eleanor of Aquitaine on affairs of state and of the spirit, warning her correspondents not to let their virtue, or their *viridity*, dry up. Good people were brimming with *viriditas*.

Unlike any of her Christian predecessors, Hildegard recognized a decidedly feminine aspect of the divine. In the twelfth century, the Virgin Mary, whom Hildegard called the *"Viridissima Virga,"* was not yet a cult figure, and Eve was still blamed for humanity's exile from Paradise. Hildegard made an unprecedented effort to celebrate the feminine side of Christianity.

As she saw it, while everyone had *viridity*, no one had more than virgins.

The nuns of Hildegard's abbey, glowing with *viriditas*, dressed all in white, with their long hair loose, and wearing gold filigree crowns, looked like princesses on a feast day. They entered the church in a procession, singing edgy, harmonic chants that the abbess had composed herself. "O sweetest lover, O sweetest hugger, help us keep our virginity," begins a song from her *Symphonium Virginum*. "How very hard to hold out against whatever tastes of the Apple."

Backlash came from a rival canoness, the reformer Tenxwind of Andernach, who was shocked by the wanton display at Bingen. Hildegard defended her nuns, explaining in a letter that while a married woman shouldn't indulge in vanity, it was okay for virgins. Such strictures "do not apply to a virgin, for she stands in the unsullied purity of paradise, lovely and unwithering, and she always remains in the full vitality of the budding rod."

WANDERERS

Those who have a roving nature

A new generation of female adventurers set out to see the world in the 1920s and 1930s, as traveling became easier, and as the hardline morality that kept women at home crumbled. They weren't explorers—there wasn't much territory left to discover—but "unconducted wanderers," as Rosita Forbes (1890–1967) put it. And they set out in search of something far less tangible than the picturesque.

Forbes left England to write about China, Tibet, New Guinea, Fiji, Syria, Sudan, and Libya, where she went disguised as a Bedouin, claiming a Cicassian mother to explain away her poor Arabic. Sheikhs found her too scrawny for their harems, but as a frequent guest of honor at their tables she was served the local delicacy— sheep eyeballs, "glazed and often semi-raw," which, she reported, tasted like oysters and were best swallowed in a single gulp. She faced sandstorms in the desert, difficult camels, and low rations. She was held prisoner in her own tent, as the tribesmen outside decided her fate. She was drugged in a coffeehouse, and later escaped through a window. She carried a revolver, and she wasn't afraid to use it.

What puzzled Forbes's critics, though, was why she went through any of it. As one lamented, "why this experienced traveler should go out of her way to make herself quite unnecessarily uncomfortable on her journeys is always a matter of surprise." He suggested that those trekking across Abyssinia needn't sleep in their clothes, or eat doubtful eggs, or "drive a caravan for ten or twelve hours a day continuously over that mountainous country."

British adventuress Freya Stark (1893–1993), Forbes's contemporary, and a great, prolific writer, gave a better idea of what drove these wanderers. Stark moved to Baghdad in her mid-thirties, learned Persian, Turkish, Kurdish, and Arabic, and traveled, Leica in hand, until she was ninety years old, suffering exotic diseases and pulling herself out of impossible scrapes along the way. "The great and almost only comfort about being a woman, is that one can always pretend to be more stupid than one is, and no one is surprised," she wrote.

She took advantage of her unusual status as a foreign female, gaining access to both the sultans and to their harems. When a local official demanded her map, she demurred, and he "was pleased with the rather peculiar substitute of a tube of tooth paste." She didn't hesitate to rifle a Bronze Age tomb, boldly taking away a skull in a handkerchief, or, on another occasion pocketing a handful of pottery shards for the British Museum. "I was the first woman to travel alone in the country," she wrote of her journey following in the footsteps of Alexander the Great to Hadhramaut, in the land of frankincense, "so they had no precedent to deal with me."

Like Forbes, Stark traveled sans frills by choice. "The nicest way to know people is not to be important or wealthy," she explained.

She always took the hard way, once creeping along a crumbling slope on camelback though "the path dwindled to the exact breadth of one hoof."

As with Forbes, Stark's reviewers were baffled. "Why do people go to the East and throw their lives away on such unprofitable journeys?" one asked. But for Stark, risking her life for the sake of adventure gave her a taste of immortality. "To awaken quite alone in a strange town is one of the pleasant sensations in the world. You are surrounded by adventure," she wrote in *Baghdad Sketches*. "You have no idea what is in store for you, but you will, if you are wise and know the art of travel, let yourself go on the stream of the unknown and accept whatever comes in the spirit in which the gods may offer it."

 **WEEKEND**

A holiday period ending the workweek

The two-day weekend was a long time coming. For much of the nineteenth century, workers put in ten-to-fourteen-hour days six days a week, recovering on Sunday. Only around 1850 did Saturday become a half day for laborers in the United States and in England. Then, after strikes, rallies, union bargaining—and brave battling—the weekend concept picked up speed, and the term entered our vocabulary. American workers secured the fifty-one-hour workweek in 1920, while most Londoners were granted the two-day weekend only after 1945.

Previously, novelists like Jane Austen (1775–1817), Edith Wharton (1862–1937), and Henry James (1843–1916) romanticized the aristocratic leisure of villa living. Wharton's own weekends in the country were decidedly idyllic, "with friends tumbling in unexpectedly from everywhere, extra seats being hastily crowded into the long dining-room, fresh provisions hurried to the already groaning tea-table, spare-rooms prepared, messages telephoned, people passing in and out with a sort of smiling fatalism, no questions asked, no explanations expected," she remembered, "just a continuous surge of easy good-humored life through the big house, the broad flagged terraces and the crowded tennis-courts."

For the less fortunate masses, the rise of the institutionalized weekend promised regeneration—of body and soul. Seaside amusements entertained the newly liberated, even if for a sole sunny afternoon. Resorts, boardwalks, and promenades cropped up as the middle class got its first taste of leisure. During the 1880s some six million people a year enjoyed the cool breezes and easy pleasures at Coney Island, an hour's train ride from New York City. "Old Ocean is a grand old Democrat, and levels all petty distinctions," one reporter wrote, describing the scene. "He buffets the rich and poor alike, who, clad for bath, present very much the same appearance."

WHISTLING

A musical sound made by forcing air through the lips

As with rumbling tribal drums and smoke signals, whistling has been used as a means of communication throughout the ages. The dewy-eyed Kickapoos of Mexico used a simple whistling language to transmit flowery notions between lovers, while the Gomerans of the Canary Islands whistled a more complex vocabulary of over four thousand words. Sailors at sea communicated through the fog by whistling, as did early train conductors. And during the days of the Nazi Occupation, shepherds from the French Pyrenean village of Aäs used an obscure whistling language to help secretly usher Jewish refugees over the mountains to safety in Spain.

For the Taoists of ancient China, whistling was a way to harmonize with nature. "A good whistler commands the attention of the whole world of spirits," wrote the mid-eighth-century author of *Principles of Whistling*. The book offered careful instructions on producing spectacular sounds like the "Fleeting Cloud," which "sinks and floats, rises and disappears," like "a dragon sporting in a spring fountain." The whistle "Tiger in a Deep Ravine" conveyed "rage to the limit." "Night Demons in a Lonely Wood" evoked crickets perched in the willow trees, and "Kite on a Dead Tree" was "cold and cheerless."

Yet melodic whistling for entertainment's sake is a distinct art. For some, the nostalgic sound brings to mind the happy-go-lucky everyman, but historically Europeans have frowned on tuneful whistling. The tutor of Napoleon III's son was shocked to find students in the corridors at King's College giddily whistling away in 1871. "As in France I had never heard whistling except from the lower orders, I had some doubts as to the young gentlemen's designs," he wrote. " 'It's not a school,' said the prince to me, 'it's a nest of blackbirds.' " In the Middle East, it was said that a whistler's mouth could not be purified for forty days, and that only the devil's touch could cause a person to emit such an awful sound.

Few whistlers have been so appreciated as the chirping, hooting performers of the American big-band era, who puckered up to amaze audiences with their quavering tunes. Fred Lowery (1909–1984), the blind whistler from East Texas, warbled along with Rudy Vallée and Art Carney, and played at Carnegie Hall and at the White House for President Roosevelt. His first solo recording, "Indian Love Call" (1939), sold more than two million copies and was played on jukeboxes from coast to coast.

To Lowery, professional whistling was more than a pastime. "Sure, everyone can whistle," he wrote in his memoirs. "But they can pick up a violin and get some kind of sound out of that, too."

WHITE PAINT

White pigment used on a dwelling's interior walls

If the walls of your home are bright and white, thank Elsie de Wolfe (1865–1950). The first professional interior decorator, de Wolfe did away with Victorian gloom at the end of the nineteenth century, reimagining the modern home by what she tossed out. She pulled down the heavy drapes, stripped away the dark patterned wallpapers, swept out the clutter, painted the walls of her house ivory and pale gray, and replaced dour Victorian furniture with the lighter designs of eighteenth-century France. "I believe in plenty of optimism and white paint," she proclaimed, "comfortable chairs with lights beside them, open fires on the hearth and flowers wherever they 'belong,' mirrors and sunshine in all rooms." In no time, de Wolfe was overwhelmed with clients, and established an airy style that called for billowing glazed chintz, neat tiled floors, and wicker chairs.

De Wolfe famously described herself as "an ugly child" living in "an ugly age," but as an adult she surrounded herself with beauty. Born in New York, she was presented at court to Queen Victoria, as well-to-do young women were, and went on to become a Broadway actress, living on Irving Place and setting up a sizzling salon there with her partner, Elisabeth Marbury. De Wolfe's parties—on both sides of the Atlantic—were epic, full of the film stars, social lions, politicians, and artistes of the era. She went up in Wilbur Wright's plane in 1908. She shocked Paris by turning handsprings on her way into a costume ball, and she was known to tint her hair green or blue on occasion.

But de Wolfe was a tough businesswoman all the same. She charged steep fees for her decorating, and handled her mogul clients firmly. When Henry Clay Frick said he'd like to see an alternate set of plans for the redesign de Wolfe had proposed for his Fifth Avenue mansion, she explained, "When I draw up a set of plans there is no second choice. There is only what I show you. The best."

Naturally, de Wolfe's own houses showcased the best of the best. Her bathroom was "moonshine and glamour, white orchids and rock crystal, silver tissue and white furs, reflected in many mirrors," she wrote in her memoir. Still, that didn't mean her approach wasn't adaptable to a more modest scale—say, to that of a small apartment. "Let me beg of you to demand only the actual essentials: a decent neighborhood, good light and air, and at least one reasonably large room," she implored budget-conscious readers in her best-selling book *The House in Good Taste* (1913). "Don't demand perfection, for you won't find it." A smaller apartment should be decorated with suitability, simplicity, and proportion in mind. "There never was a house so bad that it couldn't be made over into something worthwhile," de Wolfe insisted. She advocated spending on new wallpaper instead of buying a new hat, and going without in general rather than buying what she called "sham things." No bric-a-brac or "huge and frightful paintings"—and lots of "dignified" white walls.

"Don't buy massive furniture for your apartment," she cautioned. "You must have a place where you can breathe and fling your arms about!"

XENIA

Ancient Greek hospitality

In ancient Greece, the rules of *xenia* meant welcoming any stranger, especially a foreigner, as an honored guest, and treating him to a good meal without even asking his name until after he'd finished eating.

The practice was exemplified in *The Odyssey*, when Odysseus arrived at the Phaiakian palace and hurled himself at the queen's feet, clasping her knees and begging for help in returning home to Ithaca. "But come, have the guest get up and sit on a silver-studded throne, and you bid the heralds mix wine," commanded one of her elder kinsmen, offering the anonymous visitor a fine meal and the best seat in the house. But *xenia* wasn't merely a rich man's obligation. During another episode in the epic poem, Odysseus, disguised as a beggar, finally reached Ithaca and was taken in, unrecognized, by his own former servant. "Eat now, stranger, the food that a servant is able to give you," the humble man said, offering a simple meal of pork, bread, and wine.

At Rome's height, expressions of *xenia* reflected the opulence of the times. The dining rooms in Roman villas were painted with frescoes of the delicacies the guests might be served there, fresh eggs, peaches, and handsome vegetables. The fabled Roman banquet began in the midafternoon, after a bath, and ended the next morning when the sun came up. During the feast, inedible scraps were thrown to the floor, a crude inspiration for the clever mosaics called *asarôtos oikos*, or "unswept pavement," depicting in vivid trompe l'oeil the detritus a fabulous dinner would leave behind— scattered fish bones, lobster claws, nutshells, fruit peels, grape stalks, and chestnut husks. Guests took home carefully wrapped leftovers at the end of the night, as well as all sorts of gifts, also called *xenia*, from lamps to musical instruments and from drinking goblets to ivory backscratchers.

Poetry was often served with the meal. As a poet, Martial (38/41–103), who came from Spain to Rome to seek his fortune during Emperor Nero's reign, was something of a professional guest, amusing wealthy patrons and their dinner partners with his epigrams and a peppery mix of flattery and mockery. Poets kept a stingy host in check by demanding *xenia* for all. "Yesterday you invited sixty of us to dinner, Mancinus, yet there was nothing more than a boar placed before us . . ." Martial howled. "Just a miserable boar, and so small that it could have been killed by an unarmed dwarf."

If anyone knew about *xenia*, it was Martial, who dined out with the rich Romans for more than thirty years. When he, in turn, invited friends for a meal, he promised not only "Cappadocian lettuces and strong-smelling leeks, and tuna hidden beneath slices of egg," along with raisins, pears, roasted chestnuts, and fine wine, but also the kind of *xenia* that money can't buy. "The dinner is humble—who can deny it?" he wrote, asking a friend to supper. "But you will have no need to invent falsehoods, nor to hear them, and you can repose just as you are . . ."

XIGUO JIFA

A sixteenth-century text detailing memorization techniques of the Italian monasteries

The Italian Jesuit missionary Matteo Ricci (1552–1610) introduced the Chinese literati to the latest in Western mathematics, astronomy, and geography, all of which he hoped would convert them to Catholicism. But he stunned them with his memorization techniques, described in his popular text *Xiguo jifa*.

Like his fellow European monk-scholars, Ricci relied on a mnemonic technique that used vivid spatial visualization to organize everything he wanted to remember in his mind. In *Xiguo jifa*, he described how to employ coded visual cues to create an imaginary image for each thing to be memorized, and then how to "file" each image in an exact location within a vast storage facility, a "memory palace." A practitioner of the technique recalled a piece of information by imagining walking to a certain location within his memory palace and retrieving it. The most ambitious of such palaces consisted of hundreds of imaginary buildings, organized into separate halls and floors where scholars could store some 100,000 visual images, each one encoding detailed information. For example, historian Jonathan D. Spence suggests that a young doctor might house an image representing an anagram for the names of the bones of the leg in the medical wing of his memory palace, in the hall of anatomy.

Various adherents personalized their imaginary architecture. The fifteenth-century Franciscan scholar Lodovico da Pirano diagrammed the rows of storage towers he used to store his memories. In 1520 the Dominican Johannes Romberch described his memory palace with illustrations of an abbey.

Ricci didn't invent the method, but he used it to his advantage once he'd arrived in China in 1583. Ricci hired a Confucian tutor, rapidly mastered the language, and translated Euclid and the Ten Commandments into Chinese—the first Christian text in the language—and translated into Latin the first texts by the Chinese philosopher K'ung Fu-tzu, whom Ricci renamed Confucius. Ricci wore flowing purple robes while carried through the streets by porters, and was invited to lush banquets to discuss philosophy. He entranced those he met with outlandish Bible stories. "More than once have I told the Chinese that Jesus Christ moved the house in which he and his mother used to live [from the Holy Land] to the vicinity of my hometown," he wrote to a fellow Jesuit back in Rome. "Whenever I told them about the various kinds of miracles God produced in the West, they were simply stupefied." Ricci showed off his imported collection of prisms, hourglasses, and a world map that contradicted the local notions that the Earth was flat and that China occupied most of it. He made sundials for friends, and gave the emperor a clavichord and a pair of clocks that rang out the hours, as well as paintings of Christ and the Madonna. (At first, the emperor found the paintings fascinating, as they were done in a realistic, three-dimensional style. But soon he ordered the frightening images removed from his chambers.)

What impressed the Chinese most, however, were Ricci's phenomenal mnemonic skills. During one banquet, his host asked for a demonstration and a servant brought a book to Ricci, who read in it a poem consisting of some five hundred characters. Then, handing the book back, Ricci stood up at the table and recited it word for word. For a time, the other guests sat in silence, awed. But then someone suggested that he could have seen the book before. Ricci ordered a brush, ink, and paper brought into that hall and asked the other guests to list as many as five hundred random characters. He read through the list once before repeating it back to the crowd. The scholars applauded—they asked for more. As an encore, Ricci recited the list again—backward.

"Once your places are all fixed in order, then you can walk through the door and make your start," he explained in *Xiguo jifa*. "Turn to the right and proceed from there. As with the practice of calligraphy, in which you move from the beginning to the end, as with fish who swim along in ordered schools, so is everything arranged in your brain, and all the images are ready for whatever you seek to remember."

YES

A word used to express willingness or agreement

In the early 1960s, Yoko Ono (1933–) was a young New York artist living in a cheap loft on Chambers Street. She was known for witty artworks like *Ceiling Painting*: a white ladder leading to a picture frame hung on the ceiling that displayed one minuscule, three-lettered "YES," to be viewed with a dangling magnifying glass. Sometimes just reading the word feels good.

Born in Tokyo into a prominent banking family of samurai and aristocrats, Ono was rigorously schooled in classical music. But she was hardly the conservatory type. In New York, she joined Fluxus, a loosely knit group of artists with clever ways. (As one critic put it, "both the zany and the Zen-y.") They did installations in shop windows and built fun-house mazes. One member dipped his head in paint and drew with it. Ono handed out written instructions, suggesting, for example, that the recipient light a match and watch it until it went out.

Some of her pieces exposed a destructive edge. In *Smoke Painting*, she presented a canvas and invited people to burn it. In *Cut Piece*, an example of early performance art, she sat passively onstage as people snipped off her clothes.

Her optimism was just as radical. She designed a vending machine to dispense bits of sky. Her *A Box of Smile* was a hinged box with a mirror inside. Another piece, from 1960, encouraged her audience to think the word "yes," preferably all the time.

Of course, in every era, optimism grates on those who don't share it. For his part, the German philosopher and mathematician Gottfried Wilhelm Leibniz (1646–1716) proposed the cheerful idea that the world must be perfect, because God created it, and suffered a bookful of Voltaire's rabid parody in *Candide*. American writer Ambrose Bierce (1842–1914) called optimism "the doctrine that everything is beautiful, including what is ugly," and assured his readers that optimism was "hereditary, but fortunately not contagious." In the twentieth century, critics publicly chastised artists Yoko Ono and John Lennon (1940–1980) for their positive thinking.

But it was optimism that brought them together. In 1966 Lennon went to see Ono's show at the Indica Gallery in London and climbed the ladder to see *Ceiling Painting*. "I felt relieved," he said later. "It's a great relief when you get up the ladder and you look through the spyglass and it doesn't say 'no' or 'fuck you' or something. It said 'yes.'"

He asked to meet the artist. Ono didn't know who he was, but the gallery's owner pushed her to go "say hello to the millionaire." She handed him a card printed with the instruction "Breathe." After a few shy encounters around town, she gave him a book she'd done, which he kept next to his bed. They wrote letters to each other. They stayed up late talking.

After they became a couple, they collaborated on deliriously optimistic projects, from their famous bed-ins to the creation of a conceptual country called Nutopia. The skeptics were incensed, and the duo withstood all the criticism slung at prominent optimists of the past, though it hardly slowed them down. "Some critic recently commented on us, John and I, as being lollipop artists who are preoccupied with blowing soap-bubbles forever," Ono wrote. "I thought that was beautiful."

ACKNOWLEDGMENTS

I'm grateful to those who have offered their support, kind encouragement, and guidance throughout this project, including Nico Jenkins, Nan Talese, Ronit Feldman, David Kuhn, Susan Kerwin, Nancy Harmon Jenkins, Eve MacSweeney, Hampton Fancher, Bridget Foley, Bobbi Queen, Joanna Bober, Jaya Ashmore, Gemma Polo, and Ajay Singh. I'd further like to thank Sinclair S. Smith for his keen eye, Anne Greene for giving me a boost early on, and Misha Litvinov for schooling me on Tolstoy's love of origami.

Along the way, I've been helped by legions of librarians, including those at the New York Public Library and at the Metropolitan Museum of Art's Watson Library, Merle Thompson at the Fairchild Archive, and the librarians of the Condé Nast archives, as well as those working within the Maine library system, especially in Blue Hill and in Belfast. Thanks to the archivist at the Morgan Library & Museum who allowed me to peruse Lord Byron's letters, and to the team at Google Books, who made it possible for me to see so many rare, out-of-print, and fascinating old books which I never would have found otherwise.

BIBLIOGRAPHY

AEROSTATION

Christopher, John. *Riding the Jetstream: The Story of Ballooning, from Montgolfier to Breitling*.
   London: John Murray, 2001.

Coombs, Charles. *Hot-Air Ballooning*. New York: William Morrow, 1981.

Gillespie, Richard. "Ballooning in France and Britain, 1783–1786: Aerostation and Adventur-
   ism." *Isis* 75:2 (June 1984): 249–268.

Marion, Fulgence. *Wonderful Balloon Ascents; or, the Conquest of the Skies. A History of Balloons
   and Balloon Voyages*. New York: Scribner, Armstrong, 1874.

Shayler, David J., and Ian A. Moule. *Women in Space—Following Valentina*. Chichester; New
   York: Praxis, 2005.

ALFRESCO

Batterberry, Michael, and Ariane Batterberry. *On the Town in New York: The Landmark History
   of Eating, Drinking, and Entertainments from the American Revolution to the Food Revolution*.
   New York: Routledge, 1999.

Hern, Mary Ellen W. "Picnicking in the Northeastern United States, 1840–1900." *Winterthur
   Portfolio* 24:2/3 (Summer–Autumn 1989):139–152.

Latham, Jean. *The Pleasure of Your Company: A History of Manners & Meals*. London: A. and C.
   Black, 1972.

Osmundson, Theodore. *Roof Gardens: History, Design, and Construction*. New York: W. W.
   Norton, 1999.

"Roof Garden In Again," *New York Times*, June 20, 1920.

Wilkins, John, and Shaun Hill. *Food in the Ancient World*. Malden, MA; Oxford: Blackwell,
   2006.

Young, Carolin C. *Apples of Gold in Settings of Silver: Stories of Dinner as a Work of Art*. New York;
   London: Simon & Schuster, 2002.

AMORINI

Dempsey, Charles. *Inventing the Renaissance Putto*. Chapel Hill: University of North Carolina
　　Press, 2001.
Hall, James. *Dictionary of Subjects and Symbols in Art*. Boulder: Westview Press, 2008.
Meyer, Alfred Gotthold. *Donatello*. Trans. P. G. Konody. Bielefeld; Leipzig: Velhagen &
　　Klasing, 1904.
Nagel, Alexander. *Cherubs: Angels of Love*. Boston: Bulfinch, 1994.
Sirén, Osvald. "The Importance of the Antique to Donatello." *American Journal of Archaeology*
　　18:4 (Oct.–Dec. 1914): 438–461.
Worth, Peter J. Review of *The Transformation of Eros*, by Josef Kunstmann. *Art Bulletin* 49:2
　　(June 1967): 188–191.

ATTITUDES

Bermingham, Ann. "The Aesthetics of Ignorance: The Accomplished Woman in the Culture
　　of Connoisseurship." *Oxford Art Journal* 16:2 (1993): 3–20.
Edinger, George. "Emma's 'Attitudes.'" *Ballet Magazine*, Feb. 1947.
Fraser, Flora. *Emma, Lady Hamilton*. New York: Knopf: Distributed by Random House, 1986.
May, Gita. *Elisabeth Vigée Le Brun: The Odyssey of an Artist in an Age of Revolution*. New Haven:
　　Yale University Press, 2005.
Peakman, Julie. *Emma Hamilton*. London: Haus, 2005.
Penny, Nicholas. "Review of Sir William Hamilton. London." *Burlington Magazine* 138:119
　　(June 1996): 415–417.
"Portraits of Lady Hamilton," *Anglo-Saxon Review* 6 (Sept. 1900).
Sichel, Walter Sydney. *Emma Lady Hamilton, From New and Original Sources and Documents,
　　Together With an Appendix of Notes and New Letters*. New York: Dodd, Mead, 1907.
Vigée-Lebrun, Louise-Elisabeth. *The Memoirs of Elisabeth Vigée-Le Brun*. Trans. Sian Evans.
　　Bloomington: Indiana University Press, 1989.

BLACK

Bernhardt, Sarah. *My Double Life: The Memoirs of Sarah Bernhardt*. Trans. Victoria Tietze
　　Larson. Albany: State University of New York Press, 1999.
Fields, Jill. *An Intimate Affair: Women, Lingerie, and Sexuality*. Berkeley: University of Califor-
　　nia Press, 2007.
Kerwin, Jessica. "Tough Chic." *Women's Wear Daily*, Nov. 11, 2003, Eye Page.
Miller, Brandon Marie. *Dressed for the Occasion: What Americans Wore 1620–1970*. Minneapolis:
　　Lerner Publications, 1999.
Schneider, Jane. "Peacocks and Penguins: The Political Economy of European Cloth and
　　Colors." *American Ethnologist* 5:3 (Aug. 1978): 413–447.
Steele, Valerie. *Paris Fashion: A Cultural History*. Oxford: Berg, 1999.

BLANCMANGE

Babcock, Merton C. "The Vocabulary of Social Life on the American Frontier." *Western Folklore* 9:2 (April 1950): 136–143.

Chaucer, Geoffrey. *The Canterbury Tales*. Trans. Nevill Coghill. Harmondsworth: Penguin Books, 1977.

Hirschfelder, Arlene B. *Photo Odyssey: Solomon Carvalho's Remarkable Western Adventure, 1853–54*. New York: Clarion Books, 2000.

Kelly, Ian. *Cooking for Kings: The Life of Antonin Carême, the First Celebrity Chef*. New York: Walker, 2004.

Metzner, Paul. *Crescendo of the Virtuoso: Spectacle, Skill, and Self-promotion in Paris During the Age of Revolution*. Berkeley: University of California Press, 1998.

Moynihan, Ruth B. Review of *Wagon Wheel Kitchens: Food on the Oregon Trail*, by Jacqueline Williams. *The Journal of American History* 81:3 (Dec. 1994): 1297–1298.

Palmquist, Peter E., and Thomas R. Kailbourn. *Pioneer Photographers from the Mississippi to the Continental Divide: A Biographical Dictionary, 1839–1865*. Stanford: Stanford University Press, 2005.

BOB

"Bobbed Hair Barred," *New York Times*, Aug. 10, 1921.

"Bobbed Hair Parts Couple," *New York Times*, Aug. 30, 1921.

"Bobbed Hair Plea Unheeded; Mystery Man Does Job," *New York Times*, Dec. 21, 1922.

"Bobbed Heads Unbowed," *New York Times*, Sept. 4, 1921.

Castle, Irene, Robert Lipscomb Duncan, and Wanda Duncan. *Castles in the Air*. New York: Da Capo Press, 1958.

Charles-Roux, Edmonde. *Chanel and Her World; Friends, Fashion, and Fame*. New York: Vendome Press, 2005.

Fitzgerald, F. Scott. *Before Gatsby: The First Twenty-six Stories*. Matthew J. Bruccoli, ed., with the assistance of Judith S. Baughman. Columbia: University of South Carolina Press, 2001.

———. *Bernice Bobs Her Hair*. Whitefish, MT: Kessinger Publishing, 2004.

———. *Flappers and Philosophers*. James L. W. West III, ed. New York: Cambridge University Press, 2000.

" 'Giddy' Teachers Taboo," *New York Times*, Feb. 23, 1922.

Golden, Eve. *Vernon and Irene Castle's Ragtime Revolution*. Lexington: University Press of Kentucky, 2007.

"Hair-Clipper Story Upheld by Father," *New York Times*, Oct. 31, 1921.

"Irene Castle, Dancer, Dies at 75; Was Toast of World War I Era," *New York Times*, Jan. 26, 1969.

Roberts, Mary Louise. "Samson and Delilah Revisited: The Politics of Women's Fashion in 1920s France." *American Historical Review* 98:3 (June 1993): 657–684.

Simpson, John, ed. *Oxford English Dictionary*. Oxford: Oxford University Press, 2009.

"South Draws Hair Line," *New York Times,* July 9, 1921.

"Vogue of Bobbed Hair," *New York Times,* June 27, 1920.

Wayne, Helen M. "Bobbed Hair and Maiden Names for Wives!" *New York Times*, March 30, 1919.

BON CHRÉTIEN

Alban, Butler. *Lives of the Saints, with Reflections for Every Day in the Year, Compiled from the 'Lives of the Saints,' by Rev. Alban Butler, to Which Are Added Lives of the American Saints Placed on the Calendar for the United States by Special Petition of the Third Plenary Council of Baltimore.* New York: Benziger Brothers, 1894.

Andrews, Marian. *The Life of Louis XI, the Rebel Dauphin and the Statesman King, from his Original Letters and Other Documents.* By Christopher Hare [pseud.]. London; New York: Harper, 1907.

Farmer, James Eugene. *Versailles and the Court Under Louis XIV.* New York: The Century Co., 1905.

Ghezzi, Bert. *Mystics & Miracles: True Stories of Lives Touched by God.* Chicago: Loyola Press, 2002.

Grigson, Jane. *Jane Grigson's Fruit Book.* New York: Atheneum, 1982.

The History of Paris from the Earliest Period to the Present Day: Containing a Description of Its Antiquities, Public Buildings, Civil, Religious, Scientific, and Commercial Institutions. London: G. B. Whittaker; Paris: A. and W. Galignani, 1825.

La Quintinie, Jean Baptiste de. "Instructions pour les jardins fruitiers et potagers, La Quintinie, 1690." France Diplomatie. http://www.diplomatie.gouv.fr/fr/actions-france_830/livre-ecrit_1036/collection-textes_5281/quintinie-potager-du-roi_5676/instructions-pour-les-jardins-fruitiers-potagers_5677/index.html (accessed Jan. 16, 2010).

Lanzi, Fernando, and Gioia Lanzi. *Saints and Their Symbols: Recognizing Saints in Art and in Popular Image.* Trans. Matthew J. O'Connell. Collegeville, MN: Liturgical Press, 2004.

Smedley, Edward. *The History of France: From the Final Partition of the Empire of Charlemagne, A.D. 843, to the Peace of Cambray, A.D. 1529.* London: Baldwin, 1836.

Toussaint-Samat, Maguelonne. *A History of Food.* Trans. Anthea Bell. Chichester; Malden, UK: Wiley-Blackwell, 2009.

Whitmore, P. J. S. *The Order of Minims in Seventeenth-Century France.* The Hague: Martinus Nijhoff, 1967.

BOUDOIR

Beasley, Faith Evelyn. *Salons, History, and the Creation of Seventeenth-Century France: Mastering Memory.* Burlington, VT: Ashgate, 2006.

Caillot, Antoine. *Mémoires pour servir à l'histoire des moeurs et usages des Français, depuis les plus hautes conditions, jusqu'aux classes inférieures de la société, pendant le règne de Louis XVI, sous le Directoire Exécutif, sous Napoléon Bonaparte, et jusqu'à nos jours.* Paris: Dauvin, 1827.

Cooper, Robert Leon. *Language Planning and Social Change*. Cambridge; New York: Cambridge University Press, 1989.

De Wolfe, Elsie. *The House in Good Taste*. Salem, NH: Ayer, 1990.

Duby, Georges, and Michelle Perrot, eds. *A History of Women in the West*. Cambridge: Belknap Press of Harvard University Press, 1992–1994.

Goodman, Dena, and Kathryn Norberg, eds. *Furnishing the Eighteenth Century: What Furniture Can Tell Us About the European and American Past*. New York: Routledge, 2006.

Ladd, Mary-Sargent. *The Frenchwoman's Bedroom*. New York: Doubleday, 1991.

Oberkirch, Henriette Louise von Waldner (Baronne d'). *Memoirs of the Baroness d'Oberkirch, Countess de Montbrison, Volume 1*. London: Colburn, 1852.

Thornton, Peter. *Authentic Decor; The Domestic Interior, 1620–1920*. New York: Viking, 1984.

CAROUSEL

Browne, Ray B., and Pat Browne, eds. *The Guide to United States Popular Culture*. Bowling Green: Bowling Green State University Popular Press, 2001.

Fried, Frederick. *A Pictorial History of the Carousel*. New York: Bonanza Books, 1964.

Mulryne, J. R., Helen Watanabe-O'Kelly, and Margaret Shewring, eds. *Europa Triumphans; Court and Civic Festivals in Early Modern Europe*. Burlington, VT: Ashgate, 2004.

Rilke, Rainer Maria. *Selected Poems*. Trans. C. F. MacIntyre. Berkeley: University of California Press, 2001.

Voltaire. *Oeuvres complètes de Voltaire*. Paris: Hachette, 1859–1862.

CHAMPAGNE

Gronow, Jukka. *Caviar with Champagne; Common Luxury and the Ideals of the Good Life in Stalin's Russia*. Oxford: Berg, 2003.

Hessler, Julie. Review of *Caviar with Champagne: Common Luxury and the Ideals of the Good Life* by Jukka Gronow. *Slavic Review* 64:4 (Winter 2005): 910–911.

Kladstrup, Don, and Petie Kladstrup. *Champagne; How the World's Most Glamorous Wine Triumphed Over War and Hard Times*. New York: William Morrow, 2005.

Vizetelly, Henry. *A History of Champagne; With Notes on the Other Sparkling Wines of France*. London: Southeran, 1882.

CLAUDE GLASS

Briggs, Asa. *Victorian Things*. Stroud, UK: Sutton, 2003.

Danius, Sara. *The Senses of Modernism; Technology, Perception, and Aesthetics*. Ithaca: Cornell University Press, 2002.

Jennett, Seán. *Deserts of England*. London: Heinemann, 1964.

Gilpin, William. *Three Essays: On Picturesque Beauty; On Picturesque Travel; and on Sketching Landscape: with a Poem on Landscape Painting*. London: T. Cadell and W. Davies, 1808.

Hunt, John Dixon, and Faith M. Holland, eds. *The Ruskin Polygon; Essays on the Imagination of John Ruskin*. Manchester: Manchester University Press, 1982.

Maillet, Arnaud. *The Claude Glass; Use and Meaning of the Black Mirror in Western Art*. Trans. Jeff Fort. New York: Zone Books, 2004.

Pace, Claire. "Claude the Enchanted: Interpretations of Claude in England in the Earlier Nineteenth Century." *Burlington Magazine* 111:801 (Dec. 1969): 733–740.

Shepard, Paul. *Man in the Landscape; A Historic View of the Esthetics of Nature*. New York: Knopf, 1967.

Stainton, Lindsay. *Nature into Art; English Landscape Watercolours*. London: British Museum Press, 1991.

CONFETTI

"Coney's Mardi Gras Ends in Rowdyism," *New York Times*, Sept. 23, 1906.

Dahlquist, Allan. *Megasthenes and Indian Religion; a Study in Motives and Types*. Delhi: Motilal Banarsidass, 1977.

Hawthorne, Nathaniel. *Passages from the French and Italian Note-Books of Nathaniel Hawthorne*. Boston: Houghton, Mifflin, 1883.

Levillain, Philippe, ed. *The Papacy; An Encyclopedia*. New York: Routledge, 2002.

Redon, Odile, Françoise Sabban, and Silvano Serventi. *The Medieval Kitchen; Recipes from France and Italy*. Trans. Edward Schneider. Chicago: University of Chicago Press, 1998.

Roy, Christian. *Traditional Festivals; A Multicultural Encyclopedia*. Santa Barbara: ABC-CLIO, 2005.

Van Praagh, David. *The Greater Game: India's Race with Destiny and China*. Montreal: McGill-Queen's University Press, 2003.

Walsh, William Shepard. *Curiosities of Popular Customs and of Rites, Ceremonies, Observances, and Miscellaneous Antiquities*. Philadelphia: Lippincott, 1925.

COUNTESS DE CASTIGLIONE, AND POSTHUMOUSLY

Apraxine, Pierre, and Xavier Demange; with the collaboration of Françoise Heilbrun, and Michele Falzone del Barbarò. *La Divine Comtesse: Photographs of the Countess de Castiglione*. Trans. Caroline Beamish. New Haven: Yale University Press, in association with the Metropolitan Museum of Art, 2000.

Apter, Emily, and William Pietz, eds. *Fetishism as Cultural Discourse*. Ithaca: Cornell University Press, 1993.

Dakers, Caroline. *The Holland Park Circle: Artists and Victorian Society*. New Haven: Yale University Press, 1999.

Decaux, Alain. *La Castiglione; Dame de coeur de l'Europe; d'après sa correspondance et son journal intime inédits*. Paris: Perrin, 1964.

"Ganna Walska Has Debut as Actress," *New York Times*, June 2, 1929.

Kael, Pauline. *The Citizen Kane Book: Raising Kane*. Boston: Little, Brown, 1971.

LLL. "A Foreigner in Florence." *The Century*, Oct. 1883.

Loliée, Frédéric. *The Gilded Beauties of the Second Empire*. Adapted by Bryan O'Donnell. London: J. Long, 1909.

———. *Women of the Second Empire; Chronicles of the Court of Napoleon III, Compiled from Unpublished Documents by Frédéric Loliée*. Trans. Alice M. Ivimy. London; New York: J. Lane, 1907.

Munhall, Edgar. *Whistler and Montesquiou: The Butterfly and the Bat*. New York: Frick Collection; Paris: Flammarion, 1995.

Owens, Mitchell. "Garden of the Slightly Macabre." *New York Times*, Aug. 22, 1966.

Ryersson, Scot D., and Michael Orlando Yaccarino. *Infinite Variety: The Life and Legend of the Marchesa Casati*. Minneapolis: University of Minnesota Press, 2004.

Solomon-Godeau, Abigail. "The Legs of the Countess." *October* 39 (Winter 1986): 65–108.

Swartley, Ariel. "A Diva Who Loved High Drama." *Los Angeles Times*, March 10, 2005.

Walska, Ganna. *Always Room at the Top*. New York: R. R. Smith, 1943.

CRICKETS

Hearn, Lafcadio. *Exotics and Retrospectives*. Rutland, VT: C. E. Tuttle, 1971.

Laufer, Berthold. *Insect-Musicians and Cricket Champions of China*. Chicago: Field Museum of Natural History, 1927.

Simoons, Frederick J. *Food in China: A Cultural and Historical Inquiry*. Boca Raton: CRC Press, 1991.

CUMULONIMBUS

Avery, John. *Information Theory and Evolution*. River Edge, NJ: World Scientific, 2003.

Esmeijer, Ank C. "Cloudscapes in Theory and Practice." *Simiolus: Netherlands Quarterly for the History of Art* 9:3 (1977): 123–148.

Hamblyn, Richard. *The Invention of Clouds: How an Amateur Meteorologist Forged the Language of the Skies*. New York: Farrar, Straus & Giroux, 2001.

Lamarck, Jean-Baptiste-Pierre-Antoine de Monet de. *The Lamarck Manuscripts at Harvard*. William Morton Wheeler and Thomas Barbour, eds. Cambridge: Harvard University Press, 1933.

Packard, A. S. *Lamarck, the Founder of Evolution; His Life and Work, with Translations of His Writings on Organic Evolution*. New York: Longmans, Green, 1901.

Pretor-Pinney, Gavin. *The Cloudspotter's Guide: The Science, History, and Culture of Clouds*. New York: Perigee Book, 2006.

Slater, A. W. "Luke Howard, F.R.S. (1772–1864) and His Relations with Goethe." *Notes and Records of the Royal Society of London* 27:1 (Aug. 1972): 119–140.

Williams, John R. *The Life of Goethe: A Critical Biography*. Oxford; Malden: Blackwell Publishers, 1998.

DAHLIAS AND GLADIOLI

Davis, Linda H. *Onward and Upward: A Biography of Katharine S. White*. New York: Harper &
Row, 1987.
Glendinning, Victoria. *Vita: A Biography of Vita Sackville-West*. New York: Knopf, 1983.
Nicolson, Harold George, Sir. *Diaries and Letters*. Nigel Nicolson, ed. New York: Atheneum,
1966–1968.
Sackville-West, V. *Country Notes in Wartime*. London: Hogarth Press, 1940.
———. *Even More for Your Garden*. London: M. Joseph, 1958.
———. *More for Your Garden*. London: M. Joseph, 1955.
Sackville-West, V., and Robin Lane Fox. *The Illustrated Garden Book*. New York: Atheneum,
1986.
White, Katharine Sergeant Angell. *Onward and Upward in the Garden*. New York: Farrar, Straus
& Giroux, 1979.

DARK TOWER

Bundles, A'Lelia Perry. *Madam C. J. Walker: Entrepreneur*. New York: Chelsea House, 2008.
———. *On Her Own Ground: The Life and Times of Madam C. J. Walker*. New York: Scribner, 2001.
Hughes, Langston. *The Big Sea: An Autobiography*. New York: Hill & Wang, 1993.
Kerwin, Jessica. "Uptown Girl." *Women's Wear Daily*, April 14, 2003.
Lewis, David L. *When Harlem Was in Vogue*. New York: Penguin Books, 1997.

DIVAN

Campbell, Margaret. "From Cure Chair to 'Chaise Longue': Medical Treatment and the Form
of the Modern Recliner." *Journal of Design History* 12:4 (1999): 327–343.
Corelli, Marie. *Ziska; The Problem of a Wicked Soul*. New York: F. A. Stokes, 1898.
Decorator & Furnisher, "How to Sit on a Divan," Oct. 1891.
Gloag, John. *English Furniture*. London: A. & C. Black, Ltd., 1934.
Hoganson, Kristin L. *Consumers' Imperium: The Global Production of American Domesticity,
1865–1920*. Chapel Hill: University of North Carolina Press, 2007.
Laclos, Choderlos de. *Les Liaisons dangereuses*. Harmondsworth, UK: Penguin Books, 1961.
McMahon, Gary. *Camp in Literature*. Jefferson, NC: McFarland, 2006.
Peradotto, John, and J. P. Sullivan, eds. *Women in the Ancient World: The Arethusa Papers*.
Albany: State University of New York Press, 1984.
Roller, Matthew B. *Dining Posture in Ancient Rome: Bodies, Values, and Status*. Princeton:
Princeton University Press, 2006.
Simpson, John, ed. *Oxford English Dictionary*. Oxford: Oxford University Press, 2009.
Wilkins, John, and Shaun Hill. *Food in the Ancient World*. Malden; Oxford: Blackwell, 2006.

ELEPHANTINE COLOSSUS

Barrère, Albert, and Charles G. Leland, eds. *A Dictionary of Slang, Jargon & Cant Embrac-*
ing English, American, and Anglo-Indian Slang, Pidgin English, Tinker's Jargon and Other
Irregular Phraseology. London: The Ballantyne Press, 1889–1890.
Buonaventura, Wendy. *Something in the Way She Moves: Dancing Women from Salome to*
Madonna. Cambridge, MA: Da Capo Press, 2004.
Çelik, Zeynep, and Leila Kinney. "Ethnography and Exhibitionism at the Expositions Univer-
selles." *Assemblage* 13 (Dec. 1990): 34–59.
Denson, Charles. *Coney Island: Lost and Found*. Berkeley: Ten Speed Press, 2002.
McMahon, William. *The Story of Lucy the Elephant*. Margate, NJ: Save Lucy Committee Inc.,
1988.

ENTHUSIASM

Clark, Timothy. *The Theory of Inspiration: Composition as a Crisis of Subjectivity in Romantic and*
Post-Romantic Writing. Manchester; New York: Manchester University Press, 1997.
Goldstein, Jan. "Enthusiasm or Imagination? Eighteenth-Century Smear Words in Com-
parative National Context." *Huntington Library Quarterly* 60:1/2 (1997): 29–49.
Gray, Francine du Plessix. *Madame de Staël: The First Modern Woman*. New York; London:
Atlas, 2008.
Kennedy, Rick. Review of *Enthusiasm and Enlightenment in Europe, 1650–1850*, by Lawrence E.
Klein and Anthony J. La Vopa. *Church History Source* 69:1 (March 2000): 188–190.
Klein, Lawrence E. "Sociability, Solitude, and Enthusiasm." *Huntington Library Quarterly*
60:1/2 (1997): 153–177.
Lewis, Linda M. *Germaine de Staël, George Sand, and the Victorian Woman Artist*. Columbia:
University of Missouri Press, 2003.
Potkay, Adam. Review of *Elations: The Poetics of Enthusiasm in Eighteenth-Century Britain*, by
Shaun Irlam. *Modern Philology* 99:4 (May 2002): 640–643.
Sheriff, Mary D. "Passionate Spectators: On Enthusiasm, Nymphomania, and the Imagined
Tableau." *Huntington Library Quarterly* 60:1/2 (1997): 51–83.
Simpson, John, ed. *Oxford English Dictionary*. Oxford: Oxford University Press, 2009.
Tymieniecka, Anna-Teresa. *Enjoyment: From Laughter to Delight in Philosophy, Literature, the*
Fine Arts, and Aesthetics. Boston: Kluwer Academic, 1998.

FANFARE

Bellman, Jonathan, ed. *The Exotic in Western Music*. Boston: Northeastern University Press,
1998.
Bowles, Edmund A. "Musical Instruments at the Medieval Banquet." *Revue Belge de Musicolo-*
gie/Belgisch Tijdschrift voor Muziekwetenschap 12:1/4 (1958): 41–51.
———. *The Timpani: A History in Pictures and Documents*. New York: Pendragon Press, 2002.

Montagu, Jeremy. *Timpani and Percussion*. New Haven: Yale University Press, 2002.

Quataert, Donald. *The Ottoman Empire, 1700–1922*. Cambridge; New York: Cambridge University Press, 2005.

Visser, Margaret. *The Rituals of Dinner: The Origins, Evolution, Eccentricities, and Meaning of Table Manners*. New York: Grove Weidenfeld, 1991.

FAR NIENTE

Chard, Chloe. *Pleasure and Guilt on the Grand Tour: Travel Writing and Imaginative Geography 1600–1830*. Manchester; New York: Manchester University Press, 1999.

Gelber, Steven M. "A Job You Can't Lose: Work and Hobbies in the Great Depression." *Journal of Social History* 24:4 (Summer 1991): 741–766

Hunt, Alan. *Governance of the Consuming Passions: A History of Sumptuary Law*. New York: St. Martin's Press, 1996.

James, Henry. *Daisy Miller: A Study; Four Meetings; Longstaff's Marriage; Benvolio*. London: Macmillan, 1887.

Jameson, Anna. *The Diary of an Ennuyée*. Boston: J. R. Osgood, 1875.

Sévigné, Marie de Rabutin-Chantal (Marquise de). *Selected Letters*. Trans. Leonard Tancock. Harmondsworth; New York: Penguin Books, 1982.

Spacks, Patricia Meyer. *Boredom: The Literary History of a State of Mind*. Chicago: University of Chicago Press, 1996.

Steele, Valerie. *Paris Fashion: A Cultural History*. Oxford: Berg, 1999.

Stevenson, Robert Louis. *An Apology for Idlers*. East Aurora, NY: The Roycrofters, 1917.

Wagner, Ann. "Idleness and the Ideal of the Gentlemen." *History of Education Quarterly* 25:1/2 (Spring–Summer 1985): 41–55.

Wenzel, Siegfried. *The Sin of Sloth; Acedia in Medieval Thought and Literature*. Chapel Hill: University of North Carolina Press, 1967.

FAUX JEWELS

Campbell, Gordon, ed. *The Grove Encyclopedia of Decorative Arts*. New York: Oxford University Press, 2006.

Della Porta, Giambattista. *Natural Magick (transcribed from 1658 English edition) (Magiae Naturalis) by John Baptista Porta (Giambattista della Porta) (1535–1615): A Neapolitane: In Twenty Books (1584 A.D.): Wherein Are Set Fourth All the Riches and Delights of the Natural Sciences*. Sioux Falls: NuVision Publications, 2005.

Donkin, R. A. *Beyond Price: Pearls and Pearl-Fishing: Origins to the Age of Discoveries*. Philadelphia: American Philosophical Society, 1998.

Emanuel, Harry. *Diamonds and Precious Stones: Their History, Value, and Distinguishing Characteristics*. London: J. C. Hotten, 1865.

Opie, Amelia Alderson. *Illustrations of Lying, in All Its Branches*. Boston: D. S. King, 1841.

Page, Jutta-Annette. *Beyond Venice: Glass in Venetian Style, 1500–1750*. Corning, NY: The Corning Museum of Glass, 2004.

"Pearls and Gems," *Harper's New Monthly Magazine* 21 (June–Nov. 1860): 764–776.

Scarisbrick, Diane, Christophe Vachaudez, and Jan Walgrave. *Royal Jewels: From Charlemagne to the Romanovs*. New York: Vendome Press, 2008.

Steele, Valerie, ed. *Encyclopedia of Clothing and Fashion*. Farmington Hills, MI: Charles Scribner's Sons, 2005.

Webster, Robert, and Peter G Read. *Gems: Their Sources, Descriptions, and Identification*. Amsterdam; Boston: Elsevier, 2006.

Wells, David Ames, ed. *The Annual of Scientific Discovery; or, Year-Book of Facts in Science and Art*. Boston: Gould & Lincoln, 1862.

White, Carolyn L. *American Artifacts of Personal Adornment, 1680–1820: A Guide to Identification and Interpretation*. Lanham, MD: AltaMira Press, 2005.

Wilkinson, John Gardner. *The Manners and Customs of the Ancient Egyptians*. London: J. Murray, 1879.

FELINES

Appiah, Kwame Anthony, and Henry Louis Gates Jr., eds. *Africana: The Encyclopedia of the African and African American Experience*. Oxford; New York: Oxford University Press, 2005.

Dalton, Karen C. C., and Henry Louis Gates Jr. "Josephine Baker and Paul Colin: African American Dance Seen Through Parisian Eyes." *Critical Inquiry* 24:4 (Summer 1998): 903–934.

Golden, Eve. *Golden Images: 41 Essays on Silent Film Stars*. Jefferson, NC: McFarland, 2001.

Kete, Kathleen. *The Beast in the Boudoir: Petkeeping in Nineteenth-Century Paris*. Berkeley: University of California Press, 1994.

"The Legend Named Baker Comes Home," *New York Times*, Feb. 2, 1936.

Negri, Pola. *Memoirs of a Star*. Garden City: Doubleday, 1970.

Sunquist, Melvin E., and Fiona Sunquist. *Wild Cats of the World*. Chicago: University of Chicago Press, 2002.

Vreeland, Diana. *D.V.* George Plimpton and Christopher Hemphill, eds. New York: Vintage Books, 1984.

Zierold, Norman J. *Sex Goddesses of the Silent Screen*. Chicago: H. Regnery, 1973.

FIREWORKS

Bergeron, David M. "Venetian State Papers and English Civic Pageantry, 1558–1642." *Renaissance Quarterly* 23:1 (Spring 1970): 37–47.

Biringuccio, Vannoccio. *Pirotechnia*. Trans. Cyril Stanley Smith and Maria Teach Cnudi. Cambridge, MA: MIT Press, 1966.

Boorsch, Suzanne. "Fireworks! Four Centuries of Pyrotechnics in Prints & Drawings." *Metropolitan Museum of Art Bulletin* 58:1 (Summer 2000): 3–52.

Hall, David. "Reviving a Forgotten Pyrotechnical Art Form: Pyrotechnics and Twentieth-Century Performance Art." *Leonardo* 24:5 (1991): 531–534.

Ling, Wang. "On the Invention and Use of Gunpowder and Firearms in China." *Isis* 37:3/4 (July 1947): 160–178.

Plimpton, George. *Fireworks*. New York: Anchor Books, 1984.

Salatino, Kevin. *Incendiary Art: The Representation of Fireworks in Early Modern Europe*. Santa Monica: The Getty Research Institute for the History of Art and the Humanities, 1997.

FOLLY

Albright, John Brannon. "The Legacy of Mad King Ludwig: Wild Castles and Wagner's Music." *New York Times*, Dec. 3, 1972.

Broyard, Anatole. "Last of the Cathedral Builders." *New York Times*, June 11, 1971.

Gladstone, Valerie. "Gaudi's Unfinished Masterpiece Is Virtually Complete." *New York Times*, Aug. 22, 2004.

Martinell, César. *Gaudí: His Life, His Theories, His Work*. Trans. Judith Rohrer. Cambridge, MA: MIT Press, 1975.

McIntosh, Christopher. *The Swan King, Ludwig II of Bavaria*. London: A. Lane, 1982.

Rall, Hans, and Michael Petzet. *King Ludwig II: Reality and Mystery*. Trans. Leslie Owen, Anthony Rich, and Veronica Leary. Regensburg, Ger: Schnell & Steiner, 2001.

Robinson, William H., Jordi Falgàs, and Carmen Belen Lord. *Barcelona and Modernity: Picasso, Gaudí, Miró, Dalí*. Cleveland: Cleveland Museum of Art, in association with Yale University Press, 2006.

Trumbauer, Lisa. *King Ludwig's Castle: Germany's Neuschwanstein*. New York: Bearport, 2005.

FRILLY LINGERIE

Buckley, Cheryl, and Hilary Fawcett. *Fashioning the Feminine: Representation and Women's Fashion from the Fin de Siècle to the Present*. London; New York: I. B. Tauris, 2002.

Caldwell, Doreen. *And All Was Revealed: Ladies' Underwear, 1907–1980*. New York: St. Martin's Press, 1981.

Cunnington, C. Willett, and Phillis Cunnington. *The History of Underclothes*. London; Boston: Faber & Faber, 1981.

Fields, Jill. *An Intimate Affair: Women, Lingerie, and Sexuality*. Berkeley: University of California Press, 2007.

Glyn, Elinor. *The Visits of Elizabeth*. Leipzig: B. Tauchnitz, 1900.

Kaplan, Joel H., and Sheila Stowell. *Theatre and Fashion: Oscar Wilde to the Suffragettes*. Cambridge; New York: Cambridge University Press, 1994.

Panhael, Marquise de. "How to be Beautiful, *Les Dessous*." *Vogue*, Dec. 27, 1894.

Pritchard, Mrs. Eric, and Rose Le Quesne. *The Cult of Chiffon*. London: Richards, 1902.
Tobin, Shelley. *Inside Out: A Brief History of Underwear*. London: The National Trust, 2000.

GIOCHI D'AQUA

Bedini, Silvio A. "The Role of Automata in the History of Technology." *Technology and Culture*
    5:1 (Winter 1964): 24–42.
Elliot, Charles. "Water Jokes." *Horticulture, The Magazine of American Gardening*, Dec. 1995.
Knox, Tim. "The Artificial Grotto in Britain." *Antiques*, June 2002.
Maitland, Sara, and Peter Matthews. "Gardens: Ground Farce." *The Independent*, June 11,
    2000.
Miller, Naomi. *Heavenly Caves: Reflections on the Garden Grotto*. New York: G. Braziller, 1982.
Werrett, Simon. "Wonders Never Cease: Descartes's 'Météores' and the Rainbow Fountain."
    British Journal for the History of Science 34 (June 2001): 129–147.

GLOVES

Beck, S. William. *Gloves, Their Annals and Associations. A Chapter of Trade and Social History*.
    Detroit: Singing Tree Press, 1969.
Boehn, Max von. *Ornaments: Lace, Fans, Gloves, Walking-sticks, Parasols, Jewelry, and Trinkets*.
    New York: B. Blom, 1929.
"Gloves, Past and Present," *Frank Leslie's Popular Monthly* 18 (July–Dec. 1884): 26.
Hull, William. *The History of the Glove Trade, with the Customs Connected with the Glove: To Which
    Are Annexed Some Observations on the Policy of the Trade Between England and France, and
    Its Operation on the Agricultural and Manufacturing Interests*. London: E. Wilson, 1834.
Smith, Willard M. *Gloves, Past and Present*. New York: The Sherwood Press, 1917.
Stallybrass, Peter, and Ann Rosalind Jones. "Fetishizing the Glove in Renaissance Europe."
    Critical Inquiry 28:1 (Autumn 2001): 114–132.

HEELS

Churchwell, Sarah Bartlett. *The Many Lives of Marilyn Monroe*. New York: Metropolitan Books,
    2005.
"History of Boots and Shoes," *Godey's Magazine and Lady's Book* 45 (1852).
Mink, Eric. *This Is Today: A Window on Our Times*. Laurie Dolphin, ed. Kansas City: Andrews
    McMeel, 2003.
Pedersen, Stephanie. *Shoes: What Every Woman Should Know*. Devon, UK: David & Charles,
    2005.
Redfern, W. B. *Royal and Historic Gloves and Shoes*. London: Methuen, 1904.
Rollyson, Carl E. *Female Icons: Marilyn Monroe to Susan Sontag*. New York: Iuniverse, 2005.
———. *Marilyn Monroe: A Life of the Actress*. Ann Arbor: UMI Research Press, 1986.
Stallybrass, Peter, and Ann Rosalind Jones. "Fetishizing the Glove in Renaissance Europe."
    Critical Inquiry 28:1 (Autumn 2001): 114–132.

HELLO

Adams, Mildred. "And Now 'Thank You' Saves Time for Us." *New York Times*, June 19, 1927.
Dunn, Mark. *Zounds! A Browser's Dictionary of Interjections*. New York: St. Martin's Press, 2005.
"Good Telephone Service," *The Manufacturer and Builder*, July 1892.
" 'Hello' On Phone Is Called Taboo," *New York Times*, Aug. 14, 1937.
"The Passing of the Telephone Girl: A Retrospect," *New York Times*, March 4, 1906.
Simpson, John, ed. *Oxford English Dictionary*. Oxford: Oxford University Press, 2009.
Van Dyke, Henry. "Fisherman's Luck." *The Century Magazine*, June 1899, 1.
"We Make Politeness Pay Dividends," *New York Times*, March 31, 1929.
Webb, Herbert Laws. "The Telephone of To-Day." *New England Magazine*, June 1894.
Wink, Josh. "The Advanced Telephone Girl." *New York Times*, Nov. 13, 1901.

ITALICS

"Aldus Manutius at UCLA." UCLA Library Department of Special Collections. UCLA. http://
    unitproj.library.ucla.edu/special/misc/aldexhibit.htm (accessed Jan. 19, 2010).
Haines, John, and Randall Rosenfeld, eds. *Music and Medieval Manuscripts: Paleography and
    Performance: Essays Dedicated to Andrew Hughes*. Aldershot; Burlington, VT: Ashgate,
    2004.
Lawson, Alexander S. *Anatomy of a Typeface*. Boston: David R. Godine, 1990.
Mason, William Albert. *A History of the Art of Writing*. New York: Macmillan, 1920.
Oliphant, Mrs. (Margaret). *The Makers of Venice, Doges, Conquerors, Painters, and Men of Letters*.
    London; New York: Macmillan, 1889.
Petrarch, Francesco. *Rerum Familiarium Libri*. Trans. Aldo S. Bernardo. New York: Italica
    Press, 2005.
Updike, Daniel Berkeley. *Printing Types, Their History, Forms, and Use; A Study in Survivals*.
    Cambridge, MA: The Belknap Press, 1962.

JESTER

Doran, John. *The History of Court Fools*. London: R. Bentley, 1858.
Fools and Jesters: With a Reprint of Robert Armin's Nest of Ninnies, 1608. London, Printed for the
    Shakespeare Society, 1842.
Janik, Vicki K., ed. *Fools and Jesters in Literature, Art, and History: A Bio-bibliographical Source-
    book*. Westport; London: Greenwood Press, 1998.
Otto, Beatrice K. *Fools Are Everywhere: The Court Jester Around the World*. Chicago: University of
    Chicago Press, 2001.
Southworth, John. *Fools and Jesters at the English Court*. Gloucestershire, UK: Sutton, 1998.

KIMONO

Dalby, Liza Chrihfield. *Kimono: Fashioning Culture*. New Haven: Yale University Press, 1993.

Gerstle, Andrew, ed. *Eighteenth Century Japan: Culture and Society*. Richmond, UK: Curzon, 1999.

Hahn, Tomie. *Sensational Knowledge: Embodying Culture Through Japanese Dance*. Middletown: Wesleyan University Press, 2007.

Keene, Donald. "Japanese Aesthetics." *Philosophy East and West* 19:3 (July 1969): 293–306.

Nakagawa, Keiichiro, and Henry Rosovsky. "The Case of the Dying Kimono: The Influence of Changing Fashions on the Development of the Japanese Woolen Industry." *Business History Review* 37:1/2 (Spring–Summer 1963): 59–80.

Nara, Hiroshi, with essays by J. Thomas Rimer and Jon Mark Mikkelsen. *The Structure of Detachment: The Aesthetic Vision of Kuki Shūzō*. Honolulu: University of Hawaii Press, 2004.

Pincus, Leslie. *Authenticating Culture in Imperial Japan: Kuki Shūzō and the Rise of National Aesthetics*. Berkeley: University of California Press, 1996.

Seigle, Cecilia Segawa. *Yoshiwara: The Glittering World of the Japanese Courtesan*. Honolulu: University of Hawaii Press, 1993.

KUMARI

Allen, Michael R. *The Cult of Kumari; Virgin Worship in Nepal*. Kathmandu: Institute of Nepal and Asian Studies, Tribhuvan University, 1975.

Bearak, Barry. "When Life as a Goddess Ends, Life as a Girl Begins." *New York Times*, Dec. 12, 1998.

Guo, Jerry. "In Search of Nepal's Living Goddesses." *Christian Science Monitor*, June 26, 2008.

Sangraula, Bikash. "Nepal's Goddesses: Religious Abuse?" *Christian Science Monitor*, Jan. 2, 2007.

Sullivan, Tim. "Nepal's Goddess Stumbles into Modernity." *USA Today*, Dec. 23, 2007.

L'ART POUR L'ART

Adams, Elsie Bonita. *Bernard Shaw and the Aesthetes*. Columbus: Ohio State University Press, 1971.

Bell-Villada, Gene H. *Art for Art's Sake & Literary Life: How Politics and Markets Helped Shape the Ideology & Culture of Aestheticism, 1790–1990*. Lincoln: University of Nebraska Press, 1996.

Cheetham, Mark A. *Abstract Art Against Autonomy: Infection, Resistance, and Cure Since the '60s*. New York: Cambridge University Press, 2006.

Cooper, Barbara T., and Mary Donaldson-Evans, eds. *Modernity and Revolution in Late Nineteenth-Century France*. Newark: University of Delaware Press; London: Associated University Presses, 1992.

Craven, David. "Ruskin vs. Whistler: The Case Against Capitalist Art." *Art Journal* 37:2 (Winter 1977–1978): 139–143.

Kimmelman, Michael. "Robert Rauschenberg, American Artist, Dies at 82." *New York Times*, May 14, 2008.

Merrill, Linda. *A Pot of Paint: Aesthetics on Trial in Whistler v. Ruskin*. Washington: Smithsonian Institution Press, in collaboration with the Freer Gallery of Art, Smithsonian Institution, 1992.

Parkes, Adam. "A Sense of Justice: Whistler, Ruskin, James, Impressionism." *Victorian Studies* 42:4 (Summer 1999–Summer 2000): 593–629.

Pennell, Elizabeth Robins. *The Life of James McNeill Whistler*. Philadelphia: J. B. Lippincott; London: W. Heinemann, 1908.

Schjeldahl, Peter. "Whistler's Chic." *The New Yorker*, May 12, 2003.

LAZZI

Gordon, Mel. *Lazzi: The Comic Routines of the Commedia Dell'Arte*. New York: Performing Arts Journal Publications, 1983.

Madden, David. "Harlequin's Stick, Charlie's Cane." *Film Quarterly* 22:1 (Autumn 1968): 10–26.

McPherson, Edward. *Buster Keaton: Tempest in a Flat Hat*. New York: Newmarket Press, 2004.

Meade, Marion. *Buster Keaton: Cut to the Chase*. New York: HarperCollins, 1995.

O'Connor, John. "TV Reviews; 'Buster Keaton: Hard Act to Follow.'" *New York Times*, Nov. 18, 1987.

"The Reminiscences of Buster Keaton." The Columbia University Oral History Research Office. Columbia University. http://www.fathom.com/course/10701030/session2.html (accessed on Jan. 19, 2010).

LIGHTNING

Cheney, Margaret, Robert Uth, and Jim Glenn. *Tesla, Master of Lightning*. New York: Barnes & Noble, 1999.

Cohen, Bernard I. "The Two Hundredth Anniversary of Benjamin Franklin's Two Lightning Experiments and the Introduction of the Lightning Rod." *Proceedings of the American Philosophical Society* 96:3 (June 20, 1952): 331–366.

Dommermuth-Costa, Carol. *Nikola Tesla: A Spark of Genius*. Minneapolis: Lerner Publications, 1994.

O'Neill, John J. *Prodigal Genius: The Life of Nikola Tesla*. New York: I. Washburn, 1944.

LOVE NOTES

Catherine II, Empress of Russia, and Prince Grigory Potemkin. *Love and Conquest: Personal Correspondence of Catherine the Great and Prince Grigory Potemkin*. Trans. and ed. Douglas Smith. DeKalb: Northern Illinois University Press, 2004.

Montefiore, Simon Sebag. "An Affair to Remember." *New York Review of Books*, Feb. 24, 2005.

——. *Potemkin: Catherine the Great's Imperial Partner*. New York: Vintage, 2005.

——. *Prince of Princes: The Life of Potemkin*. New York: Thomas Dunne, 2000.

Rounding, Virginia. *Catherine the Great: Love, Sex and Power*. New York: St. Martin's Press, 2006.

MARAVIGLIA

Barolsky, Paul. "Cellini, Vasari, and the Marvels of Malady." *Sixteenth Century Journal* 24:1 (Spring 1993): 41–45.

Barthes, Roland, and Achille Bonito Oliva. *Arcimboldo*. Trans. John Shepley. Milan: F. M. Ricci, 1980.

Carney, Jo Eldridge, ed. *Renaissance and Reformation, 1500–1620: A Biographical Dictionary*. Westport: Greenwood Press, 2001.

Fara, Amelio, *Bernardo Buontalenti*. Milan: Electa, 1995.

Ferino Pagden, Sylvia. *Arcimboldo*. Paris: Gallimard, 2007.

Johns, Pamela Sheldon. *Gelato! Italian Ice Creams, Sorbetti & Granite*. Berkeley: Ten Speed Press, 2000.

Kriegeskorte, Werner. *Giuseppe Arcimboldo 1527–1593*. London; Los Angeles; Madrid; Paris; Tokyo: Taschen, 2004.

Lotz, Wolfgang. *Architecture in Italy, 1500–1600*. New Haven: Yale University Press, 1995.

Mullaney, Steven. "Strange Things, Gross Terms, Curious Customs: The Rehearsal of Cultures in the Late Renaissance." *Representations* 3 (Summer 1983): 40–67.

Mulryne, J. R., Helen Watanabe-O'Kelly, and Margaret Shewring, eds. *Europa Triumphans: Court and Civic Festivals in Early Modern Europe*. Burlington, VT: Ashgate, 2004.

MASQUERADE

Caillois, Roger. *Man, Play, and Games*. Trans. Meyer Barash. New York: Free Press of Glencoe, 1961.

Castle, Terry. *The Female Thermometer: Eighteenth-Century Culture and the Invention of the Uncanny*. New York: Oxford University Press, 1995.

——. *Masquerade and Civilization: The Carnivalesque in Eighteenth-Century English Culture and Fiction*. Stanford: Stanford University Press, 1986.

DeMaria, Robert, Jr. *British Literature, 1640–1789: An Anthology*. Malden, MA: Blackwell, 2008.

Michaelson, Patricia Howell. *Speaking Volumes: Women, Reading, and Speech in the Age of Austen*. Stanford: Stanford University Press, 2002.

Munns, Jessica, and Penny Richards, eds. *The Clothes That Wear Us: Essays on Dressing and Transgressing in Eighteenth-Century Culture*. Newark: University of Delaware Press, 1999.

Pfister, Manfred, and Barbara Schaff, eds. *Venetian Views, Venetian Blinds: English Fantasies of Venice*. Atlanta: Rodopi, 1999.

Steward, James Christen. *The Mask of Venice: Masking, Theater & Identity in the Art of Tiepolo & His Time*. Berkeley: University of California, Berkeley Art Museum, in association with the University of Washington Press, 1996.

MILK BATHS

Bingham, Colin, compiler. *The Affairs of Women: A Modern Miscellany*. Sydney: Currawong Publishing Co., 1969.

Birchard, Robert S. *Cecil B. DeMille's Hollywood*. Lexington: University Press of Kentucky, 2004.

Forester, C. S. *Napoleon and His Court*. New York: Dodd, Mead, 1924.

Gerhard, William Paul. *Modern Baths and Bath Houses*. New York: John Wiley & Sons, 1908.

Golden, Eve. *Anna Held and the Birth of Ziegfeld's Broadway*. Lexington: University Press of Kentucky, 2000.

Griffin, Miriam T. *Nero: The End of a Dynasty*. New Haven: Yale University Press, 1985.

Gyles, Mary Francis. "Nero Fiddled While Rome Burned." *Classical Journal* 42:4 (Jan. 1947): 211–217.

Kakutani, Michiko. "Claudette Colbert Still Tells DeMille Stories." *New York Times*, Nov. 16, 1979.

Kehr, Dave. "Critic's Choice: New DVD's." *New York Times*, May 23, 2006.

Louvish, Simon. *Man on the Flying Trapeze: The Life and Times of W. C. Fields*. London: Faber, 1997.

Page, Eric. "Claudette Colbert, Unflappable Heroine of Screwball Comedies, Is Dead at 92." *New York Times*, July 31, 1996.

Solomon, Jon. *The Ancient World in the Cinema*. New Haven: Yale University Press, 2001.

"Uses Milk in Baths," *New York Times*, Oct. 10, 1896.

MIRACLES

Barber, Richard W. *Pilgrimages*. Rochester: Boydell Press, 1991.

Coleman, Simon. *Pilgrimage: Past and Present: Sacred Travel and Sacred Space in the World Religions*. London: British Museum Press, 1995.

Finucane, Ronald C. *Miracles and Pilgrims: Popular Beliefs in Medieval England*. New York: St. Martin's Press, 1995.

Staunton, Michael. *Thomas Becket and His Biographers*. Rochester: Boydell Press, 2006.

MISERERE

Boursy, Richard. "The Mystique of the Sistine Chapel Choir in the Romantic Era." *Journal of Musicology* 11:3 (Summer 1993): 277–329.

Milner, Anthony. "The Sacred Capons." *Musical Times* 114:1561 (March 1973): 250–252.

Rosselli, John. "The Castrati as a Professional Group and a Social Phenomenon, 1550–1850." *Acta Musicologica* 60, Fasc. 2 (May–Aug. 1988): 143–179.

Solomon, Maynard. "Mozart: The Myth of the Eternal Child." *19th-Century Music* 15:2 (Autumn 1991): 94–106.

MORITSUKE

Ashkenazi, Michael, and Jeanne Jacob. *The Essence of Japanese Cuisine: An Essay on Food and Culture*. Richmond, UK: Curzon, 2000.

——. *Food Culture in Japan*. Westport: Greenwood Press, 2003.

Hosking, Richard. *A Dictionary of Japanese Food: Ingredients & Culture*. Rutland; Tokyo: Charles E. Tuttle, 1996.

Keene, Donald. "Japanese Aesthetics." *Philosophy East and West* 19:3 (July 1969): 293–306.

Lowry, Dave. *The Connoisseur's Guide to Sushi : Everything You Need to Know About Sushi Varieties and Accompaniments, Etiquette and Dining Tips, and More*. Boston: Harvard Common Press, 2005.

Nishiyama, Matsunosuke. *Edo Culture: Daily Life and Diversions in Urban Japan, 1600–1868*. Trans. and ed. Gerald Groemer. Honolulu: University of Hawaii Press, 1997.

Saito, Yuriko. "Japanese Aesthetics of Packaging." *Journal of Aesthetics and Art Criticism* 57:2 (Spring 1999): 257–265.

Tsuchiya, Yoshio. *A Feast for the Eyes: The Japanese Art of Food Arrangement*. Trans. Juliet Winters Carpenter. Tokyo; New York: Kodansha International, 1985.

MOUCHES

Fairholt, F. W. "Costume in England." *The Living Age* 10:118. (Aug. 15, 1846): 324–326.

Lester, Katherine Morris, and Bess Viola Oerke. *An Illustrated History of Those Frills and Furbelows of Fashion Which Have Come to Be Known as: Accessories of Dress*. Peoria: Chas. A. Bennett, 1940.

Pointer, Sally. *The Artifice of Beauty: A History and Practical Guide to Perfumes and Cosmetics*. Stroud, UK: Sutton, 2005.

Romm, Sharon. *The Changing Face of Beauty*. St. Louis: Mosby Year Book, 1992.

Saisselin, Remy G. "The Rococo as a Dream of Happiness." *Journal of Aesthetics and Art Criticism* 19:2 (Winter 1960): 145–152.

NEBULA, THE POWDERED SUGAR PRINCESS

Cornell, Joseph. "Joseph Cornell Papers, 1804–1986 bulk 1939–1972." The Smithsonian Archives of American Art. http://www.aaa.si.edu/collectionsonline/cornjose/ (accessed Jan. 16, 2010).

Hennessey, Christine. "Joseph Cornell: A Balletomane." *Archives of American Art Journal* 23:3 (1983): 6–12.

Lawson, Thomas. "Silently, by Means of a Flashing Light." *October* 15 (Winter 1980): 49–60.

The Museum of Modern Art. *MoMA Highlights*. New York: The Museum of Modern Art, 2004.

Pennington, Estill Curtis (Buck). "Joseph Cornell: Dime Store Connoisseur." *Archives of American Art Journal* 23:3 (1983): 13–20.

Simic, Charles. "Forgotten Games." *New York Review of Books*, April 27, 2000.

Solomon, Deborah. *Utopia Parkway: The Life and Work of Joseph Cornell*. New York: Farrar,
Straus & Giroux, 1997.
Waldman, Diane. *Joseph Cornell: Master of Dreams*. New York: Harry N. Abrams, 2002.

NECTAR AND AMBROSIA

Andrews, Tamra. *Nectar & Ambrosia: An Encyclopedia of Food in World Mythology*. Santa Barbara;
Oxford: ABC-CLIO, 2000.
De Almeida, Hermione. *Romantic Medicine and John Keats*. New York: Oxford University
Press, 1991.
Morton, Mark Steven. *Cupboard Love: A Dictionary of Culinary Curiousities*. Winnipeg: Bain &
Cox, 1996.
Onians, Richard Broxton. *The Origins of European Thought; About the Body, the Mind, the Soul,
the World, Time, and Fate*. New York: Arno Press, 1973.
Ransome, Hilda M. *The Sacred Bee in Ancient Times and Folklore*. Mineola, NY: Dover, 2004.
Toussaint-Samat, Maguelonne. *A History of Food*. Trans. Anthea Bell. Chichester, UK; Malden,
MA: Wiley-Blackwell, 2009.

OBELISK

Bellori, Giovan Pietro. *The Lives of the Modern Painters, Sculptors and Architects*. Trans. Alice
Sedgwick Wohl. Notes by Hellmut Wohl. New York: Cambridge University Press,
2005.
D'Alton, Martina. "The New York Obelisk or How Cleopatra's Needle Came to New York and
What Happened When It Got Here." *Metropolitan Museum of Art Bulletin* 50:4 (Spring
1993): 1–72.
Fazio, Michael W., Marian Moffett, and Lawrence Wodehouse. *A World History of Architecture*.
Boston: McGraw-Hill, 2008.
"The Influnce of Obelisks" [sic.], *New York Times*, Oct. 10, 1877.
Knight, Charles, ed. *The English Cyclopaedia, Volume 6*. London: Bradbury, Evans, 1867.
"The Obelisk in Position," *New York Times*, Jan. 23, 1881.
"Obelisks," *New York Times*, Oct. 29, 1879.

OBSIDIAN

Dee, John. *The Diaries of John Dee*. Edward Fenton, ed. Charlbury, UK: Day Books, 1998.
Harkness, Deborah E. "Shows in the Showstone: A Theater of Alchemy and Apocalypse in the
Angel Conversations of John Dee (1527–1608/9)." *Renaissance Quarterly* 49:4 (Winter
1996): 707–737.
"The Magical Speculum of Dr Dee (British Museum)," *Burlington Magazine* 110:778 (Jan.
1968): 42–43.
Paddock, John. "Tezcatlipoca in Oaxaca." *Ethnohistory* 32:4 (Autumn 1985): 309–325.

Saunders, Nicholas J. "A Dark Light: Reflections on Obsidian in Mesoamerica." *World Archae-ology* 33:2 (Oct. 2001): 220–236.

Trattner, Walter I. "God and Expansion in Elizabethan England: John Dee, 1527–1583." *Journal of the History of Ideas* 25:1 (Jan.–March 1964): 17–34.

Woolley, Benjamin. *The Queen's Conjurer: The Science and Magic of Dr. John Dee, Advisor to Queen Elizabeth I.* New York: Henry Holt, 2001.

OGI

Bingham, Colin, compiler. *The Affairs of Women: A Modern Miscellany.* Sydney: Currawong, 1969.

Boehn, Max von. *Ornaments; Lace, Fans, Gloves, Walking-sticks, Parasols, Jewelry, and Trinkets.* New York: B. Blom, 1970.

Rhead, G. Woolliscroft. *History of the Fan.* London: Kegan Paul, Trench, Trübner, 1910.

Sayers, Lesley-Anne. "From the Ballroom to Hell: Grace and Folly in Nineteenth-Century Dance." *Dance Now* 3:1 (Spring 1994): 71–72.

OMELET

Ayto, John. *The Glutton's Glossary: A Dictionary of Food and Drink Terms.* London; New York: Routledge, 1990.

Brillat-Savarin, Jean-Anthelme. *The Physiology of Taste; or, Meditations on Transcendental Gastronomy.* Trans. M. F. K. Fisher. San Francisco: Arion Press, 1994.

David, Elizabeth. *Italian Food.* Foreword by Julia Child. New York: Penguin Books, 1999.

———. *An Omelette and a Glass of Wine.* New York: Viking, 1985.

Dodd, Anna Bowman. *In and Out of Three Normandy Inns.* New York; London: G. P. Putnam's Sons, 1929.

"Food at the International Exhibition," *Food Journal* 4 (May 1873): 121–126.

ORIGAMI

Gardner, Martin. *The Universe in a Handkerchief: Lewis Carroll's Mathematical Recreations, Games, Puzzles, and Word Plays.* New York: Copernicus, 1996.

Houdini, Harry. *Houdini's Paper Magic: The Whole Art of Performing with Paper, Including Paper Tearing, Paper Folding and Paper Puzzles.* New York: E. P Dutton, 1922.

Jahn, Gary R. "The Aesthetic Theory of Leo Tolstoy's What Is Art?" *Journal of Aesthetics and Art Criticism* 34:1 (Autumn 1975): 59–65.

Lister, David. "History of Origami." British Origami Society. http://www.britishorigami.info/academic/lister/basichistory.php (accessed Jan. 16, 2010).

Litvinov, Misha, and Sergei Mamin. "Tolstoy and Origami." *British Origami* 186 (Oct. 1997).

Maude, Aylmer. Review of *What Is Art?* by Leo Tolstoy. *Burlington Magazine for Connoisseurs* 5:17 (Aug. 1904): 504.

Robinson, Nick, and David Lister. *The Origami Bible*. London: Collins & Brown; Cincinnati: Distributed by North Light Books, 2004.

Sosnoski, Daniel, ed. *Introduction to Japanese Culture*. Rutland, VT; Tokyo: Tuttle, 1996.

"Tolstoy Timeline." Public Broadcasting Service. http://www.pbs.org/wgbh/masterpiece/ anna/timeline_text.html (accessed Jan. 16, 2010).

PAINTED LADIES

Baldwin, Neil. *Man Ray, American Artist*. New York: Da Capo Press, 2001.

Davis, Anna. "The Queen of Bohemia." *The Guardian*, Feb. 7, 2007.

Gammel, Irene. *Baroness Elsa: Gender, Dada, and Everyday Modernity—A Cultural Biography*. Cambridge, MA: MIT Press, 2002.

Glassco, John. *Memoirs of Montparnasse*. Toronto; New York: Oxford University Press, 1970.

Jiminez, Jill Berk, ed. *Dictionary of Artists' Models*. London; Chicago: Fitzroy Dearborn, 2001.

Prin, Alice. *Kiki's Memoirs*. Trans. Samuel Putnam. Edited, annotated, and with a foreword by Billy Klüver and Julie Martin. Hopewell: The Ecco Press, 1996.

Reilly, Eliza Jane. "Elsa von Freytag-Loringhoven." *Woman's Art Journal* 18:1 (Spring–Summer 1997): 26–33.

PELL-MELL

Adams, William Howard. *The Paris Years of Thomas Jefferson*. New Haven: Yale University Press, 1997.

Jefferson, Thomas. *The Jeffersonian Cyclopedia; A Comprehensive Collection of the Views of Thomas Jefferson Classified and Arranged in Alphabetical Order Under Nine Thousand Titles Relating to Government, Politics, Law, Education, Political Economy, Finance, Science, Art, Literature, Religious Freedom, Morals, etc.* John P. Foley, ed. New York: Russell & Russell, 1967.

———. *The Writings of Thomas Jefferson*. Washington, D.C., issued under the auspices of the Thomas Jefferson Memorial Association of the United States, 1903–1904.

Judson, Harry Pratt. *The Growth of the American Nation*. New York: Macmillan, 1899.

Kukla, Jon. *Mr. Jefferson's Women*. New York: Alfred A. Knopf, 2007.

Larus, Joel. "Growing Pains of the New Republic: III, Pell-Mell Along the Potomac." *William and Mary Quarterly* 17:3 (July 1960): 349–357.

"Precedence." *Encyclopedia Britannica*. New York: The Encyclopedia Britannica Company, 1911.

Probert, W. G. "Some Variations of Etiquette." *The Living Age*, June 1894.

PENTIMENTO

Courbet, Gustave. *Letters of Gustave Courbet*. Trans. and ed. Petra ten-Doesschate Chu. Chicago: University of Chicago Press, 1992.

Font-Réaulx, Dominique, Laurence des Cars, Michel Hilaire, Bruno Mottin, and Bertrand Tillier. *Gustave Courbet*. New York: The Metropolitan Museum of Art; Ostfildern: Hatje Cantz, 2008.

Mack, Gerstle. *Gustave Courbet*. New York: Alfred A. Knopf, 1951.

PERFUME

Aftel, Mandy. *Essence and Alchemy: A Book of Perfume*. New York: North Point Press, 2001.

Allen, Brooke. "Colette: The Literary Marianne." *Hudson Review* 53:2 (Summer 2000): 193–207.

Barry, Joseph A. "La Grande Colette—Aging, Ailing, Adored." *New York Times*, Jan. 22, 1950.

Burckhardt, Jacob. *The Civilization of the Renaissance in Italy*. Trans. S. G. C. Middlemore. London; New York: Penguin Books, 1990.

Capote, Truman. *Answered Prayers: The Unfinished Novel*. New York: Vintage, 1994.

Groom, N. St. J. *The New Perfume Handbook*. London; New York: Blackie Academic & Professional, 1997.

Lester, Katherine Morris, and Bess Viola Oerke. *An Illustrated History of Those Frills and Furbelows of Fashion Which Have Come to be Known as: Accessories of Dress*. Peoria: Chas. A. Bennett, 1940.

Sell, Charles, ed. *The Chemistry of Fragrances: From Perfumer to Consumer*. Cambridge, UK: Royal Society of Chemistry, 2006.

Stamelman, Richard Howard. *Perfume: Joy, Obsession, Scandal, Sin: A Cultural History of Fragrance from 1750 to the Present*. New York: Rizzoli, 2006.

Thompson, C. J. S. *The Mystery and Lure of Perfume*. Detroit: Singing Tree Press, 1969.

Thurman, Judith. *Secrets of the Flesh: A Life of Colette*. New York: Alfred A. Knopf, Distributed by Random House, 1999.

PILLOWBOOK

Fukumori, Naomi. "Sei Shōnagon's Makura No Sōshi: A Re-Visionary History." *Journal of the Association of Teachers of Japanese* 31:1 (April 1997): 1–44.

Miner, Earl. "Splendid Things." Review of *The Pillow Book of Sei Shōnagon* by Ivan Morris, and *Essays in Idleness: The Tsurezuregusa of Kenko* by Donald Keene. *Hudson Review* 21:3 (Autumn 1968): 575–579.

Morris, Mark. "Sei Shōnagon's Poetic Catalogues." *Harvard Journal of Asiatic Studies* 40:1 (June 1980): 5–54.

Saito, Yuriko. "The Japanese Aesthetics of Imperfection and Insufficiency." *Journal of Aesthetics and Art Criticism* 55:4 (Autumn 1997): 377–385.

Shōnagon, Sei. *The Pillow Book of Sei Shōnagon*. Trans. and ed. Ivan Morris. New York: Columbia University Press, 1991.

Birley, Derek. *Sport and the Making of Britain*. Manchester, UK: Manchester University Press; distributed in the USA by St. Martin's Press, 1993.

Boga, Steve. *Badminton*. Mechanicsburg, PA: Stackpole Books, 1996.

Crego, Robert. *Sports and Games of the 18th and 19th Centuries*. Westport: Greenwood Press, 2003.

Guest, Antony. "Some Old English Games." *Badminton Magazine of Sports & Pastimes* 2. (Jan.–June 1896): 158–174.

Guillain, Jean-Yves. *Badminton: An Illustrated History*. Les Éditions Publibook. http://books.google.com/books?id=9a8ykrpScKcC&source=gbs_navlinks_s (accessed Jan. 16, 2010.)

Liu, James T. C. "Polo and Cultural Change: From T'ang to Sung China." *Harvard Journal of Asiatic Studies* 45:1 (June 1985): 203–224.

Tennyson, Charles. "They Taught the World to Play." *Victorian Studies* 2:3 (March 1959): 211–222.

Weir, Robert; Henry Charles Fitz Roy, eighth Duke of Somerset Beaufort; Henry Charles Howard, Earl of Suffolk and Berkshire; William Hillier Onslow, fourth Earl of Onslow; Edward L. Anderson; and Alfred Edward Thomas Watson. *Riding*. London; Bombay: Longmans, Green, 1902.

POUF

Daniels, Margaret H. "French Engraved Portraits." *Metropolitan Museum of Art Bulletin* 20:3 (March 1925): 72–74.

Delpierre, Madeleine. *Dress in France in the Eighteenth Century*. Trans. Caroline Beamish. New Haven: Yale University Press, 1997.

Erickson, Carolly. *To the Scaffold: The Life of Marie Antoinette*. New York: St. Martin's Press, 2004.

Feydeau, Elisabeth de. *A Scented Palace: The Secret History of Marie Antoinette's Perfumer*. Trans. Jane Lizop. London: I. B. Tauris; distributed in the USA by Palgrave Macmillan, 2006.

Jones, Jennifer Michelle. *Sexing La Mode: Gender, Fashion and Commercial Culture in Old Regime France*. Oxford; New York: Berg, 2004.

La Rocheterie, Maxime de. *The Life of Marie Antoinette*. Trans. Cora Hamilton Bell. New York: Dodd, Mead, 1893.

Oberkirch, Henriette Louise von Waldner (Baronne d'). *Memoirs of the Baroness d'Oberkirch, Countess de Montbrison, Volume 1*. London: Colburn, 1852.

Sennett, Richard. *The Fall of Public Man: The Forces Eroding Public Life and Burdening the Modern Psyche with Roles It Cannot Perform*. New York: Alfred A. Knopf, 1977.

Ward, Harry M. *The War for Independence and the Transformation of American Society*. London: UCL Press, 1999.

Ward, Marion. *The Du Barry Inheritance*. London: Chatto & Windus, 1967.

Weber, Caroline. *Queen of Fashion: What Marie Antoinette Wore to the Revolution*. New York: Henry Holt, 2006.

PUNTO IN ARIA

Beck, S. William. *Gloves, Their Annals and Associations: A Chapter of Trade and Social History.* Detroit: Singing Tree Press, 1969.

Berger, Ronald M. *The Most Necessary Luxuries: The Mercer's Company of Coventry, 1550–1680.* University Park: Pennsylvania State University Press, 1993.

Boehn, Max von. *Ornaments; Lace, Fans, Gloves, Walking-sticks, Parasols, Jewelry, and Trinkets.* New York: B. Blom, 1970.

Campbell, Gordon, ed. *The Grove Encyclopedia of Decorative Arts*. New York: Oxford University Press, 2006.

C. F. W. "A Flounce of Point De France Lace." *Bulletin of the Pennsylvania Museum* 19:81 (Dec. 1923): 49–50.

Datta, Satya Brata. *Women and Men in Early Modern Venice: Reassessing History*. Burlington, VT: Ashgate, 2003.

Earnshaw, Pat. *A Dictionary of Lace*. Mineola, NY: Dover, 1999.

Harrison, Emily Leland. "Ancient Lace." *Bulletin of the Pennsylvania Museum* 3:9 (Jan. 1905): 1–5.

Jackson, F. Nevill. "Ecclesiastical Lace Ancient and Modern: A Comparison. Part I." *Burlington Magazine for Connoisseurs* 4:10 (Jan. 1904): 54–64.

Palliser, Mrs. Bury. *History of Lace*. London: Sampson Los, Son & Marston, 1865.

Stevenson, Mrs. Cornelius. "Old Point de Venise." *Bulletin of the Pennsylvania Museum* 7:28 (Oct. 1909): 72–76.

QABUS NAMA

Bloom, Jonathan, and Sheila Blair. *Islam: A Thousand Years of Faith and Power*. New York: TV Books, 2000.

Bosworth, C. E. "An Early Arabic Mirror for Princes: Tāhir Dhū l-Yaminain's Epistle to His Son Abdallāh (206/821)." *Journal of Near Eastern Studies* 29:1 (Jan. 1970): 25–41.

Coulton, G. G. *Medieval Panorama, the English Scene from Conquest to Reformation*. New York: Meridian, 1960.

Gelder, G. J. H. van. *Of Dishes and Discourse: Classical Arabic Literary Representations of Food.* Richmond, UK: Curzon, 2000.

Gutas, Dimitri. "Classical Arabic Wisdom Literature: Nature and Scope." *Journal of the American Oriental Society* 101:1 (Jan.–March 1981): 49–86.

Iskandar, Kai-Kāus ibn, Prince of Gurgān. *A Mirror for Princes; The Qābūs Nāma*. Translated from the Persian by Reuben Levy. London: Cresset Press, 1951.

Marlow, Louise. "Kings, Prophets and the 'Ulamā' in Mediaeval Islamic Advice Literature." *Studia Islamica*, 81 (1995): 101–120.

Richter-Bernburg, Lutz. "Plato of Mind and Joseph of Countenance. The Notion of Love and the Ideal Beloved in Kay Kāus b. Iskandar's Andarznāme." *Oriens* 36 (2001): 276–287.

QUADRILLE NATURALISTE

Camus, Renée. "Cancan: Blurring the Line Between Social Dance and Stage Performance." *Society of Dance History Scholars (U.S.). Conference 2001 Proceedings* (2001): 6–10.
Guest, Ivor. "Bal Mabille." *Ballet*, Feb. 1947.
———. "Cancan." *Dancing Times*, Jan. 1999.
———. "Queens of the Cancan." *Dance and Dancers*, Dec. 1952.
Majdalany, Fred. "Truth About the Can Can." *Dancing Times*, June 1935.
Marrus, Michael R. "Modernization and Dancing in Rural France: From la Bourree to le Fox-Trot." *Dance Research Journal* 8:2 (Spring–Summer 1976): 1–9.
Michel, Artur. "Polka—The Dance Sensation of 1844." *Dance*, Jan. 1944.
———. "Polka—The Dance Sensation of 1844, Part 2." *Dance*, Feb. 1944.
"Parisian Sketches," *Harper's New Monthly Magazine*, Dec. 1867.
"Polka," *Folk Dance Scene*, March 1994.
Price, David. *Cancan!* London: Cygnus Arts; Madison, NJ: Fairleigh Dickinson University Press, 1998.
Richardson, P. J. S. *The Social Dances of the Nineteenth Century in England.* London: H. Jenkins, 1960.
"Scandalous Dances. Brought from French Casinos to American Parlors," *International Magazine of Literature, Art, and Science*, 2:3 (Feb. 1, 1851): 333–334.

QUINTESSENCE

Cockren, Archibald. *Alchemy Rediscovered and Restored.* Charleston: Forgotten Books, 2007.
Craig, Edward, ed. *Routledge Encyclopedia of Philosophy.* London; New York: Routledge, 1998.
Dobbs, Betty Jo Teeter. *The Foundations of Newton's Alchemy; or, "The Hunting of the Greene Lyon."* Cambridge; New York: Cambridge University Press, 1975.
———. *The Janus Faces of Genius: The Role of Alchemy in Newton's Thought.* Cambridge; New York: Cambridge University Press, 1991.
———. "Newton's Alchemy and His Theory of Matter." *Isis* 73:4 (Dec. 1982): 511–528.
Gleick, James. *Isaac Newton.* New York: Vintage, 2004.
"Lost Newton Manuscript Rediscovered at Royal Society." Royal Society. http://royalsociety .org/News.aspx?id=1400 (accessed Jan. 16, 2010).
Radford, Tim. "Newton the Alchemist Revealed in Lost Papers." *The Guardian*, July 2, 2005.
Westfall, Richard S. *Never at Rest: A Biography of Isaac Newton.* Cambridge; New York: Cambridge University Press, 1980.

RED LIPSTICK

"Cosmetics Go to Britain Too," *New York Times*, Nov. 11, 1941.
"Cosmetic Supply Is Held Adequate," *New York Times*, Jan. 27, 1942.
Delano, Page Dougherty. "Making Up for War: Sexuality and Citizenship in Wartime Culture."*Feminist Studies* 26:1 (Spring 2000): 33–68.
"Italy Aids Women to Keep Looks While Nazis Impose Dowdiness," *New York Times*, June 3, 1942.
Last, Nella, Richard Broad, and Suzie Fleming. *Nella Last's War*. London: Profile Books, 2006.
Long, Tania. "Cosmetics Benefit Morale in Britain." *New York Times*, April 28, 1942.
"Nazis Ban Cosmetics," *New York Times*, Aug. 8, 1933.
Pointer, Sally. *The Artifice of Beauty: A History and Practical Guide to Perfumes and Cosmetics.* Stroud, UK: Sutton, 2005.
Waller, Maureen. *London 1945: Life in the Debris of War.* New York: St. Martin's Press, 2004.

ROSARIAN

Batey, Mavis. "Landscape with Flowers: West Surrey: The Background to Gertrude Jekyll's Art." *Garden History* 2:2 (Spring 1974): 12–21.
Gessert, George. "Bastard Flowers."*Leonardo* 29:4 (1996): 291–298.
Jekyll, Gertrude. *Gertrude Jekyll: The Making of a Garden: An Anthology: A Collection of Gertrude Jekyll's Writings, Illustrated with Her Own Photographs and Drawings, and Paintings and Watercolours by Contemporary Artists*. Compiled and edited by Cherry Lewis. Woodbridge, UK: Garden Art Press, 2000.
––––––. *Wood and Garden: Notes and Thoughts, Practical and Critical, of a Working Amateur*. Introduced and revised by Graham Stuart Thomas. Salem, NH: Ayer, 1983.
Schnare, Susan E., and Rudy J. Favretti. "Gertrude Jekyll's American Gardens." *Garden History* 10:2 (Autumn 1982): 149–167.
Thomas, Graham. "The Influence of Gertrude Jekyll on the Use of Roses in Gardens and Garden Design." *Garden History* 5:1 (Spring 1977): 53–65.
Valkenburgh, Michael R. "The Flower Gardens of Gertrude Jekyll and Their Twentieth-Century Transformations." *Design Quarterly* 137 (1987): 1–32.

RUFF AND CRAVAT

Breward, Christopher, Edwina Ehrman, and Caroline Evans. *The London Look: Fashion from Street to Catwalk.* New Haven: Yale University Press, in association with the Museum of London, 2004.
Chambers, William, and Robert Chambers. *Chambers's Information for the People: A Popular Encyclopaedia, Volume 1*. Philadelphia: J. L. Gihon, 1854.
Craik, George L., and Charles MacFarlane, assisted by other contributors. *The Pictorial History*

of England: Being a History of the People, as Well as a History of the Kingdom. London: C. Knight, 1849.

"Curiosities of Fashion," *London Society* 4 (1863): 232–240.

Jesse, William. *The Life of George Brummell, Esq., Commonly Called Beau Brummell.* London: J. C. Nimmo, 1886.

Jones, Ann Rosalind, and Peter Stallybrass. *Renaissance Clothing and the Materials of Memory.* Cambridge; New York: Cambridge University Press, 2000.

Lewis, Theresa, Lady. *Lives of the Friends and Contemporaries of Lord Chancellor Clarendon: Illustrative of Portraits in His Gallery.* London: J. Murray, 1852.

Lockyer, Roger. *Buckingham, the Life and Political Career of George Villiers, First Duke of Buckingham, 1592–1628.* London; New York: Longman, 1981.

Luijten, Ger. "Frills and Furbelows: Satires on Fashion and Pride Around 1600." *Simiolus: Netherlands Quarterly for the History of Art* 24:2/3 (1996): 140–160.

Murray, Venetia. *An Elegant Madness: High Society in Regency England.* New York: Viking, 1999.

Scott, Sir Walter. *The Waverley Novels, Volume 27.* Edinburgh: Adam & Charles Black, 1879.

Smith, Thomas Spence. "Aestheticism and Social Structure: Style and Social Network in the Dandy Life." *American Sociological Review* 39:5 (Oct. 1974): 725–743.

SAFFRON

Adamson, Melitta Weiss. *Food in Medieval Times.* Westport: Greenwood Press, 2004.

Beckmann, Johann, William Johnston, William Francis, and J. W. Griffith. *A History of Inventions, Discoveries, and Origins.* London: H. G. Bohn, 1846.

Fletcher, Nichola. *Charlemagne's Tablecloth: A Piquant History of Feasting.* New York: St. Martin's Press, 2005.

Humphries, John. *The Essential Saffron Companion.* London: Grub Street, 1996.

Jenkins, Marjorie. "Medicines and Spices, with Special Reference to Medieval Monastic Accounts." *Garden History* 4:3 (Autumn 1976): 47–49.

Krueger, Hilmar C. "The Wares of Exchange in the Genoese-African Traffic of the Twelfth Century." *Speculum* 12:1 (Jan. 1937): 57–71.

Toussaint-Samat, Maguelonne. *A History of Food.* Trans. Anthea Bell. Chichester, UK; Malden, MA: Wiley-Blackwell, 2009.

Willard, Pat. *Secrets of Saffron: The Vagabond Life of the World's Most Seductive Spice.* Boston: Beacon Press, 2001.

SEQUINS

Bruhn, Jutta-Annette. *Coins and Costume in Late Antiquity.* Washington, D.C.: Dumbarton Oaks Research Library and Collection, 1993.

Gostelow, Mary. *Blackwork.* Mineola, NY: Dover, 1998.

Guest, Ivor. "Theophile Gautier on Spanish Dancing." *Dance Chronicle* 10:1 (1987): 1–104.

Leslie, Catherine Amoroso. *Needlework Through History: An Encyclopedia.* Westport: Greenwood Press, 2007.

Maguire, Henry. "Magic and Money in the Early Middle Ages." *Speculum* 72:4 (Oct. 1997): 1037–1054.

Marsh, Gail. *18th Century Embroidery Techniques*. Lewes, UK: Guild of Master Craftsman Publications, 2006.

Planché, J. R. *A Cyclopaedia of Costume or Dictionary of Dress, Including Notices of Contemporaneous Fashions on the Continent; A General Chronological History of the Costumes of the Principal Countries of Europe, from the Commencement of the Christian Era to the Accession of George the Third*. London: Chatto & Windus, 1876–1879.

Wallace, David. *Hollywoodland*. New York: St. Martin's Press, 2002.

SHABBY CHIC

Broome, Peter, and Graham Chesters. *The Appreciation of Modern French Poetry, 1850–1950*. Cambridge; New York: Cambridge University Press, 1976.

Diderot, Denis. *Rameau's Nephew and Other Works*. New York: Doubleday, Anchor Books, 1956.

Douglas, George H. *Women of the 20s: Aimee Semple McPherson, Edna St. Vincent Millay, Dorothy Parker, Amelia Earhart, Martha Graham, Anita Loos*. San Francisco: Saybrook; distributed in New York by W. W. Norton, 1986.

Epstein, Daniel Mark. *What Lips My Lips Have Kissed: The Loves and Love Poems of Edna St. Vincent Millay*. New York: Henry Holt, 2001.

"Intersections: Patti Smith, Poet Laureate of Punk." National Public Radio, *Morning Edition*. http://www.npr.org/templates/story/story.php?storyId=1814648 (accessed Jan. 16, 2010).

Milford, Nancy. *Savage Beauty: The Life of Edna St. Vincent Millay*. Waterville, ME: Thorndike Press, 2002.

Millay, Edna St. Vincent. *A Few Figs from Thistles*. New York; London: Harper & Brothers, 1922.

Starkie, Enid. *Arthur Rimbaud*. New York: New Directions, 1961.

Welters, Linda, and Patricia A. Cunningham. *Twentieth-Century American Fashion*. Oxford; New York: Berg, 2005.

Wilson, Edmund. *I Thought of Daisy*. New York: Farrar, Straus & Young, 1953.

SHOWSTOPPERS

"The Dance: New Musical Comedy Talent," *New York Times*, July 22, 1928.

Encyclopaedia of Hindi Cinema. New Delhi: Encyclopaedia Britannica (India) Pvt. Ltd., 2003.

Hanley, Robert. "Busby Berkeley, the Dance Director, Dies." *New York Times*, March 15, 1976.

Joshi, Lalit Mohan. *Bollywood: Popular Indian Cinema*. London: Dakini, 2002.

Kohli, Suresh. "Helen of Bollywood." *The Hindu*, April 14, 2006.

Murray, William. "The Return of Busby Berkeley." *New York Times*, March 2, 1969.

Robertson, Pamela. *Guilty Pleasures: Feminist Camp from Mae West to Madonna*. Durham, NC: Duke University Press, 1996.

Rubin, Martin. *Showstoppers: Busby Berkeley and the Tradition of Spectacle*. New York: Columbia University Press, 1993.

Snyder, Robert W. Review of *Showstoppers: Busby Berkeley and the Tradition of Spectacle* by Martin Rubin. *Journal of American History* 81:2 (Sept. 1994): 773–774.

SILENCE

Ackerley, C. J., and S. E. Gontarski. *The Grove Companion to Samuel Beckett: A Reader's Guide to His Works, Life, and Thought*. New York: Grove Press, 2004.
Bryden, Mary, ed. *Samuel Beckett and Music*. New York: Clarendon Press, 1997.
Cage, John. *Silence, Lectures and Writings*. Middletown: Wesleyan University Press, 1973.
Cohn, Ruby. *A Beckett Canon*. Ann Arbor: University of Michigan Press, 2001.
J.B. "Look, No Hands! And It's 'Music.' " *New York Times*, April 15, 1954.
Kahn, Douglas. *Noise, Water, Meat: A History of Sound in the Arts*. Cambridge, MA: MIT Press, 1999.
Knowlson, James. *Images of Beckett*. Cambridge; New York: Cambridge University Press, 2003.
Pattie, David. *The Complete Critical Guide to Samuel Beckett*. London; New York: Routledge, 2000.
Sim, Stuart, *Manifesto for Silence*, Edinburgh: Edinburgh University Press, 2007.

SOTELTIE

Andrews, Julia C. *Breakfast, Dinner, and Tea: Viewed Classically, Poetically, and Practically. Containing Numerous Curious Dishes and Feasts of All Times and All Countries. Besides Three Hundred Modern Receipts*. New York: D. Appleton, 1859.
Bentley, Richard. "Curiosities of Cookery." *Bentley's Miscellany* 33 (1853): 209–220.
Hieatt, Constance B., Brenda Hosington, and Sharon Butler. *Pleyn Delit: Medieval Cookery for Modern Cooks*. Toronto; Buffalo: University of Toronto Press, 1996.
Hutchings, John B. *Expectations and the Food Industry: The Impact of Color and Appearance*. New York: Kluwer Academic/Plenum Publishers, 2003.
Redon, Odile, Françoise Sabban, and Silvano Serventi. *The Medieval Kitchen: Recipes from France and Italy*. Trans. Edward Schneider. Chicago: University of Chicago Press, 1998.
Scully, Terence. *The Art of Cookery in the Middle Ages*. Woodbridge; Rochester, NY: Boydell Press, 1995.
Visser, Margaret. *The Rituals of Dinner: The Origins, Evolution, Eccentricities, and Meaning of Table Manners*. New York: Grove Weidenfeld, 1991.
Withington, Robert. *English Pageantry; An Historical Outline*. New York: B. Blom, 1963.
Woloson, Wendy A. *Refined Tastes: Sugar, Confectionery, and Consumers in Nineteenth-Century America*. Baltimore: Johns Hopkins University Press, 2002.

STRING

Fleure, H. J. "Alfred Cort Haddon. 1855–1940." *Obituary Notices of Fellows of the Royal Society* 3:9 (Jan. 1941): 449–465.

Haddon, Kathleen. *Artists in String, String Figures: Their Regional Distribution and Social Signifi-gance*. London: Methuen, 1930.

———. *Cat's Cradles from Many Lands*. London; New York: Longmans, Green, 1911.

———. *String Games for Beginners*. Cambridge, UK: Heffer, 1934.

Maude, Honor. "Cradles of Civilisation." *RAIN* 16 (Oct. 1976): 6.

Quiggin, A. H., and E. S. Fegan. "Alfred Cort Haddon, 1855–1940." *Man* 40 (July 1940): 97–100.

Rivers, W. H. R., and A. C. Haddon. "A Method of Recording String Figures and Tricks." *Man* 2 (1902): 146–153.

SUBAQUATIC

"Dalí Surrealistic Show to Provide Fun at Fair," *New York Times*, April 23, 1939.

Eggener, Keith L. "An Amusing Lack of Logic." *American Art* 7:4 (Autumn 1993): 31–45.

Eldredge, Charles C. "Wet Paint: Herman Melville, Elihu Vedder, and Artists Undersea." *American Art* 11:2 (Summer 1997): 106–135.

Gosse, Philip Henry. *A Handbook to the Marine Aquarium*. London: John Van Voorst, 1856.

Hibberd, Shirley. *Rustic Adornments for Homes of Taste: Contains Suggestions for the Floral Embellishment of the Home, the Garden, Balcony, Window, Greenhouse and Conservatory: With Hints on the Formation and Management of Fresh-Water and Marine Aquariums, Vivariums, etc.* London: W. H. & L. Collingridge, 1895.

Kete, Kathleen. *The Beast in the Boudoir: Petkeeping in Nineteenth-Century Paris*. Berkeley: University of California Press, 1994.

Kino, Carol. "Venus on Red Satin: Salvador Dalí's House in Queens." *New York Times*, June 22, 2003.

Kinzer, Stephen. "Memory Persists in a Dalí Pavilion Revisited." *New York Times*, April 8, 2002.

Logan, Thad. *The Victorian Parlour*. Cambridge; New York: Cambridge University Press, 2001.

SWING

Baillio, Joseph. "Hubert Robert's Decorations for the Château de Bagatelle." *Metropolitan Museum Journal* 27 (1992): 149–182.

Bernier, Olivier. "The Refinements of France in an Age of Elegance." *New York Times*, Dec. 6, 1987.

Bremmer, Jan, ed. *From Sappho to De Sade: Moments in the History of Sexuality*. New York: Routledge, 1991.

Hubert, Renee Riese. "The Fleeting World of Humor from Watteau to Fragonard." *Yale French Studies* 23 (1959): 85–91.

Nevill, Ralph. *French Prints of the Eighteenth Century*. London: Macmillan, 1908.

Posner, Donald. "The Swinging Women of Watteau and Fragonard." *Art Bulletin* 64:1 (March 1982): 75–88.

Saint-Laurent, Cécil. *A History of Ladies Underwear*. London: Joseph, 1968.
Saisselin, Remy G. "The Rococo as a Dream of Happiness." *Journal of Aesthetics and Art Criticism* 19:2 (Winter 1960): 145–152.
Sheriff, Mary D. "For Love or Money? Rethinking Fragonard." *Eighteenth-Century Studies* 19:3 (Spring 1986): 333–354.
Tymieniecka, Anna-Teresa, ed. *Enjoyment: From Laughter to Delight in Philosophy, Literature, the Fine Arts, and Aesthetics*. Boston: Kluwer Academic, 1998.

TALK

Della Casa, Giovanni. *Galateo; or, a Treatise on Politeness and Delicacy of Manners*. Baltimore: G. Hill, 1811.
Genlis, Stéphanie Félicité (Comtesse de). *Memoirs of the Countess de Genlis: Illustrative of the History of the Eighteenth and Nineteenth Centuries*. New York: Wilder & Campbell; Philadelphia: R. H. Small, 1825.
Goodman, Dena. *The Republic of Letters: A Cultural History of the French Enlightenment*. Ithaca, NY: Cornell University Press, 1996.
Goodman, Dena, and Elizabeth C. Goldsmith. *Going Public: Women and Publishing in Early Modern France*. Ithaca, NY: Cornell University Press, 1995.
Gray, Francine du Plessix. *Madame de Staël: The First Modern Woman*. New York; London: Atlas, 2008.
Hall, Evelyn Beatrice. *The Women of the Salons, and Other French Portraits, by S. G. Tallentyre [pseud.]*. New York: G. P. Putnam & Sons, 1926.
Kale, Steven D. *French Salons: High Society and Political Sociability from the Old Regime to the Revolution of 1848*. Baltimore: Johns Hopkins University Press, 2004.
Mowat, R. B. *The Age of Reason*. Alcester, UK: Read Country Books, 2006.
Necker, Suzanne. *Mélanges, extraits des manuscrits de Mme Necker, Volume II*. Paris: Charles Pougens, 1798.
———. *The Salon of Madame Necker, Volume II*. Trans. Henry M. Trollope. London: Chapman & Hall, 1882.
Post, Emily. *Etiquette in Society, in Business, in Politics and at Home*. New York: Cosmo Classics, 2007.
Visser, Margaret. *The Rituals of Dinner: The Origins, Evolution, Eccentricities, and Meaning of Table Manners*. New York: Grove Weidenfeld, 1991.

TASSEL

Bonfante, Larissa. *Etruscan Dress*. Baltimore: Johns Hopkins University Press, 2003.
Budge, E. A. Wallis. *Amulets and Superstitions*. New York: Dover, 1978.
Campbell, Gordon, ed. *The Grove Encyclopedia of Decorative Arts*. New York: Oxford University Press, 2006.
Condra, Jill, ed. *The Greenwood Encyclopedia of Clothing Through World History*. Westport: Greenwood Press, 2008.

Cooke, Edward S., Jr. *Upholstery in America & Europe: From the Seventeenth Century to World War I.* New York: W. W. Norton, 1987.

Crowston, Clare Haru. *Fabricating Women: The Seamstresses of Old Regime France, 1675–1791.* Durham, NC: Duke University Press, 2001.

Eberlein, Harold Donaldson. "The Decorative Value of Chinese and Japanese Tassels." *House Beautiful* 36 (June–Nov. 1914): 29–32.

Gonzalez-Wippler, Migene. *The Complete Book of Amulets & Talismans.* St. Paul: Llewellyn Worldwide, 1991.

Jenkins, David, ed. *The Cambridge History of Western Textiles.* Cambridge; New York: Cambridge University Press, 2003.

Pile, John F. *A History of Interior Design.* Hoboken: J. Wiley & Sons, 2005.

Silverman, Eric Kline. *From Abraham to America: A History of Jewish Circumcision.* Lanham, MD: Rowman & Littlefield, 2006.

Welters, Linda, ed. *Folk Dress in Europe and Anatolia: Beliefs About Protection and Fertility.* Oxford: Berg, 1999.

TEA

Broomfield, Andrea. *Food and Cooking in Victorian England: A History.* Westport: Praeger, 2007.

Dumoulin, Heinrich. *Zen Buddhism: A History.* Trans. James W. Heisig and Paul Knitter. Bloomington, IN: World Wisdom, 2005.

Fukukita, Yasunosuke. *Tea Cult of Japan.* Boston: Bruce Humphries, 1935.

Isao, Kumakura, and Peter McMillan. "Reexamining Tea: 'Yuisho,' 'Suki,' 'Yatsushi,' and 'Furumai.'" *Monumenta Nipponica* 57:1 (Spring 2002): 1–42.

Ludwig, Theodore M. "Before Rikyu. Religious and Aesthetic Influences in the Early History of the Tea Ceremony." *Monumenta Nipponica* 36:4 (Winter 1981): 367–390.

Morris, Dixon, and Veronica Taylor. Review of *The Japanese Way of Tea: From Its Origins in China to Sen Rikyu* by Sen Soshitsu. *Pacific Affairs* 73:4 (Winter 2000–2001): 605–607.

Saito, Yuriko. "The Japanese Aesthetics of Imperfection and Insufficiency." *Journal of Aesthetics and Art Criticism* 55:4 (Autumn 1997): 377–385.

Toussaint-Samat, Maguelonne. *A History of Food.* Trans. Anthea Bell. Chichester, UK; Malden, MA: Wiley-Blackwell, 2009.

Ukers, William H. *The Romance of Tea: An Outline History of Tea and Tea-Drinking Through Sixteen Hundred Years.* New York; London: Alfred A. Knopf, 1936.

Varley, Paul, and Kumakura Isao, eds. *Tea in Japan: Essays on the History of Chanoyu.* Honolulu: University of Hawaii Press, 1994.

TEMPEST

Andronik, Catherine M. *Wildly Romantic: The English Romantic Poets—The Mad, the Bad, and the Dangerous.* New York: Henry Holt, 2007.

Beattie, Andrew. *The Alps: A Cultural History*. Oxford; New York: Oxford University Press, 2006.

Bieri, James. *Percy Bysshe Shelley: A Biography*. Baltimore: Johns Hopkins University Press, 2008.

Byron, George Gordon. *The Works of Lord Byron Complete in One Volume*. Frankfurt: H. L. Broenner, 1837.

Rousmaniere, John. *After the Storm: True Stories of Disaster and Recovery at Sea*. Camden, ME: International Marine/McGraw-Hill, 2002.

Rousseau, Jean-Jacques. *La Nouvelle Héloïse: Julie; or, the New Eloise: Letters of Two Lovers, Inhabitants of a Small Town at the Foot of the Alps*. Translated and abridged by Judith H. McDowell. University Park: Pennsylvania State University Press, 1987.

Senici, Emanuele. *Landscape and Gender in Italian Opera: The Alpine Virgin from Bellini to Puccini*. Cambridge; New York: Cambridge University Press, 2005.

Shakespeare, William. *The Tempest*. Richard Preiss, ed. London: Methuen Drama/A. & C. Black, 2008.

Thompson, Carl. *The Suffering Traveller and the Romantic Imagination*. New York: Oxford University Press, 2007.

Woodman, Ross Greig. *Sanity, Madness, Transformation: The Psyche in Romanticism*. Toronto; Buffalo: University of Toronto Press, 2005.

THAUMATROPE

Herbert, Stephen. *A History of Pre-Cinema, Volume 1*. New York: Routledge, 2000.

Paris, Ayrton John. *Philosophy in Sport Made Science in Earnest: Being an Attempt to Implant in the Young Mind the First Principles of Natural Philosophy by the Aid of the Popular Toys and Sports of Youth*. London: John Murray, 1853.

Wade, Nicholas J. *Destined for Distinguished Oblivion: The Scientific Vision of William Charles Wells (1757–1817)*. New York: Kluwer Academic/Plenum Publishers, 2003.

TOPPER

Amphlett, Hilda. *Hats: A History of Fashion in Headwear*. Chalfont St. Giles, UK: Sadler, 1974.

Bard, Solomon. *Voices from the Past: Hong Kong, 1842–1918*. Hong Kong: Hong Kong University Press [u.a.], 2002.

Clark, Fiona. *Hats*. London: B. T. Batsford, 1982.

Dickens, Charles. *Selected Journalism, 1850–1870*. David Pascoe, ed. London; New York: Penguin, 1997.

Hoffmann, Frank W., and William G. Bailey. *Fashion & Merchandising Fads*. New York: Haworth Press, 1994.

Hurlock, Elizabeth Bergner. *The Psychology of Dress; An Analysis of Fashion and Its Motive*. New York: B. Blom, 1971.

Nevill, Ralph. *Fancies, Fashions, and Fads*. New York: Brentano's, 1914.

Picard, Liza. *Victorian London: The Life of a City, 1840–1870*. New York: St. Martin's Press, 2006.

Robinson, Fred Miller. *The Man in the Bowler Hat: His History and Iconography*. Chapel Hill: University of North Carolina Press, 1993.

Skeat, Walter William. *The Past at Our Doors; or, the Old in the New Around Us*. London: Macmillan, 1912.

Thackeray, William Makepeace, Albert Smith, Gilbert Abbott À. Beckett, Horace Mayhew, and Henry Mayhew. *The Comic Almanack: An Ephemeris in Jest and Earnest, Containing Merry Tales, Humorous Poetry, Quips, and Oddities*. New York: Scribner, Welford, 1853.

TRAJE DE LUCES

Chrisman-Campbell, Kimberly. Review of *Goya: Images of Women* by Janis A. Tomlinson, and *Whistler, Women, & Fashion* by Margaret F. MacDonald, Susan Grace Galassi, Aileen Ribeiro, and Patricia de Montfort. *Woman's Art Journal* 26:2 (Autumn 2005–Winter 2006): 46–50.

De Oliva, Mari. "Matador's Garb Part of Bull-Ring Spectacle." *New York Times*, May 28, 1961.

Du Gué Trapier, Elizabeth. "Only Goya." *Burlington Magazine* 102:685 (April 1960): 158, 160–161.

Fuchs, Dale. "Illuminating the 'Suit of Lights.'" *International Herald Tribune*, May 31, 2006.

Hagen, Rainer, and Rose-Marie Hagen. *What Great Paintings Say*. Köln, Ger.; London: Taschen, 2003.

Kennedy, A. L. *On Bullfighting*. New York: Anchor, 2001.

Marvin, Garry. *Bullfight*. Urbana: University of Illinois Press, 1994.

McCormick, John. *Bullfighting: Art, Technique & Spanish Society*. New Brunswick: Transaction Publishers, 1998.

Noyes, Dorothy. "La Maja Vestida: Dress as Resistance to Enlightenment in Late-18th-Century Madrid." *Journal of American Folklore* 111:440 (Spring 1998): 197–217.

Pink, Sarah. *Women and Bullfighting: Gender, Sex and the Consumption of Tradition*. Oxford; New York: Berg, 1997.

Pitt-Rivers, Julian. "The Spanish Bull-Fight: And Kindred Activities." *Anthropology Today* 9:4 (Aug. 1993):11–15.

Shubert, Adrian. *Death and Money in the Afternoon: A History of the Spanish Bullfight*. New York: Oxford University Press, 1999.

Wolff, H. Drummond. "Madrilenia." *Bentley's Miscellany* 28 (1850).

TRAPEZE

Cullen, Frank, Florence Hackman, and Donald McNeilly. *Vaudeville, Old & New: An Encyclopedia of Variety Performers in America*. New York: Routledge, 2007.

"Leona Dare, Acrobat, Dead." *New York Times*, May 25, 1922.

"Leona Dare's Trapeze," *New York Times*, June 9, 1879.

"Nervous Dare," *New York Times*, Nov. 23, 1884.

Raser. Timothy, ed. *Peripheries of Nineteenth-Century French Studies: Views from the Edge*. Newark: University of Delaware Press; London: Associated University Presses, 2002.

Stoddart, Helen. *Rings of Desire: Circus History and Representation*. Manchester, UK; New York: Manchester University Press, 2000.

Tait, Peta. *Circus Bodies: Cultural Identity in Aerial Performance*. New York: Routledge, 2005.

TRUFFLES

Brillat-Savarin, Jean-Anthelme. *The Physiology of Taste; or, Meditations on Transcendental Gastronomy*. Translated from the French by M. F. K. Fisher. San Francisco: Arion Press, 1994.

Burnett, John. *England Eats Out: A Social History of Eating Out in England from 1830 to the Present*. New York: Pearson/Longman, 2004.

Casanova de Seingalt, Jacques. *The Memoirs of Casanova, Volume 1: Venetian Years*. Trans. Arthur Machen. Teddington, UK: Echo Press, 2007.

Clermont, B. *The Professed Cook; or, the Modern Art of Cookery, Pastry, & Confectionary, Made Plain and Easy; Consisting of the Most Approved Methods in the French, as Well as English Cookery*. London: C. Richards, 1812.

Fielding, Daphne. *The Duchess of Jermyn Street; The Life and Good Times of Rosa Lewis of the Cavendish Hotel*. Boston: Little, Brown, 1964.

Francatelli, Charles Elmé. *The Modern Cook*. London: Macmillan, 1911.

James, Ken. *Escoffier: The King of Chefs*. London; New York: Hambledon & London, 2002.

Kelly, Ian. *Casanova: Actor, Spy, Lover, Priest*. London: Hodder & Stoughton, 2008.

Masters, Anthony. *Rosa Lewis, an Exceptional Edwardian*. London: Weidenfeld & Nicolson, 1977.

Mudrick, Marvin. "The Great Lover." Review of *History of My Life by Giacomo Casanova*, by Willard R. Trask. *Hudson Review* 20:4 (Winter 1967–1968): 681–686.

Saint-Ange, Madame E., and Paul Aratow. *La Bonne Cuisine de Madame E. Saint-Ange: The Original Companion for French Home Cooking*. Berkeley: Ten Speed Press, 2005.

Toussaint-Samat, Maguelonne. *A History of Food*. Trans. Anthea Bell. Chichester, UK; Malden, MA: Wiley-Blackwell, 2009.

Young, Carolin C. *Apples of Gold in Settings of Silver: Stories of Dinner as a Work of Art*. New York; London: Simon & Schuster, 2002.

TURBAN

Anthony, Carl Sferrazza. *First Ladies: The Saga of the Presidents' Wives and Their Power, 1789–1961*. New York: Quill/William Morrow, 1990.

Benito, Carmel. "Paris Milliners at Work." *Vogue*, Nov. 1944.

Boller, Paul F. *Presidential Wives*. New York: Oxford University Press, 1998.

Breskin, Isabel. "On the Periphery of a Greater World: John Singleton Copley's 'Turquerie' Portraits." *Winterthur Portfolio* 36:2/3 (Summer–Autumn 2001): 97–123.

Dean, Elizabeth Lippincott. *Dolly Madison, the Nation's Hostess*. Boston: Lothrop, Lee &
    Shepard, 1928.
Desmond, Alice Curtis. *Glamorous Dolly Madison*. New York: Dodd, Mead, 1946.
Goodwin, Maud Wilder. *Dolly Madison*. New York, Scribner, 1896.
Scott, Georgia. *Headwraps: A Global Journey*. New York: Public Affairs, 2003.
Simpson, John, ed. *Oxford English Dictionary*. Oxford: Oxford University Press, 2009.
Sorel, Nancy Caldwell. "When Isak Dinesen Met Marilyn Monroe." *The Independent*, Dec. 23,
    1995.
Steele, Valerie. *Paris Fashion: A Cultural History*. Oxford: Berg, 1999.
"Turquerie," *Metropolitan Museum of Art Bulletin* 26:5 (Jan. 1968): 225–239.
Varon, Elizabeth R. Review of *These Fiery Frenchified Dames: Women and Political Culture in
    Early National Philadelphia* by Susan Branson, and *Parlor Politics: In Which the Ladies of
    Washington Help Build a City and a Government* by Catherine Allgor. *William and Mary
    Quarterly* 58:3 (July 2001): 764–769.
Watanabe, Toshio. "Exotic Worlds–European Fantasies. Stuttgart." *Burlington Magazine*
    129:1016 (Nov. 1987): 763–764.

TWILIGHT

Donoghue, Denis. "Wallace Stevens, Imperator." *New York Review of Books*, Dec. 1, 1966.
Doreski, William. "Wallace Stevens in Connecticut." *Twentieth Century Literature* 39:2
    (Summer 1993): 152–165.
Hudson, Deatt. "Wallace Stevens." *Twentieth Century Literature* 1:3 (Oct. 1955): 135–138.
Millard, Christopher. *Bibliography of Oscar Wilde*. London: Rota, 1967.
Miller, Christopher R. *The Invention of Evening: Perception and Time in Romantic Poetry*. Cam-
    bridge; New York: Cambridge University Press, 2006.
Shepard, Paul. *Man in the Landscape: A Historic View of the Esthetics of Nature*. College Station:
    Texas A&M University Press, 1991.
Stevens, Wallace. *The Collected Poems of Wallace Stevens*. New York: Vintage, 1990.
Stevens, Wallace. *Letters of Wallace Stevens*. Holly Stevens, ed. Berkeley; London: University of
    California Press, 1996.

UMBRELLA

Beer, Robert. *The Handbook of Tibetan Buddhist Symbols*. Boston: Shambhala, 2003.
Hartwig, G. *The Aerial World: A Popular Account of the Phenomena and Life of the Atmosphere*. New
    York: D. Appleton, 1875.
Lougheed, Victor. *Vehicles of the Air; A Popular Exposition of Modern Aeronautics, with Working
    Drawings*. Chicago: Reilly & Briton, 1911.
Marion, Fulgence. *Wonderful Balloon Ascents; or, the conquest of the Skies. A History of Balloons
    and Balloon Voyages*. New York: Scribner, Armstrong, 1874.
Poleski, Steve. "Art and Flight: Historical Origins to Contemporary Works." *Leonardo* 18:2
    (1985): 69–80.

Russell, R. V. *The Tribes and Castes of the Central Provinces of India*. London: Macmillan, 1916.

Sangster, William. *Umbrellas and Their History*. London: Effingham Wilson, 1855.

Simpson, John, ed. *Oxford English Dictionary*. Oxford: Oxford University Press, 2009.

White, Lynn, Jr. "The Invention of the Parachute." *Technology and Culture* 9:3 (July 1968): 462–467.

UNICORN

Châtelet-Lange, Liliane. Trans. Renate Franciscond. "The Grotto of the Unicorn and the Garden of the Villa di Castello." *Art Bulletin* 50:1 (March 1968): 51–58.

Cohen, Claudine. *The Fate of the Mammoth: Fossils, Myths, and History*. Trans. William Rodarmor. Chicago: University of Chicago Press, 2002.

Grigson, Geoffrey, and Charles Harvard Gibbs-Smith, eds. *Things: A Volume of Objects Devised by Man's Genius Which Are the Measure of His Civilization*. New York: Hawthorne Books, 1957.

Nickel, Helmut. "Presents to Princes: A Bestiary of Strange and Wondrous Beasts, Once Known, for a Time Forgotten, and Rediscovered." *Metropolitan Museum Journal* 26 (1991): 129–138.

Schoenberger, Guido. "A Goblet of Unicorn Horn." *Metropolitan Museum of Art Bulletin* 9:10 (June 1951): 284–288.

Shepard, Odell. *The Lore of the Unicorn*. New York: Dover, 1993.

Suhr, Elmer G. "An Interpretation of the Unicorn." *Folklore* 75:2 (Summer 1964): 91–109.

"The Unicorn Tapestries," *Metropolitan Museum of Art Bulletin* 32:1 (1973–1974): 177–224.

VELOCITY

Carter, William C. *Marcel Proust: A Life*. New Haven: Yale University Press, 2000.

——. *Proust in Love*. New Haven: Yale University Press, 2006.

——. *The Proustian Quest*. New York: New York University Press, 1992.

Danius, Sara. *The Senses of Modernism: Technology, Perception, and Aesthetics*. Ithaca, NY: Cornell University Press, 2002.

Mortimer, Armine Kotin, and Katherine Kolb, eds. *Proust in Perspective: Visions and Revisions*. Urbana: University of Illinois Press, 2002.

Proust, Marcel. "Impressions de Route en Automobile." *Le Figaro*, Nov. 19, 1907.

VIRIDITAS

Boyce-Tillman, Joyce. "Hildegard of Bingen at 900. The Eye of a Woman." *Musical Times* 139:1865 (Winter 1998): 31–36.

Cahill, Thomas. *Mysteries of the Middle Ages: And the Beginning of the Modern World*. New York: Anchor, 2006.

Hildegard, Saint, and Carmen Acevedo Butcher. *Hildegard of Bingen: A Spiritual Reader*. Brewster, MA: Paraclete Press, 2007.

Hildegard, Saint, Joseph L. Baird, and Radd K. Ehrman. *The Letters of Hildegard of Bingen, Volume. 1*. New York: Oxford University Press, 1998.

John, Helen J. "Hildegard of Bingen: A New Twelfth-Century Woman Philosopher?" Review of *Sister of Wisdom: St. Hildegard's Theology of the Feminine* by Barbara Newman; *Scivias* by Hildegard of Bingen, Columba Hart, and Jane Bishop; and *Hildegard of Bingen, 1098–1179: A Visionary Life* by Sabina Flanagan. *Hypatia* 7:1 (Winter 1992): 115 123.

Newman, Barbara. "Hildegard of Bingen: Visions and Validation." *Church History* 54:2 (June 1985): 163–175.

———. *Voice of the Living Light: Hildegard of Bingen and Her World*. Berkeley [u.a.]: University of California Press, 1998.

Roche-Mahdi, Sarah. "The Sibyl of the Rhine." Review of *Scivias/Know the Ways* by Hildegard of Bingen and Bruce Hozeski. *Women's Review of Books* 4:2 (Nov. 1986): 14–15.

Schipperges, Heinrich. *The World of Hildegard of Bingen: Her Life, Times, and Visions*. Collegeville, MN: Liturgical Press, 1998.

Storey, Ann. "A Theophany of the Feminine: Hildegard of Bingen, Elisabeth of Schönau, and Herrad of Landsberg." *Woman's Art Journal* 19:1 (Spring–Summer 1998): 16–20.

Witts, Richard. "How to Make a Saint: On Interpreting Hildegard of Bingen." *Early Music* 26:3 (Aug. 1998): 478–485.

WANDERERS

B.G.C. Review of *Unconducted Wanderers* by Rosita Forbes. *Geographical Journal* (Nov. 1919): 317–318.

Edmonds, C. J. Review of *The Valleys of the Assassins, and Other Persian Travels* by Freya Stark. *Geographical Journal* (Aug. 1934): 156–157.

Forbes, Rosita. *Adventure; Being a Gypsy Salad—Some Incidents, Excitements and Impressions of Twelve Highly-Seasoned Years*. London: Cassell, 1928.

———. *Women Called Wild*. New York: Dutton, 1937.

Middleton, Dorothy. "Obituaries: Dame Freya Stark 1893–1993." *Geographical Journal* 159:3 (Nov. 1993): 368–369.

Prescott, E. N. Review of *Baghdad Sketches* by Freya Stark. *Journal of Bible and Religion* 6:3 (Summer 1938): 169.

Ruthven, Malise. *Traveller Through Time: A Photographic Journey with Freya Stark*. New York: Viking, 1986.

Stark, Freya. "The Assassins' Valley and the Salambar Pass." *Geographical Journal* (Jan. 1931): 48–60.

Stark, Freya. *The Journey's Echo*. London: J. Murray, 1963.

WEEKEND

"Flocking to Summer Resorts," *New York Times*, June 27, 1909.

"Hotels at the Shore Busiest Since 1929," *New York Times*, Aug. 11, 1935.

King, Anthony D. *Buildings and Society: Essays on the Social Development of the Built Environment*. New York: Routledge, 1984.

Sterngass, Jon. *First Resorts: Pursuing Pleasure at Saratoga Springs, Newport, & Coney Island*. Baltimore: Johns Hopkins University Press, 2001.

Wharton, Edith. *A Backward Glance*. New York: Simon & Schuster, 1998.

WHISTLING

Borgen, Robert. *Sugawara no Michizane and the Early Heian Court*. Honolulu: University of Hawaii Press, 1994.

Braun, Hans-Joachim, ed. *Music and Technology in the Twentieth Century*. Baltimore: John Hopkins University Press, 2002.

Calero, Henry H. *The Power of Nonverbal Communication: How You Act Is More Important Than What You Say*. Los Angeles: Silver Lake Publishing, 2005.

Edwards, E. D. " 'Principles of Whistling'—Hsiao Chih—Anonymous." *Bulletin of the School of Oriental and African Studies* 20 (1957): 217–229.

Engel, Carl. *An Introduction to the Study of National Music; Comprising Researches into Popular Songs, Traditions, and Customs*. London: Longmans, Green, Reader, & Dyer, 1866.

Lowery, Fred, and John R. McDowell. *Whistling in the Dark*. Gretna, LA: Pelican, 1983.

Ritzenthaler, Robert E., and Frederick A. Peterson. "Courtship Whistling of the Mexican Kickapoo Indians," Part 1. *American Anthropologist* 56:6 (Dec. 1954): 1088–1089.

Robb, Graham. *The Discovery of France: A Historical Geography from the Revolution to the First World War*. New York: W. W. Norton, 2007.

Stern, Theodore. "Drum and Whistle 'Languages': An Analysis of Speech Surrogates." *American Anthropologist* 59:3 (June 1957): 487–506.

Thompson, Francis M. L. *The University of London and the World of Learning: 1836–1986*. London: Hambledon, 1990.

Williams, Frederick Smeeton. *Our Iron Roads: Their History, Construction and Administration*. London: Bemrose & Sons, 1883.

WHITE PAINT

De Wolfe, Elsie. *After All*. London: Heinemann, 1935.

———. *The House in Good Taste*. Salem, NH: Ayer, 1990.

Flanner, Janet. "Handsprings Across the Sea." *The New Yorker*, Jan. 15, 1938.

Franklin, Ruth. "A Life in Good Taste." *The New Yorker*, Sept. 27, 2004.

Hobart, Christy. "Elsie in Amber." *House & Garden*, May 2007.

Munhall, Edgar. "Elsie de Wolfe." *Architectural Digest*, Jan. 2000.

Smith, Jane S. *Elsie de Wolfe: A Life in the High Style*. New York: Atheneum, 1982.

XENIA

Albrecht, Michael von, and Gareth L. Schmeling. *A History of Roman Literature: From Livius Andronicus to Boethius*. New York: E. J. Brill, 1997.
Anthon, Charles. *A Classical Dictionary: Containing an Account of the Principal Proper Names Mentioned in Ancient Authors and Intended to Elucidate All the Important Points Connected with the Geography, History, Biography, Mythology, and Fine Arts of the Greeks and Romans*. New York: Harper & Brothers, 1892.
Bagnan, Gilbert. "The House of Trimalchio." *American Journal of Philology* 75:1 (1954): 16–39.
Boardman, John, Jasper Griffin, and Oswyn Murray, eds. *The Oxford Illustrated History of the Roman World*. Oxford; New York: Oxford University Press, 2001.
Bober, Phyllis Pray. *Art, Culture, and Cuisine: Ancient and Medieval Gastronomy*. Chicago: University of Chicago Press, 1999.
Bryson, Norman. *Looking at the Overlooked: Four Essays on Still Life Painting*. Cambridge, MA: Harvard University Press, 1990.
Budin, Stephanie Lynn. *The Ancient Greeks: New Perspectives*. Santa Barbara: ABC-CLIO, 2004.
Fitzgerald, William. *Martial: The World of the Epigram*. Chicago: University of Chicago Press, 2007.
Gowers, Emily. *The Loaded Table: Representations of Food in Roman Literature*. Oxford: Clarendon Press; New York: Oxford University Press, 1993.
Gozzini Giacosa, Ilaria. *A Taste of Ancient Rome*. Trans. Anna Herklotz. Chicago: University of Chicago Press, 1992.
Homer. *The Odyssey*. Trans. Rodney Merrill. Ann Arbor: University of Michigan Press, 2002.

XIGUO JIFA

Aldrich, M. A. *The Search for a Vanishing Beijing: A Guide to China's Capital Through the Ages*. Hong Kong: Hong Kong University Press, 2007.
Bernard, Miguel A. *Five Great Missionary Experiments and Cultural Issues in Asia*. Manila: Cardinal Bea Institute, Loyola School of Theology, Ateneo de Manila University, 1991.
Cronin, Vincent. *The Wise Man from the West*. New York: E. P. Dutton, 1955.
Gross, John. Review of *The Memory Palace of Matteo Ricci* by Jonathan D. Spence. *New York Times*, Nov. 21, 1984.
Leys, Simon. *The Burning Forest: Essays on Chinese Culture and Politics*. New York: Holt, Rinehart & Winston, 1986.
Mungello, David E. Review of *The Memory Palace of Matteo Ricci* by Jonathan D. Spence. *American Historical Review* 91:2 (April 1986): 444–445.
Robinson, Paul. "Ming Mnemonics." *New York Times*, Nov. 25, 1984.
Schwartz, Harry. "Western Winds in the East." *New York Times*, May 5, 1973.
Spence, Jonathan D. *The Memory Palace of Matteo Ricci*. New York: Viking, 1984.
Young, John D. *East-West Synthesis: Matteo Ricci and Confucianism*. Hong Kong: Centre of Asian Studies, University of Hong Kong, 1980.

Zhang, Qiong. "About God, Demons, and Miracles: The Jesuit Discourse on the Supernatural in Late Ming China." *Early Science and Medicine* 4:1 (1999): 1–36.

YES

Bierce, Ambrose. *The Collected Works of Ambrose Bierce*. New York; Washington: The Neale Publishing Company, 1909–1911.
Kimmelman, Michael. "Art Review." *New York Times*, Oct. 27, 2000.
——. "Yoko Ono on Her Own, Storming the Barricades." *New York Times*, Feb. 10, 1989.
Lennon, John. *Lennon Remembers*. Introduction by Jann S. Wenner. London; New York: Verso, 2000.
Ono, Yoko. *Grapefruit: A Book of Instructions + Drawings*. Introduction by John Lennon. New York: Simon & Schuster, 2000.
Silberman, Robert. "Review: 'In the Spirit of Fluxus.' Minneapolis." *Burlington Magazine* 135:1083 (June 1993): 432–433.
Wallach, Amel. "The Widow." *New York Times*, Sept. 24, 2000.

Jessica Kerwin Jenkins was a reporter and editor at *Women's Wear Daily* in New York, and worked in Paris as the European editor of *W* magazine. She currently lives on the coast of Maine and writes for *Vogue*.

A NOTE ABOUT THE TYPE

The text of this book was set in Filosofia, a typeface designed by Zuzana Licko in 1996 as a revival of the typefaces of Giambattista Bodoni (1740–1813). Basing her design on the letterpress practice of altering the cut of the letters to match the size for which they were to be used, Licko designed Filosofia Regular as a rugged face with reduced contrast to withstand the reduction to text sizes, and Filosofia Grand as a more delicate and refined version for use in larger display sizes.

Licko, born in Bratislava, Czechoslovakia, in 1961, is the cofounder of Emigre, a digital type foundry and publisher of *Emigre* magazine, based in Northern California. Founded in 1984, coinciding with the birth of the Macintosh, Emigre was one of the first independent type foundries to establish itself centered around personal computer technology.